Three Elegies of Ch'u

Geoffrey R. Waters

Three Elegies of Ch'u

An Introduction
to the Traditional
Interpretation of the *Ch'u Tz'u*

The University of Wisconsin Press

Published 1985

The University of Wisconsin Press
114 North Murray Street
Madison, Wisconsin 53715

The University of Wisconsin Press, Ltd.
1 Gower Street
London WC1E 6HA, England

First printing

Printed in the United States of America

For LC CIP information see the colophon

ISBN 0-299-10030-8

To my family

Thus, the gentleman follows his virtuous nature in carrying on his inquiries and studies; he masters the broad and profound to penetrate the subtle and abstruse; he attains the heights of intelligence in order to live by the Golden Mean; he keeps the past alive as a key to understand the present; and he is honest and generous in his reverence for what is right.

Chung Yung 27:6

Contents

Preface

This book is an exercise in philology. I define philology as the scientific study of literature in its widest sense, including literary criticism and the relationship of literature and history: "Philology is not a mere matter of grammar, but is, in the largest sense, a master-science, whose duty is to present to us the whole of ancient life, and to give archaeology its just place by the side of literature" (*Athenæum*, June 25, 1892).

In order to place our text, three Elegies from the *Ch'u Tz'u*, in its proper context, we must first survey the historical, social, and literary background to the way the Elegies were read. Only then can we proceed to a discussion of method, and after that to the text itself. This is not a literary evaluation in the usual sense of an appreciative conspectus. Close explication must precede literary evaluation. Approaching the *Ch'u Tz'u* the other way round has led to confusions, the unravelling of which is my present aim.

I was first introduced to the polytropic nature of Chinese writing by Friedrich A. Bischoff in his seminars in Classical and in Medieval Chinese Literature at Indiana University. These seminars spanned a decade, from the mid-sixties through the mid-seventies. When I joined the group, in 1972, they had already begun their study of the allusive rhymed essay known as *fu*. The work of the seminars proceeded from Bischoff's Prime Directive: "The author meant what he said." Or, put another way: "Why did he choose *this* word over another?" The sense of discovery we shared while participating in what I feel to be the literary revelation of the generation was reinforced by Professor Bischoff's insistence on intellectual honesty and slow, careful, and thorough training. The result, augmented by the books of those of us who learned the method from him, is Bischoff's pioneering series of works on the interpretation of the *fu*.

This book is based on my Ph.D. thesis, written for Professor Bischoff.

It grew from some notes we made during our year-long reading of Su Shih's "First Fu on the Red Cliff" (v. Bischoff, pp. 193–318). Su's *fu*, written in 1082 A.D., is a savage criticism of the conduct of the wars against the Tanguts, a non-Chinese kingdom to the northwest. That year, after decades of war, the Tanguts had inflicted a humiliating and disastrous defeat on the Sung army. When Su made his political points by means of allusions to the official Classics we were on fairly solid ground in interpreting them and fitting them into the fabric of his indictment. However, when he alluded to the *Ch'u Tz'u*, and he especially favored the Nine Elegies, we found ourselves at sea. Accepted interpretations of the *Ch'u Tz'u* gave us no help at all: a volunteer was required to establish the rudiments of an allusive key to the *Ch'u Tz'u*. I was the volunteer.

Out of expedience, I chose the Nine Elegies. Though the *Li Sao*, the masterpiece of the *Ch'u Tz'u*, would have been the obvious place to begin, it was simply too long. A manuscript of the *Li Sao*, annotated and presented in the format I use for the Elegies, would have exceeded two thousand typewritten pages. Heeding sage advice not to confuse a thesis with a *magnum opus*, I decided to test the method on the first three of the Nine Elegies.

The method of rediscovering the essential nature of the Elegies and of verifying the political interpretation is sufficiently demonstrated here in the analysis of these three poems. The necessary spadework to complete the set (there are eleven poems in the Nine Elegies) has been finished as well, and I hope that a subsequent volume may make the scientific study of the *Ch'u Tz'u* easier by providing a complete decoding of the allusive context of the Elegies.

Next, logically, the study of the *Ch'u Tz'u* must focus on the *Li Sao*. The recent appearance of the *Li Sao Tsuan I* (*Collected Annotations on the Li Sao*) of Yu Kuo-en finally makes such an effort feasible. I can only hope that while I am laboring on the *Li Sao*, my colleagues (with Yu's forthcoming similar encyclopedia of Nine Elegies annotations open on their desks) will carry the study of the Elegies as far beyond where I leave it as I have tried to go beyond the banalities of the appreciative school. That kind of constant renewal is what makes Chinese literature such a lively field, including the study of such "irrelevant" things as poems two millennia old.

In offering the result of my work, I must acknowledge some debts. Elizabeth Steinberg, Peter Givler, and the editors at the University of Wisconsin Press graciously agreed to read a manuscript pressed unsolicited into Mr. Givler's hand at a convention. Their patience in correspondence, and in preparing the manuscript of a globe-trotting banker, has been enormous. I am grateful to my predecessors in the seminars, especially Bill Nienhauser, Charles Hartman, and Brad Langley, for their contribution to the seminars, their encouragement of a latecomer, and their help in seeing this book published.

Professor Liu Wu-chi generously offered a number of suggestions to help make the work of a young heretic more palatable.

Above all, Professor Friedrich A. Bischoff, now Chairman at the University of Hamburg, made this book possible by teaching me the craft of philology.

GRW
Hong Kong
May 1983

Abbreviations

(For fuller notices of books and articles, see the bibliography.)

ANC	Ancient Chinese (ca. 600 A.D.)
ARC	Archaic Chinese (early Chou, ca. 800 B.C.)
Barnard	Noel Barnard. *The Ch'u Silk Manuscript.*
Biallas	F. X. Biallas. "K'ü Yüan, His Life and Poems."
Bischoff	Friedrich A. Bischoff. *Interpreting the Fu.*
BMFEA	*Bulletin of the Museum of Far Eastern Antiquities,* Stockholm.
Chu Hsi	Chu Hsi. *Ch'u Tz'u Chi Chu.*
CMH	Smith & Stuart. *Chinese Medicinal Herbs.*
CW	*Chung Wen Ta Tz'u Tien.*
DK	*Dai Kan-wa Jiten.*
Five Ministers	Their commentary, from Hsiao T'ung, ed. *Sung Pen Liu Ch'en Chu Wen Hsüan.*
Giles	Herbert A. Giles. *Gems of Chinese Literature.*
GSR	Bernhard Karlgren. *Grammata Serica Recensa.*
Harlez	C. de Harlez. "La Poesie chinoise."
Hawkes	David Hawkes. *Ch'u Tz'u: Songs of the South.*
Hung Hsing-tsu	Hung Hsing-tsu. *Ch'u Tz'u Pu Chu.*
Legge	James Legge. *The Chinese Classics.*
Liu	Liu Wu-chi. *An Introduction to Chinese Literature.*
MSC	Modern Standard Chinese.
Odes	*Shih Ching* (in Legge).
OED	*The Oxford English Dictionary.*
Pfizmaier	August Pfizmaier. *Das Li-sao und die neun Gesänge.*
Shu Ching	*Shu Ching* (in Legge).
Waley	Arthur Waley. *The Nine Songs.*
Wang I	Wang I's notes in Hung Hsing-tsu.
WHTL	*Wen Hsin Tiao Lung.*

Three Elegies of Ch'u

Introduction

The Warring States

The years from 481 to 221 B.C. are known in China as the period of the "Warring States." There were three principal states: Ch'in in the northwest, Ch'u in the Yangtze valley, and Ch'i in the northeast. Four others, Chao, Han, Wei, and Chin, made up the seven important states whose wars gave the period its name. These states traced their authority over their respective regions back through enfeoffments to the kings of the Chou dynasty, which had come to power in the twelfth century B.C. From that time until the era of the Warring States, with which this study is concerned, the power of the Chou court waned. First one lord and then another asserted his leadership among Chou's vassal states. Wars and diplomatic missions among them constitute the greater part of the annals of the time.

Late in the fourth century B.C., the balance of power among the states began to tip toward Ch'in. Ch'in was a northwestern state, racially quite different from the people of the central plain. By adopting the economies of a harsh totalitarian government it was able to raise a large and effective army and to mount devastating attacks on its small neighbors. Ch'in began to expand into the central plain of China.

Ch'in's major adversary was Ch'i. Ch'i itself was expanding, annexing small states throughout the fourth century. Ch'i, however, was not able to face Ch'in alone. For that reason, the major contemporary political question throughout China, and especially at the Ch'u court, was: Shall Ch'u join Ch'i to oppose "rapacious Ch'in," as it was known, or join Ch'in to oppose the confederation of states controlled by Ch'i? Those who advocated the alliance with Ch'in, even knowing Ch'in's treacher-

3

ous history of dealing with its fellow states, hoped that by aiding Ch'in now, Ch'u might be able to mitigate its eventual fate.

The alternatives were labeled the "horizontal" (east-west) and "vertical" (north-south) alliances. Much of our information concerning these matters comes from the quasi-historical book *Chan Kuo Ts'e* (*Intrigues of the Warring States*) and the earliest systematic history of China, the *Shih Chi* (*Records of the Historian*) by the Han scholar Ssu-ma Ch'ien. From these sources we learn of the intrigues at the Ch'u court as the two factions fought for the ear of the kings of Ch'u. In the *Shih Chi* we encounter Ch'ü Yüan, the putative author of the Nine Elegies, a partisan of the vertical, pro-Ch'i alliance. His alienation from King Huai of Ch'u (reigned 329–299 B.C.), the central theme of the Nine Elegies, was due to the influence of his enemies among the pro-Ch'in faction at the Ch'u court.

Ch'ü Yüan was banished from court and sent to the southern swamps. He did not live to see Ch'in, aided by the unwise kings of his native Ch'u, defeat Ch'i and then turn on and destroy its hapless allies. He drowned himself. By 221 B.C., Ch'in had completed its conquest of the feudal states. In that year the king of Ch'in declared himself emperor of the first Chinese empire.

His dynasty would last only fifteen years, yet two of his decrees would have far-reaching impact on China's traditional culture. To consolidate his control of the conquered states he ordered that the written characters of the Chinese language be standardized and simplified. To eliminate opposition from the intellectual class, he ordered the scholars buried alive and their books burned. The effect of this catastrophic interruption of Chinese literary and cultural development was to create a temporal and conceptual gulf across which traditions and texts would not pass without careful reconstruction in later eras.

Ch'ü Yüan

Ch'ü Yüan escaped the oblivion of many of his contemporaries of the late Warring States period. Some of them are now no more than names in books, such as the *Chan Kuo Ts'e* and others. For some it remains a challenge to modern scholars to prove even their simple historicity. Many have no doubt vanished completely. Ch'ü Yüan, in surviving, has become associated with a whole literary genre. An anthology of poems is attributed to him and his literary heirs.

The authorship of the older sections of the *Ch'u Tz'u* is in dispute. David Hawkes, in his Ph.D. thesis, "The Problem of Date and Authorship of Ch'u Tz'u," summarized the recent debate over attribution of parts of the collection to Ch'ü Yüan and discussed evidence for and against the assertion that such a person did in fact exist. This archaeological discussion is only incidental to a study of the traditional view of the poems in later times. The orthodox account of their supposed author is more useful in this context and has been well summarized by Burton Watson as follows:

> The story of Ch'ü Yüan, the loyal minister to King Huai of Ch'u (329–299 B.C.), was already well known to men of the early Han. A commentary, now lost, on Ch'ü Yüan's most famous poem, the *Li Sao*, was compiled by Liu An, the king of Huai-nan (d. 122 B.C.). Shortly afterwards the historian Ssu-ma Ch'ien, apparently utilizing Liu An's work, wrote a biography of Ch'ü Yüan (*Shih Chi* 84). According to his account, Ch'ü Yüan was a nobleman of Ch'u who at first enjoyed great favor under King Huai but later, due to the slander of a court rival, became estranged from the king. He remained out of favor, and was finally banished to the south by King Huai's son and successor King Ch'ing-hsiang (298–265 B.C.). There, he committed suicide by throwing himself into the Mi-lo River, a tributary of the Yangtze. His poems, outbursts of grief and anger at the injustice of his fate, were believed to have been written during the time of his estrangement and banishment. The poems were deeply admired and often imitated by Han scholars, and their reputed author came to symbolize the loyal minister who, because of the calumny of rivals and the blindness of the ruler, is rejected by his sovereign. (*Early Chinese Literature*, p. 232)

Two elements of the story require some amplification. First, the late Warring States period was characterized by the existence of a class of wandering "persuaders" who served one prince and then another, selling their advice for patronage (for an excellent treatment of these persuaders, see Crump, *Intrigues*). Thus, for Ch'ü Yüan, banishment was not the only option. The high degree of loyalty to his state that he showed by not deserting it to serve a rival was a rare example. Few men would accept banishment and drown themselves rather than dishonor a trust, especially one which had been betrayed.

Second, one must also remember that for seventy generations, from Confucius' time until the nineteenth century, it was customary for the best and most talented of the literati to serve in the government. Literary skill was the most important prerequisite, short of the patronage of a powerful mentor, to an official career. The critical combination created by having the most talented writers of the age in the most frustrating and dangerous positions—ministers to courts where intrigue was rampant, where rulers were swayed by first one faction, then another—produced an outpouring of intensely moving literary expression. A common cause of death among those officials also regarded as great writers was execution for *lèse majesté*. When a man could be executed for insulting the emperor with a poorly chosen pun, great subtlety and skill in his writing was often an author's only defense against his enemies.

The great Sung dynasty poet Su Shih is a famous example. Su Shih had angered his opponents, the men of Wang An-shih's party at the court of Emperor Shen-tsung (1068–1085). He was arrested in 1079 and put on trial for slandering the emperor in satirical poems. The trial lasted several weeks, much of the time being taken up by detailed analysis of his allusions and their alleged criticisms (v. Lin Yutang, *The Gay Genius*, pp. 187–204; and *Wu T'ai Shih An*, or *The Poetry Trial of the Raven Terrace*, by Peng Chiu-wan, which is a summary of the trial and a transcript of many of the documents introduced during it). Though he was convicted, he made excellent use of the technique of the *alibi*. In the legal sense, *alibi* (Latin for "elsewhere") is a plea that one was elsewhere at the time of some alleged action. In the context of an inquisition, such as Su's trial, one's *alibi* was an alternative interpretation of whatever allusion was being indicated as seditious, which turned the phrase from a castigation into a compliment. Su's brilliance at confounding his accusers in such a literary battle of wits could not have helped his case in what was, in any event, a star-chamber trial.

When a minister could be degraded and banished, as Su Shih was, for remarking on the ability of nature to produce so many varieties of peonies (i.e., the ability of the government to levy such a variety of taxes), it is not surprising that generations of scholar-bureaucrats preserved and admired the graceful Elegies of Ch'ü Yüan.

One interesting comment on the historicity of Ch'ü Yüan is Ssu-ma Ch'ien's failure to include his biography in what would seem to be its chronologically correct place in the *Shih Chi*. Ssu-ma Ch'ien was sometimes very conservative when deciding what matters to include in his history. He omitted the legends of Chinese antiquity on the grounds that there was not sufficient evidence to establish their validity. For Ssu-ma Ch'ien to append his biography of Ch'ü Yüan to that of the Han scholar Chia I, who died in 168 B.C., seems to indicate some doubt about the historicity, or at least the date, of Ch'ü Yüan. One explanation of the apparent anachronism might be based on the circumstances surrounding Chia I's "Tiao Ch'ü Yüan Wen," "Lament for Ch'ü Yüan," a *fu* which is the earliest datable reference to Ch'ü Yüan in an imitative work of literature.

Chia I's introductory note to the lament says:

> I became tutor of the king of Ch'ang-sha, having been banished in disgrace, and was very disappointed. When I crossed the Hsiang River en route, I made a *fu* to lament Ch'ü Yüan. Ch'ü Yüan was a virtuous minister of Ch'u who was cast out because of slander. He made the *fu* called *Li Sao*, the end of which says: "Enough! There is no true man in the kingdom! Nobody knows my talents!" Then he threw himself into the Mi-lo River and died. I was grieved by the memory of Ch'ü Yüan and wrote this in the same spirit. (*Wen Hsüan*, ch. 60)

Presumably, Ssu-ma Ch'ien attached his biography of Ch'ü Yüan to that of Chia I because the primary association of Ch'ü Yüan at that time was with Chia I's "Lament." Otherwise, we would expect to find Ch'ü Yüan's biography in the proper section: the "Basic Annals (*pen-chi*) of Ch'u."

In any case, all this is speculation. To resolve the question at this late date would be difficult. An attempt would involve, beyond a careful study of Chia I, a comparison of Ssu-ma Ch'ien's treatment of material from the *Li Sao Chuan* of Liu An to that of materials from other quasi-historical sources such as *Mu T'ien Tzu Chuan, Yen Tan Tzu*, and the *Chan Kuo Ts'e*.

Burton Watson, in the passage quoted earlier, followed conventional wisdom when he called the lost *Li Sao Chuan* a "commentary." It is possible that *chuan* should be read to mean "The Story of . . ." as in the *Mu T'ien Tzu Chuan*. I suspect that the *Li Sao Chuan* was a romance, much like the fictional parts of the *Chan Kuo Ts'e*, and not a commentary on the *Li Sao*. If Ch'ü Yüan were a fictional person, or at least a person about whom a fictional romance had been written, it would mean that the early sections of the *Ch'u Tz'u* might have been produced in the early Han era, a supposition that would explain the phonetic similarity between the early part of the *Ch'u Tz'u* and datable Han compositions, especially *fu*.

Ch'ü Yüan became the archetype of the slandered minister. This identification ensured his survival in the literary would, just as it decreed his suicide in the political world of the late Warring States period. The poems allegedly from his brush, from those writers in his train such as Sung Yü, and by later imitators, became a genre known as *tz'u*, the abbreviation of *Ch'u Tz'u*, the title of the anthology: "phrases of Ch'u." The special feature of the *tz'u* genre was that it expressed its political frustrations and presented its message in an artificial diction based on the *Li Sao*, head piece of the eponymous literary collection *Li Sao Ching*: the "*Li Sao* Classic" now better known as the *Ch'u Tz'u*. In using the "phrases of Ch'u," writers placed themselves in the literary wake of Ch'ü Yüan and his heirs. In expressing their frustrations in the form of poetry, however, they were firmly in the ancient didactic tradition of Chinese letters.

Didactic Poetry

The oldest collection of poetry in Chinese is the *Shih Ching*, also called the *Three Hundred Odes*, which contains 305 poems. The traditional account of its compilation is as follows: the Chou kings, during the period from roughly the eleventh to the seventh centuries B.C., sent officials from the Music Bureau to survey the feudal states and to collect the songs then current. When these officials returned to the Chou court, the songs were examined to determine the attitudes of the people toward their government. Confucius is credited with later editing the three thousand or so such songs, or poems. He discarded inferior pieces and duplicates, producing the *Three Hundred Odes*, actually numbering 311 (of which six were subsequently lost). It is of these songs that Confucius said:

> My disciples, why do you not study the Odes? They are useful in drawing parallels, in making observations, in categorizing, in expressing resentment. From them one learns to serve one's parents, and the wider duty of service to one's prince, as well as to recognize the names of many animals and plants. (*Lun Yü* 17:9)

> The Master said, "There are three hundred Odes, but one phrase can cover them all: the authors' thoughts were honest." (*Lun Yü* 2:2)

The *Shih Ching* was among the books banned and burned by the first emperor of the Ch'in. After the Han dynasty replaced the Ch'in at the beginning of the second century B.C., the process of reconstructing the banned texts and reestablishing the interrupted traditions began. Four versions of the *Shih Ching* text, along with commentaries and interpretation, appeared in the early Han. Three were named after the regions where they were established; Lu, Ch'i, and Han (not the Han of the dynastic title). Of them little remains except a short book called *Han Shih Wai Chuan*, or *The Exoteric Tradition of the Han Odes*. This book survived, and has been studied and translated by James R. Hightower. The fourth version of the *Shih Ching* was called the *Mao Shih*, or *Mao Odes*. It took its name from two men, Mao Ch'ang and Mao Heng. Mao Heng's commentary on the *Shih Ching*, written early in the second century B.C., was lost. Mao Ch'ang presented his edition of the *Shih Ching*, said to be based on the interpretation of Mao Heng, to the court around 130 B.C. It became the standard text at that time and has remained so until the present time.

Orthodox Confucian tradition posits a chain of transmission that connects the Mao text back through time to Confucius' disciple Tzu-hsia. The prefaces to the *Mao Shih*, as contained in the text we know today, were allegedly passed down the same chain from antiquity to Mao Ch'ang, who included them in his book. There are a number of accounts of how the explanatory material contained in the prefaces came to be in its present arrangement, but they are not crucial to this argument. The text we know today includes the *Great Preface*, which introduces the collection as a whole and explains the didactic method of the Mao School, and the *Little Prefaces*, which are brief headnotes to the individual odes placing them in the proper didactic category.

The didactic approach of the Mao tradition became the accepted interpretation of the *Shih Ching*, memorized by every candidate for the Imperial Examinations. In any case, later commentators interpreted each poem of the *Shih Ching* within the political context of the history of Chou China as it was known to them from history and legend, as categorized by Mao's commentary. The poems were satirical and critical; they castigated the unworthy and the malfeasor. They also praised paragons and celebrated the proper conduct of government both by princes and by their ministers. This was the didactic tradition in its first full flower.

The clearest statement of this didactic view is in the *Great Preface*. In the *Great Preface* (which is actually rather short, composed of only a few hundred words) poetry is the supreme instrument of a minister, the mirror of government. Because the *Great Preface* is the first clear statement of the way in which literati read poetry, it will be examined in some detail. It begins:

> Poetry is the product of earnest thought [*chih* 志]. Thought (cherished) in the mind becomes earnest; expressed in words, it becomes poetry [*shih* 詩]. The feelings move inwardly, and are embodied in words. When words are insufficient for them, recourse is had to sighs and exclamations. When sighs and exclamations are insufficient for them, recourse is had to the prolonged utterances of song. When those prolonged utterances of song are insufficient for them, unconsciously the hands begin to move and the feet to dance. (Legge 4 : 34)

These earnest expressions are combined with the five musical notes to produce the harmonious symbol of good government: elegies or "songs" [*ko* 歌]:

> The style of such pieces in an age of good order is quiet, going on to be joyful;—the government is then a harmony.

Their style in an age of disorder is resentful, going on to the expression of anger;—the government is then a discord. Their style, when a State is going to ruin, is mournful, with the expression of (retrospective) thought;—the people are then in distress. Therefore correctly to set forth the successes and failures (of government), to move Heaven and Earth, and to excite spiritual Beings to action, there is no readier instrument than poetry. (Legge 4:34)

The function of poetry was often to correct, even to castigate:

Superiors, by the Feng transformed their inferiors, and inferiors, by them, satirized their superiors. The principal thing in them was their style, and reproof was cunningly insinuated. They might be spoken without giving offence, and the hearing of them was sufficient to make men careful of their conduct;—hence they are called *Feng* (or Lessons of manners). . . . The historiographers of the States, understanding the indications of success and failure, pained by the changes in the observance of the relations of society, and lamenting the severity of punishments and of (the general) government, gave expression in mournful song to their feelings, to condemn their superiors;—they were intelligent as to the changes of circumstances, and cherished (the recollection of) the ancient customs. (Legge 4:35−36)

The essential question is: How could a poem that could be sung aloud without giving offense still remonstrate and make those in power careful of their conduct? The answer is that the poems were *feng* 風: allegorical and allusive, employing metaphors and symbols.

The duty of a minister is to enlighten his ruler. When the ruler will not be enlightened, the minister remonstrates. An extremely clever and erudite poem could be spoken without giving offense, yet through its use of allegorical devices, clearly indicate the frustration of the writer and the shortcomings of his superior. To write a poem extolling the beautiful decorations of a throne room, for example, required poetic skill. To do so while cunningly insinuating a condemnation of the extravagance of the royal court required far more skill and produced a poem of more complex beauty.

It is upon this Chinese tradition of interpreting poetry didactically that this study of the *Ch'u Tz'u* will rest.

The Southern Culture Hypothesis

Historians of Chinese literature propose two separate literary cultures in pre-Han China; the Northern, represented by the *Shih Ching* odes, written roughly between 1100 and 600 B.C., and the Southern, originating in the Kingdom of Ch'u. This Southern tradition is represented by the anthology *Ch'u Tz'u*, the contents of which date from between roughly 300 B.C. and A.D. 150. The Confucian orthodox have studied the literature ascribed to both schools, as have modern Sinologists as well, but the *Shih Ching* has been explained far more exhaustively and convincingly than the *Ch'u Tz'u*.

Advocates of the two-culture hypothesis might be better explicators of their own theories, but the essentials may be simply stated. Because the *Ch'u Tz'u* appears to come from Ch'u, which was in the south of the Chinese culture area as it stood at that time, they believe the poems of the *Ch'u Tz'u* must represent a poetic tradition separate from the *Shih Ching* of the Yellow River valley. The language and prosody differ markedly, they say, from that of the *Shih Ching*. The plants and animals mentioned in the poems are representative of what, compared with the flora and fauna of the *Shih Ching*, seems an exotic southern paradise. Some writers have proposed that the poems of the *Ch'u Tz'u* are actually samples of a Ch'u dialect as it might have existed in Ch'ü Yüan's time.

Another view, that which underlies this study, is that the *Shih Ching* and the *Ch'u Tz'u* are from one main stream of Chinese literary evolution. On close examination (e.g., with an impartial computer program) one finds that the language is quite similar. The vocabulary—for example, the botanical names used—is quite homogeneous. The prosody, while showing significant differences, is not so dissimilar as is often maintained. Most telling is the common rhyme system. The *Ch'u Tz'u* and the *Shih Ching* rhyme consistently, both internally and with each other. Hawkes and Karlgren have shown, by studying the incidence of rhyme in those texts and carefully combining words which rhyme with each other into groups, that there is both a remarkable consistency of rhyme within each text, and a substantial overlap: a given pair of words which rhyme in the *Shih Ching* will almost always rhyme in the *Ch'u Tz'u*, and vice versa. This suggests certain problems with the Ch'u dialect hypothesis. This common rhyme may be due to the reestablishment of the respective texts in the early Han, after the catastrophe of the Ch'in emperor's book-burning edict. But if so, why do they share their homogeneous rhyme system with the Ch'u Silk Manuscript, as carefully studied by Noel Barnard? This document, in its considerable rhyming sections, rhymes quite satisfactorily in the *Shih Ching*–based phonetic reconstruction of Karlgren. If the Silk Manuscript, which, safely buried in its tomb at Ch'ang-sha, avoided the Ch'in edicts, shares the rhyme system of the *Shih Ching* and the *Ch'u Tz'u*, we must look elsewhere for evidence of the two cultures.

A common assertion of the two-culture school is that the separate traditions followed separate courses of later evolution: the *Shih Ching* odes prefigured the *shih* regular metrical poetry, while the *tz'u* (also called the *sao*-style after the *Li Sao*) developed into the *fu* 賦, irregular compositions in rhymed and unrhymed lines, generally longer and more complex essays on political themes. This assertion is substantially accurate, but the notion of separateness is misleading. The development from the *Shih Ching* Odes to poetry and *tz'u* to rhapsodic essays was the development of *genres*, not geographically and temporally remote literary cultures.

The gap of several hundred years of missing literary production between the youngest ode and the oldest parts of the *Ch'u Tz'u* may explain more of the differences between the texts than creating two literary cultures where they need not exist does. Do Chaucer and Hardy come from two separate literary cultures? The fact that separate genres developed at different times in the mainstream of Chinese literary culture does nothing to support a two-culture hypothesis. It renders such a hypothesis, at the very least, moot.

My assumption of a common literary tradition in pre-Han China is tested in this study: the reader may judge. In any case, this debate is one of the most interesting and most passionately argued in the field of early Chinese literature and will probably entertain the next generation of Sinologists as much as it does us today.

The Ch'u Tz'u

The best description of the *Ch'u Tz'u*—both the history of the text and its contents—is by David Hawkes, in his General Introduction to *Ch'u Tz'u: The Songs of the South*. For convenience, the main points will be summarized here, but I encourage the interested reader to pursue these topics in more detail.

The preface to the oldest editions of the *Ch'u Tz'u* says the anthology was assembled by Wang I, a librarian at the Han court who lived in the second century A.D. Wang I himself writes that he based his compilation on an earlier collection by Liu Hsiang (77–6 B.C.), a scholar at the court who revised and collated many old books in the Imperial Library, including the *Chan Kuo Ts'e*. He wrote several famous works on government and literature and was also a student of magic. Early in the reign of Emperor Yüan Ti (48–32 B.C.), Liu Hsiang was caught up in some court intrigues. His clashes with two powerful eunuchs, and with the emperor's mother and grandmother, resulted in his expulsion from the government. He was out of favor for fifteen years, until 32 B.C., when Emperor Ch'eng Ti succeeded his father on the throne and Liu Hsiang's enemies lost much of their influence.

Though Wang I's attribution of the compilation of the *Ch'u Tz'u* to Liu Hsiang cannot be proven, the tradition of scholars, victims of intrigue expelled from court, taking up the *Ch'u Tz'u* in their enforced idleness is a persistent one. The Sung polymath Chu Hsi (1130–1200) wrote his commentary to the *Ch'u Tz'u* 1,250 years later after a similar fall from power.

The *Ch'u Tz'u* consists of seventeen sections. The earliest are traditionally said to be the work of Ch'ü Yüan himself. The later sections are ascribed to various Han writers, such as Wang I and Liu Hsiang, as well as to Tung-fang Shuo (b. 160 B.C.), Yen Chi (ca. 150 B.C.), and Wang Pao, who was a contemporary of Liu Hsiang. These later sections are generally derivative in style, imitating the older sections. They represent the genre fully established.

The first and most important section of the *Ch'u Tz'u* is the *Li Sao*. The *Li Sao* is a long narrative poem of 188 couplets. The title means "Encountering Sorrow." Because some Chinese characters have two opposite meanings, which makes reading these old texts doubly challenging, we may also read the title as "Parting from Sorrow." The former is the generally accepted translation.

In the *Li Sao*, Ch'ü Yüan speaks. He sets forth his noble ancestry and then begins an allegorical essay of political self-justification. He describes his talents and his desire to be his king's true advisor. He draws historical parallels with the contemporary political climate of Ch'u. Then he embarks on a symbolic journey to the grave of the legendary sage-king Shun, whose example he urges his king to recall: the sage-king Yao set aside his unworthy son Tan Chu and declared the virtuous Shun his chief minister and heir. Finally, Ch'ü Yüan, unable to enter heaven (i.e., return to court), delivers a final diatribe against his enemies and announces his intention to drown himself.

Much of the political sentiment is expressed through references to birds, animals, and flowers, each with a special significance or quality. The interpretation of these similes and metaphors has occupied commentators from the early Han until the present day. Yet, arguments over fine points of interpretation aside, the *Li Sao* is rightfully considered the greatest poem in pre-Han literature.

The second section of the *Ch'u Tz'u* is the *Chiu Ko*, or Nine Elegies, which will be described in a separate discussion below.

The third section is the *T'ien Wen*, or Heavenly Questions. The text is a series of riddles on mythological themes. Wang I offers the pious legend that the *T'ien Wen* is a collection of captions Ch'ü Yüan wrote to a series of frescoes on the walls of Ch'u temples. As it is the most difficult of the parts of the *Ch'u Tz'u* to read, the text being both cryptic and in some disorder, it has been the least studied. The *T'ien Wen* remains a challenge to some intrepid scholar.

The fourth section is the *Chiu Chang*, or Nine Declarations. Opinions vary as to whether there are nine or ten poems in this section (a problem of enumeration which will reappear). The poems are regarded by literary critics as of uneven quality, but in general representative of the beginning of the genre which imitated the earlier *Li Sao*. Two of the poems are frequently found in anthologies. One is "Ai Ying," a lament for the earlier glories of the Ch'u capital. The other is "Chü Sung," or "In Praise of the Orange Tree."

The remaining thirteen sections describe mystical journeys and lament personal, political, or national tragedies in increasingly formulaic

A Note on Shamans

Students of shamanism and folk religion may certainly find something useful to their researches in the *Ch'u Tz'u*. They should not, however, repeat Arthur Waley's mistake. He assumed, based on his own research and that of others (especially Aoki Masaru) that texts like the Nine Elegies were primary sources for such studies. Waley regarded them as actual liturgical relics of some Ch'u cult:

> I take them to have been a set of rites in honour of the principal deities of the land of Ch'u at a time when the territories already extended far beyond the original home-land in the basins of the Yangtze and Han rivers. There is no reason to suppose that the songs represent a complete libretto of the performances. There may very well have been prose dialogue (improvised or otherwise); for example, the shaman may during the "mantic honeymoon" (this, I ought to point out, is my own descriptive phrase and not a Chinese term) have pleaded with the Spirit on behalf of the people of Ch'u, securing promises of good harvests, immunity from floods and diseases and so on. This part of the programme would have varied according to circumstances and so not have formed a part of the fixed liturgy. There may also have been some "properties." For example, the Western Mountain (K'un-lun) may have been represented by a raised platform of some kind, and Heaven by a pole with notches cut in it to make the Nine Regions of Heaven. (Waley, p. 15)

While I find his descriptions enlightening and convincing, I feel, almost apologetically, that I simply do not believe his fundamental assumption. The amount of accurate information on shamanism one may find in the Nine Elegies must hang on one's faith in the accuracy of the poet who adopted the literary conceit of the shamanist milieu to express his political message. These Elegies occupy a similar position to the *kung-tz'u* genre, the "palace lyrics" of later periods, especially the Sung. These were artificial poems written (mostly by men) in the persona of a concubine or palace woman lamenting her lost love, isolation, un-fulfilled middle age, and the like. One may draw valid conclusions about the life of women in medieval China from them only to the extent that they are true to their predecessors: the few genuine examples of the palace lyric written by women. I fear it is the same with the *Ch'u Tz'u*: the shamans in the *Ch'u Tz'u* are literary devices, and the *Ch'u Tz'u* is only tangentially ethnographic.

Perhaps the best compromise is suggested by Waley: "The Nine Songs owe their preservation to the fact that like other early Chinese songs they were interpreted allegorically. The shaman becomes a virtuous minister who after having for a time enjoyed the favour of his prince is discarded by him" (p. 16). Though I disagree about which came first, the minister or the shaman, the basic point is true. Waley continues: "It was in this allegorical sense that the Nine Songs were understood till well into the twentieth century, although it was recognised as early as the second century A.D. onwards that the moral interpretation was only a sort of ultimate meaning, and that taken in their literal sense they were *wu* (shaman) songs" (p. 16).

The analysis of Waley and others provides us valuable insights into the Chinese culture and religions of the pre-Han period. The value of Waley's study is not diminished by the error of its false premise; the reputation and popularity of his book endure.

METHOD

The literati of ancient China were immensely learned. They knew their Histories intimately and their Classics by heart. One of the skills essential to an official career was to have a thousand books at the tip of one's writing brush. It is in this context that much traditional commentary writing and textual interpretation proceeded.

Meanings could be clarified or amplified by reference to something not mentioned: what we call "allusion." The problem we encounter today is that, while these allusions were transparent to the intended audience, they are obscure to us today. Nor is this handicap limited to Western readers or eliminated by a thorough knowledge of Chinese, as two modern scholars attest.

Noel Barnard describes the pitfalls that hinder the scientific study and translation of archaic written material:

> Except in the case of those of us who have actively engaged
> in the translation of ancient Chinese text into English (or into

other European languages) it is not, perhaps, generally appreciated that we have essentially to work directly from the original text. It is not simply a matter of translating from a modern character rendering of an archaic text as published by Kuo Mo-jo, Ch'en Meng-chia, etc. Nor may a translation be effectively accomplished by taking a step further and following the convenient "translations" made by Japanese scholars replete with *kaerigana* and *kunten*. In both cases Chinese and Japanese scholars tend to pay minimal attention to many "commonplace" characters which nonetheless are often difficult to understand in certain contexts, while seemingly straightforward text which is found on due examination to be filled with ambiguity, or to be practically incomprehensible, is left alone rather too often. Upon first reading of such passages in either Chinese or Japanese transcriptions one may gain the impression that the meaning has been fairly well understood by the transcriber. But only when it comes to the task of rendering the passages into an alien language does one begin to realize that the impression of comprehension earlier gained is not so certain as it might have first appeared. Many dormant and disregarded difficulties in interpretation make themselves painfully obvious only when the degree of precision in understanding as required by the translator is sought. (Barnard, pp. 55–56)

Friedrich Bischoff extends this caution from the exotica of fragments of archaic documents to the more familiar world of well-known literary works, the interpretation of the *fu*: "[The] method of approaching the *fu* genre through native literary criticism may be ideally desirable, but it is impracticable. The alternative method, a pragmatic and probative approach to the *fu*, although it was classical of the native commentators, has long been equally impracticable. No modern scholar, neither Han nor Hu, possesses a knowledge of the characters even faintly comparable, in extent and in depth, to that of the literati of old. In fact, our knowledge is so poor we cannot even use the *P'ei Wen Yün Fu* in routine fashion" (p. viii). Bischoff goes on to describe what he calls "the Sinologist's paradox":

It can be summarized in the following fashion. We are

perfectly aware of the astonishing amount of lexicographic
and literary knowledge that the Chinese erudites possessed.
We know they learned their Classics by heart and enjoyed
quoting from them appositely even more than Westerners a
few generations ago were fond of quoting from the Bible and
the works of Classical Roman writers. Complaints about the
lack of original thought induced by this mania for constant
quoting are well known and, apparently, justified. At the
same time, when it comes to comprehending the works of
the Chinese erudites, their grand style, the *ku-wen*, is all too
frequently treated as though it were nothing but condensed
vernacular (pai-hua), and modern pai-hua at that. Unfortunately, many scholars of Chinese Literature have never
raised, even in passing, the following question, let alone
treated it seriously: Why, if a dictionary of the Mathews
type was really sufficient, was there a need to compile the
P'ei Wen Yün Fu? (Bischoff, p. ix)

In adopting Bischoff's "pragmatic and probative approach," I have
attempted to deal with the inherent obscurity of these poems in several
ways.

Assumptions

First, I take for granted that a written character, or graph, may have
more than one correct meaning, depending upon the reader's assumptions about the context. Graphs may represent a word with more than
one meaning, they may be borrowed for other words of similar pronunciation, and they may stand for similar graphs from which they
differ only in detail: different radical, alternate form.

To help order the chaos that could result from a free application of
these assumptions, I limit myself to some conventions. One is that
borrowings and loanword hypotheses should be based on Karlgren's
Grammata Serica Recensa (GSR) as amplified by his copious notes to the
various Classics, and the phonetic loan rules set out in his series of
articles "Loan Characters in Pre-Han Texts."

Karlgren's transcriptions are taken in their algebraic sense, meaning
that his transcriptions represent a conventional set of symbols by which

one may come to some conclusions about rhyme, assonance, and phonetic loans. I do not consider them necessarily phonologically exact reproductions of the pronunciation current in the period for which the reconstruction is offered. I have also arbitrarily simplified Karlgren's transcription, in the interest of simplicity and economy. For those readers who follow my suggestion and read this book with GSR open, the GSR serial numbers are given for all important words.

Karlgren's method of verifying loans, assonances, rhymes, and equivalences was extremely conservative. He relied primarily on the rhymes of the *Shih Ching* and other pre-Han texts. Without at least one datable authority for an equivalence or borrowing, he would not admit it to his list. Neither will I. To Karlgren's conservatism I add a supplementary caveat: unless a borrowed meaning relates the phrase in question to a political or ceremonial antecedent of demonstrable applicability, I will not gratuitously adopt it merely to press a point.

I also checked the reconstructions of Tung Tung-ho and Chou Fa-kao, conveniently compiled in Chou's *A Pronouncing Dictionary of Chinese Characters*. Although there are notational differences among the three systems and certain phonetic disagreements, especially between Karlgren and Chou, for the most part they are internally consistent. In the few cases where a significant variance exists, I offer the competing reconstructions for the reader's judgment.

It is often contended, as described earlier, that the *Ch'u Tz'u* was written in a southern "Ch'u" dialect. If so, Karlgren's data on Archaic Chinese derived from the *Shih Ching* rhymes would be of little use in analyzing the *Ch'u Tz'u*. Yet, as copiously attested by both Karlgren (in the sound system of GSR) and David Hawkes (in "The Problem of Date and Authorship"), the *Ch'u Tz'u* and the *Shih Ching* rhymed with remarkable consistency. From this fact of a common rhyme system I strengthen my assumption that the reader interpreted the *Ch'u Tz'u* with the same ear as he read his *Shih Ching*, as a readily intelligible document from the mainstream of Chinese literary tradition.

My second major assumption is that much of the transitory currency of ancient political writing, especially satire, is irretrievably lost. As with aural elements and puns, references to contemporary events and quotations from contemporary persons well known to the writer and his circle of readers are impossible to decipher today unless they rest on some Classical foundation. In this effort we must rely on the commentaries, and on our own wide reading. An example of this type from our own time would be the phrase, "Let me make one thing perfectly clear." This phrase was a trademark of Richard Nixon, and may not elicit the same political associations for a reader two thousand years in the future that it does for us now (or did fifteen years ago!). For evidence of this ephemeral element of contemporary events, in the case of the *Ch'u Tz'u* we know practically nothing beyond the skeleton history already mentioned.

The third and most important assumption required for dealing with the obscurity of the text concerns the Chinese custom of making reference to the official Classics. Since the vocabulary of Classical Chinese was very limited and the style of writing very terse, writers often clarified and amplified their meanings by using phrases taken from earlier writings likely to be known to the reader. This both showed the writer's (and reader's) erudition, and was a highly respected means of expressing one's inner feelings. This has been a major characteristic of Chinese discourse since earliest times.

A relatively clear example of this is found in the first elegy, "The Magnificent One of the East, Grand Monarch," line 4. The ministrant prepares the ceremonial objects for the arrival of the Spirit. Among them are various precious stones that clash together to make a musical sound. The words and context are similar to a passage in the Book of Rites (*Li Chi*) in which the precious stones of the Prime Minister's official girdle clash together as he enters the royal presence to make a remonstrance. With similar words in similar order, the reader who was reading for political content and who knew his *Li Chi* (and who didn't?) would surely have thought of one passage upon reading the other.

A literary passage can thus carry its own meaning, yet point as well to another, the context of which may even modify the reader's perception of the words before him.

Materials

For the verification of these allusions, the study relies upon several standard sources: first, the *commentaries*.

My examination of the commentaries is limited to those written before the end of the Sung dynasty in 1280. Later Ming and Ch'ing dynasty commentaries add little to what the earlier commentaries tell us about the *Ch'u Tz'u* and are more useful as sources of information on the Ming and Ch'ing eras themselves than to the interpretation of the present study. (The same is decidedly true of most twentieth-century Chinese analyses of these poems: Ch'ü Yüan has become a modern culture hero, improbably in the same breath with the first emperor of the Ch'in, who destroyed Ch'ü Yüan's beloved Ch'u.) Four commentaries on these poems produced before 1280 survive; it is these four which are translated in full here.

(1) Wang I, the compiler of the *Ch'u Tz'u*, also annotated the poems of the collection and included a section of his own poems at the end. His commentary is terse, often giving only one-word synonyms, yet sometimes explaining the self-evident in painful detail. He occasionally relates the political context as he sees fit, but his notes mainly explain the religious element. This is to be expected when his audience was much more likely to recognize a parallel passage in the Classics than to be familiar with the images Ch'ü Yüan drew from the aboriginal religion of Ch'u. Later commentators rely heavily upon him, either assenting or dissenting in places, but never contesting the essential nature of the poems as he sets it forth.

David Hawkes, expressing the modern view, is less charitable: "The frequent imbecilities of his commentary tend to make one forget that, because of his familiarity with the dialect and traditions of Ch'u, he often provides us with the only key to what would otherwise be insoluble difficulties" (p. 170).

(2) The T'ang dynasty *Wen Hsüan* commentaries of the "Five Ministers" (Lü Hsiang, Lü Yen-chi, Liu Liang, Chang Hsien, and Li Chou-han) date from the eighth century. They add little to Wang I in their notes to the six of the Nine Elegies that are included in the *Wen Hsüan*, which means "literary selections," a massive collection of literary works in all important genres that had been compiled at the beginning of the sixth century A.D. The contribution of the Five Ministers is twofold. They often show the pronunciation of unfamiliar words or words with two or more equally possible readings by inserting a homonym in smaller writing after the word in question. Following the phonetic pointers, one or another of the five, under his own name, explains or simplifies Wang I's note, adds something original, or appends a summary judgment.

Significantly, the great T'ang scholar Li Shan chose not to write notes of his own to the *Ch'u Tz'u* sections included in the *Wen Hsüan* (among them the *Li Sao*). In his court-sponsored edition of the *Wen Hsüan*, which he annotated and published in the middle of the seventh century, he reproduced Wang I's commentary complete. This I interpret as an endorsement of Wang I by Li Shan, well respected for his own commentary, and as evidence that Wang I was regarded as authoritative by the literary establishment of the early T'ang. Perhaps if Li Shan had waited to publish his notes to the *Wen Hsüan* he might have written his own notes to the Elegies since his own experience was similar to Ch'ü Yüan's; he too was caught up in a court intrigue, slandered, and banished a few years later.

(3) Hung Hsing-tsu (1090–1155) wrote his *Ch'u Tz'u Pu Chu* to be, as the title suggests, "a supplementary annotation of the *Ch'u Tz'u*." The notes supplement Wang I. Hung often gives phonetic spellings (*fan-ch'ieh*) for ambiguous or obscure words: two characters, one providing the initial sound and the other the tone and final sound, indicate the exact pronunciation. He also amplifies Wang I's subjective comments, gives numerous Classical parallels, and discusses openly the political equivalences the reader must make: Spirit = king, sorceress = minister, and the like. Sometimes he disagrees with Wang I, and in such cases is careful to explain the basis for his disagreement in full. He is also especially fond of identifying river and place names in ample (or superabundant) detail.

(4) The *Ch'u Tz'u Chi Chu*, "Collected Annotations to the *Ch'u Tz'u*," is a late work by the Sung polymath Chu Hsi (1130–1200). His habit of making a commentary into a platform for expounding his own philosophy is less pronounced in these notes. The "collected" aspect of the commentary is not obvious, unless he means to say that his commentary is a distillation (though certainly not a collation) of the many commentaries listed in his introduction. In any case, the notes are meant to be his own offering, though frequently they are based on Wang I, the Five Ministers, and Hung Hsing-tsu. His introduction criticizes these commentaries for their inaccuracies or narrowness of vision, yet he incorporates their notes into his own. This tendency is most obvious when the four commentaries are laid out side by side, as in the translations that

make up a part of this study. His comments refer equally to the political and religious contexts. Typically, he deals with the political interpretation in summary form at the beginning or the end of a poem, leaving the religious interpretation to be scattered piecemeal among the various lines.

His commentary dates from his last years. It is interesting that late in his life, after he had himself fallen from grace in 1196 during one of the most spectacular purges in Chinese history, Chi Hsi turned to the *Ch'u Tz'u* and wrote a commentary on the poems of Ch'ü Yüan. But given the ancient connection between political frustration and didactic literature, especially the *Ch'u Tz'u*, is it any surprise?

Various reference works serve as secondary sources for the verification of the allusive nature of this text. The dictionary *Chung Wen Ta Tz'u Tien* (abbreviated CW), which was based on the monumental *Dai Kan-wa Jiten* of Morohashi Tetsuji (abbreviated DK), gives numerous early citations for every word and phrase. Although it relies heavily upon commentaries to the Classics and other literature for its definitions (leading to frustrating circularity in some cases), it is a valuable compendium of quotations and extremely useful in leading the reader to similar passages and to alternate usages in other texts. The encyclopedia of Chinese quotations *nulli secundus* is the *P'ei Wen Yün Fu*, which was published in 1711. It contains practically every phrase from every important Chinese writing (and some not so important) from antiquity up to the date of the compilation, including the Thirteen Official Classics, the entire *Wen Hsüan* and much of the various official dynastic histories, and collections of famous poems and essays. Though it has no match for tracing allusions, the difficulty lies in the mechanics of its use. The phrases are arranged by the rhyme of the last word of the phrase, according to the traditional scheme of rhymes based on the rhyming dictionaries *Kuang Yün* (601 A.D.) and *Chi Yün* (eleventh century A.D.). In the *P'ei Wen Yün Fu*, the entries are classified under 106 separate rhymes. There is an index volume attached to modern editions (though the text itself is usually a reduced photocopy of the so-called Palace edition of 1720). Even with the aid of an index, the 4,785 pages and sometimes microscopic printing are a serious barrier to its use. For passages known to be in the *Wen Hsüan*, a shortcut is the index by Shiba Rokuro, *Mongen Sakuin*. For other texts, the indexes and concordances published by the Harvard-Yenching University, by the Centre d'Études Sinologiques de Pékin, by the École Française d'Éxtrême-Orient, and others are indispensable.

The use of these aids to allusion-hunting can also provide access to the interpretations of later writers by leading one to passages in later imitative or allusive contexts for which the text we are reading is the antecedent. These later imitators can be an important barometer of the accuracy of an assumption about the text. Later writers were still familiar with the Classics, more familiar than we with the usual interpretation of the passage, and frequently produced an imitation less subtle than the model. Analysis of such later allusions can be quite valuable in expanding our understanding of the way a text was read in earlier times.

Format

Though I have analyzed the three Elegies word by word, the basic unit of text is the couplet, and the text is so divided here. For each unit, including the titles, the arrangement of the entries is as follows:

First, the Chinese text of the couplet is presented in the regular script, according to the standard edition of the *Ch'u Tz'u Pu Chu*. Below each character is given its pronunciation in Archaic Chinese (ARC), Ancient Chinese (ANC), and Modern Standard Chinese (MSC). The ARC and ANC pronunciations are from Karlgren's GSR. The MSC pronunciation is from CW. Beneath the MSC pronunciation is the series number from GSR for the convenience of the reader in checking references and phonetic assumptions, as well as in restoring the diacritical marks omitted here. Words that Karlgren does not include I have reconstructed using Karlgren's rules, or I have substituted the reconstruction of Chou Fa-kao. These words are followed by a question mark.

Beneath the pronunciations is a terse English synonym of the basic meaning of the Chinese word. These are based on Karlgren's analysis and the Han dictionary *Shuo Wen* (ca. 100 A.D.).

Below the text and pronunciations for each couplet are two translations. The first, marked "Meta," is a metaphrase, a "word-for-word translation, in contradistinction to a paraphrase" (OED VI : 385ab). The metaphrase emphasizes the religious context that serves as the vehicle for the political interpretation. The second translation, marked "Para," is a paraphrase, "an expression in other words, usually fuller and clearer, of the sense of any passage or text" (OED VII : 266b). The paraphrase amplifies and clarifies the line in the context of the political interpretation as derived from the commentaries and the supplementary analysis.

In addition to the metaphrase and paraphrase, there are occasional "brocades." A brocade is an extra meaning of some word or phrase, beyond the two basic levels of metaphrase and paraphrase, which enhances the interpretation or provides an unexpected insight into the author's counterpoint. The term was coined in Professor Bischoff's seminars on the *fu*. We borrowed it from the *Hsi Ching Tsa Chi* (Nienhauser, p. 72):

> Ssu-ma Hsiang-ju's friend Sheng Lan was a renowned scholar from Ts'ang-k'o. He inquired about writing *fu*. Hsiang-ju told him: "Combine silk ribbons and braid them to form the pattern; arrange the brocade and embroidery to make the material; a warp, a woof, a *kung*, a *shang* [a musical metaphor which might best be rendered in Western idiom by reference to counterpoint] this is the way of the *fu*. The heart of a *fu* writer embraces the universe, his glance perceives all persons and all things. This can be attained within oneself, but cannot be transmitted to others." Thereupon Lan wrote a "Combining Braids Song" and a "Fu on Arranging Brocades" and withdrew. For the rest of his life he never again presumed to speak of the spirit of *fu* composition. (Bischoff, pp. 11–12)

Following the metaphrase and paraphrase, the four commentaries are translated in full, with page references from the editions indicated in the bibliography.

The main part of each entry is the section headed "Notes," which is essentially my own commentary on the text and the earlier commentaries. The notes, representing the results of the study, discuss the text and commentaries, draw Classical and linguistic parallels, offer explanations of points in dispute, compare modern translations of the poems, and in general relate the political associations likely to have been suggested to a classically trained reader. They place the poems within the context of the didactic tradition of Chinese letters and within the bureaucratic milieu common to generations of Chinese writers.

Nine Elegies

Title

	九	歌
ARC	kiug	ka
ANC	kiəu	ka
MSC	chiu	ko
GSR	992	l
	nine	song

META: Nine Elegies

PARA: My Earnest Thoughts About This Political Nadir

The Commentaries

WANG I: The Nine Elegies were made by Ch'ü Yüan. Formerly, in the district of Ying 郢, in the south of Ch'u, between the Yüan 沅 and Hsiang 湘 rivers, it was the custom of the people to believe in ghosts and to offer sacrifices to them.

> Hung Hsing-tsu: The *Han Shu* says: "In Ch'u, the people believe in sorceresses and prize lewd sacrifices." The *Sui Shu* says: "In Ching-chou 荆州 they especially prize sacrifices." Ch'ü Yüan's creation of the Nine Elegies probably originated from this.

Their sacrifices required singing, music, drums, and dancing in order to please the spirits.

> Hung Hsing-tsu: One version omits the word "singing."

Ch'ü Yüan had been banished and was hiding, a fugitive in the border region. He was sorrowful and in a poisonous mood, sad in thoughts and in a turmoil of anxiety. He went out to see the local rituals and hear the music of their dances. The lyrics were rude and rustic. Based on them, he created the various sections of the Nine Elegies.

> Hung Hsing-tsu: Wang I's note to the title of the Nine Arguments says: "Nine is the Yang number, the fundamental principle of the Tao." The Five Ministers say: "Nine

is the ultimate Yang number. Because he refers to evil circumstances which have reached their most extreme point,
Ch'ü Yüan chose Nine as the title of these elegies." Note that
there are eleven of the Nine Elegies and nine of the Nine
Arguments, both using Nine in their titles. The meaning of
the titles is explained by reference to Shun's music and its
nine parts. The *Li Sao* says: "We played the Nine Elegies and
danced the Nine Shao Dances, oh! I wanted to snatch some
time for pleasure and amusement." The meaning is the same
here. From Sung Yü's Arguments on down, all originate in
this way.

On the surface they manifest the reverence with which the Spirits were
served. Beneath the surface can be seen Ch'ü Yüan's rancor. He uses the
Elegies to criticize and remonstrate. For this reason, the words and their
significance are not the same; the sections and lines are in disorder.
There are wide differences of opinion about the matter.

Hung Hsing-tsu: One version says: "Thus the words and
their significance are jumbled and confused." [2/1b6–2a5]

FIVE MINISTERS: Hsien says: Formerly, in the district of Ying, in the south of Ch'u,
between the Rivers Yüan and Hsiang, it was the custom of the people to
believe in ghosts and offer sacrifices to them. They drummed and
danced in order to please all the Spirits. Yüan had suffered banishment.
He was harboring bad feelings, grief, and rage. He saw the rituals of
sacrifice of the local people and heard the music of their songs and
dances. Based on them he created the sections of the Nine Elegies. The
surface words are songs of service to the Spirit. The concealed message
uses his feelings about having experienced a degrading expulsion to
remonstrate. Nine is the ultimate Yang number. Because he refers to evil
circumstances which have reached their most extreme point, he chose
Nine as the title of his elegies. Wang I's preface says: "The Nine Elegies
were created by Ch'ü Yüan. Formerly, in the district of Ying, in the south
of Ch'u, it was the custom of the people to believe in ghosts and offer
sacrifices to them. Their sacrifices required music, drumming, and
dancing. Based on them, he created the sections of the Nine Elegies and
used them to criticize and remonstrate." [32/15a1–3]

CHU HSI: The Nine Elegies were created by Ch'ü Yüan. Formerly, in the district of Ying, in the south of Ch'u, between the Rivers Yüan and Hsiang, it was the custom of the people to believe in ghosts and offer sacrifices to them. Their sacrifices required male and female sorcerers to make music, sing, and dance in order to give pleasure to the Spirits. The vulgar phrases of the barbarous people of Ching-chou 蠻荆 were crude, and in their intermediacy between Yin and Yang, man and ghost, they were unable to avoid the confusion of profanity and licentiousness. Ch'ü Yüan had been banished. Because he saw their sacrifices and was moved, he emended their words somewhat. He cast out their excesses and used the idea of serving the Spirits to express this sentiment: "I am loyal to my prince, and I love my country; my devotion to them will never diminish." For this reason, even if their words are not without some suspicious enmity beneath their harmonious intimacy, the Elegies may yet provide something for the gentleman.

> Chu Hsi's note to his own preface: In this chapter all the sections use the idea of one's service to a Spirit which does not answer and yet one does not lose one's reverence and love for it, to represent the idea of one's service to a king who is not in agreement and yet one does not lose one's loyalty to him. Furthermore, it is sufficient to see the significance of this earnest sentiment. The old explanations lost this; now, I have completely set things right again. [2/1a3–11]

Notes

We begin with the commentaries and notes to the title of the Nine Elegies. An author, by the proper choice of a title, influences the reader's perception and experience of what is to follow. The reaction of the classically trained reader to the words *chiu ko* called forth highly significant political associations and provided the framework of metaphysics, legend, history, and reference within which the reader would interpret what came after.

Chiu 九 (CW 173) is "nine." Modern readers ought immediately to be intrigued by the apparent miscounting of the elegies. There are eleven.

One popular answer is that the first nine are the Nine Elegies and the last two, "The Spirits of the Fallen" and "The Ritual Finale," are later additions. Another, advanced by Hawkes, is that "The Princess of the Hsiang" and "The Lady of the Hsiang" are alternate versions of the same elegy. "The Greater Arbiter of Fate" and "The Lesser Arbiter of Fate" are also considered such a pair. Counting each pair as one elegy yields a total of nine Nine Elegies.

More intriguing than the ingenuity of these schemes is the silence of the commentaries. That there are eleven elegies is obvious to anyone able to count, yet no early editor felt the need to alter the title to Eleven Elegies. That Wang I fails to mention the discrepancy in his introduction does not indicate that he was obtuse. Presumably, he felt the significance to be obvious. The significance of the poems, as the commentators assert, often differs from the literal sense of the words, and the same is true of the title.

The Five Ministers (writing five hundred years later), who are less coy about these matters, clarify the apparent discrepancy by stating that the number nine is used in its numerological rather than its numerical sense: the ultimate Yang must counteract the pervasive Yin.

In fact, Wang I himself is the originator of this explanation in his note to the title of the Nine Arguments, or *Chiu Pien*, another set of poems from the *Ch'u Tz'u*:

> The Nine Arguments are by the Great Officer of Ch'u, Sung Yü. *Pien* 辯 is 變, "to change." It refers to elucidating the Tao and its Te in order to persuade the king to change.
>
> Nine is the Yang number, the fundamental principle of the Tao. Thus: Heaven has the Nine Stars to regulate the North Star. Earth has the Nine Regions in order to establish the Ten Thousand States. Men have the Nine Openings to permit the passage of energy and intelligence.
>
> Ch'ü Yüan was sorrowful because, in spite of his loyal and faithful service, he had suffered from slander and treachery. He was sorely wounded at the ignorance and benightedness of his king, and that his country was on the point of extinction. Thus, he adduced the number of Heaven and Earth to make plain the critical point in human circumstance, making

the Nine Elegies and Nine Declarations in order to remonstrate with King Huai and to indicate that he should pay
attention to these words and conduct himself in accordance
with the laws of Heaven and Earth. (*Ch'u Tz'u Pu Chu*
8/1a4—1b4)

In a consideration of these notions about the number nine, two
concepts are important: qualitative numbers and polarity.

Numerology plays a far greater role in Chinese culture than in the
societies of the West. More than conventional signs to enumerate objects, the Chinese numbers have personalities and attributes. This concept is dealt with extensively by Marcel Granet in his *Pensée Chinoise*. He
explains:

> Un symbole numérique commande à tout un lot de réalitiés
> et d'emblèmes; mais, à ce même lot, peuvent être attachés
> divers nombres, que l'on considere, *en l'espèce*, comme *équi-
> valents*. A côté d'une valeur quantitive qui les distingue, mais
> qu'on tend à négliger, les Nombres possèdent une valeur
> symbolique beaucoup plus intéressante, car, n'offrant
> aucune résistance au génie opératoire, elle les laisse se
> prêter à une sorte d'alchimie. Les Nombres sont suscep-
> tibles de *mutations*. Ils le sont en raison de l'efficience
> multiple dont ils paraissent dotés et qui dérive de leur
> fonction principale; ils servent et valent en tant que *Rubri-
> ques emblématiques*. (p. 151)

These numbers with qualitative value are bound up inextricably with
the notion of polarity. Yin and Yang are the negative and positive aspects
of existence. They alternate in a perpetual cycle of increase and decrease.
Numbers are either Yin or Yang; in the *I Ching*, the oldest literary source
of this polar numerology, even numbers are Yin, odd Yang. Three and
nine are the most male, the most complete; two and eight are the most
Yin. The commentators make direct reference to this idea when they say
"Nine is the Yang number."

The poet's description of his country's political situation is also
evident in the light of these concepts of polar alternation and qualitative
numbers.

The function of the king, in exercising his power, is Yang; in listening to the advice of his ministers, in Yin. The function of ministers, conversely, is Yin when carrying out their king's orders, Yang when advising him on matters of state. The essential balance is royal power = Yang, ministerial duty = Yin. When these interdependent powers are in harmony, the state is well governed. The king exhibits the proper balance of Yang (disposing) and Yin (being advised); the ministers likewise Yin (obeying) and Yang (advising).

When a king is weak, or when a minister corrupts his king and begins to exercise royal power through his control of the king, the mechanism is thrown out of balance. Legitimate power is Yang, illegitimate power is Yin. When the government is unbalanced and Yin increases through the exercise of illegitimate power, negative influences pervade the cosmos: windstorms (emblematic of the slanderer), floods, plagues.

Hoping that matters have reached their lowest ebb, that the illegitimate exercise of royal power shall increase no further, Ch'ü Yüan names his elegies "Nine," signifying thereby and claiming for them the creative, positive, and beneficial power of Yang (in the form of his advice). His almost incantatory use of Nine is to serve as a talisman and as a qualitative symbol. His elegies contain the power to reduce Yin and increase Yang to their proper balance in the royal character. His advice, if followed, will restore the king to the rightful exercise of his royal influence and return Ch'u to a position of safety and good government.

The graph 九 may also be used to mean "to reunite," as in *Lun Yü* 14:17.2 "The Master said: 'The Duke Huan assembled 九合 all the princes together, and not with weapons of war, or chariots: it was through the influence of Kuan Chung.'" In this sense it is often glossed 九, 鳩也. *Chiu* 鳩 (CW 47620) is read **kiog* [九 = **kiug*] and is the name of a bird (GSR 992). It was loaned for a homophone **kiog*, which means "to accumulate." This word was also written 勼, 逑, or 𢢀; an example of the flexibility of the Chinese writing system in the early period.

Furthermore, Nine is the number of the king:

> La salle ou le Chef reçoit et mange forme une estrade surlevée
> de 3 pieds, s'il est un simple Officier; de 5 pieds s'il est grand
> Officier; de 7 pieds s'il est seigneur; de 9 s'il est le roi. Quand
> le roi meurt, on doit, pour lui fermer la bouche, se servir de 9
> cauris; on le pleure sans arrêt 9 jours; on continue à pleurer

pendant 9 mois; on trépigne par séries de 9 bonds; il faut,
enfin, après l'enterrement définitif, répéter 9 fois les off-
randes.... Les Sages peuvent donc réprésenter a l'aide de
Nombres l'ordre protocolaire qui régit la vie universelle.
(Granet, *Pensée chinoise*, p. 296f)

The source of this hierarchical numerology is mainly the *Li Chi*, which
is probably no earlier a work than our poems. If one is to follow the
accepted way of protocol, one must present nine elegies to the king, if
one is to present any at all. Nine is the most auspicious, the royal
number. That there are actually eleven is of no importance: Nine is the
proper number of things royal regardless of their sum.

In conclusion, it is clear that Nine has little to do with the number of
the Songs, but much to do with their significance. Numerology and
polarity dictate this significance and it is in accord with the basic theme
of the poems as uniformly expressed by the commentators.

Ko 歌 (CW 16517) means "song," or "to sing." In the specific context
of the *Ch'u Tz'u*, I have translated it "elegy." In the Classics, references
to ritual songs almost always describe them as *ko*. In the *Shu Ching* (the
Classic *Book of History*) *ko* is defined in terms which recall the *Great
Preface*: " Poetry [*shih*] is the expression of earnest thought; singing [*ko*]
is the prolonged utterance of that expression" (Legge 3:48).

As has been mentioned, the function of poetry in ancient China was
didactic and political. When the word *ko* appears, for example, in the
odes of the *Shih Ching*, the context is usually one of political comment.
Among the *Shih Ching* odes are *ko* that castigate kings (# 141, 252, 257),
and that decry slander and injustice (# 109, 139, 199, 204). It is the same
in the *Lun Yü* (e.g., 18:5), *Mencius* (e.g., 6B:6.5), and in this example
from the *Shu Ching*, "The Songs of the Five Sons": "The emperor's five
brothers had attended their mother in following him, and were waiting
for him on the north of the Lo; and, when they heard of Yi's movement,
all full of dissatisfaction, they related the cautions of the great Yü in the
form of songs" (Legge 3:157).

The *Ch'u Tz'u*, like the Six Dynasties anthology *Wen Hsüan* to follow,
was preserved and learned for the same reason that the *Shih Ching* had
been studied before: it was a guide to expressing political frustration, an
encyclopedia of the didactic style. Ch'ü Yüan became the archetype of
the loyal minister slandered and fallen from grace. He wrote poems, the

legend goes, to express his "earnest thoughts" about the political situation, and these eleven Nine Elegies are among the poems he wrote. To read them as political statements is to do them no injustice. It is to read them in the context of an ancient Chinese literary tradition, as they had been read for centuries. On this point, all the commentaries are in agreement.

It is profitable to note that the title "Nine Elegies" is older than our text. Its association with the proper regulation of government is as old as the *Shu Ching*. In the "Ta Yü Mu," or "Counsels of the Great Yü," Shun cedes his throne to Yü after Yü counsels him on good government:

> Oh! Think of these things, O emperor. Virtue is seen in the goodness of the government, and the government is tested by its nourishing of the people. There are water, fire, metal, wood, earth, and grain,—these must be duly regulated; there are the rectification of the people's virtue, the conveniences of life, and the securing abundant means of sustentation,—these must be harmoniously attended to. When the nine services thus indicated have been orderly accomplished, let that accomplishment be celebrated by songs. Caution the people with gentle words; correct them with the majesty of law; stimulate them with the songs on those nine subjects [九歌],—in order that your success may never suffer diminution. (Legge 3:55–56)

The Nine Elegies correspond to the nine functions of the government, as explained in the *Tso Chuan*, Duke Wen year 7:

> You are our chief minister, the director of all the princes; and if you do not make it your object to manifest such virtue, what will be the consequence? It is said in one of the books of Hsia, "Caution them with the majesty of law; stimulate them with the nine songs:—in order that your success may never suffer diminution." There are the virtues seen in the nine services, all of which may be sung; and they are called the nine songs. There are the six magazines and the three businesses, which are called the nine services. ... The accomplishment of them with righteousness shows the possession of propriety. The want of this propriety, leading to

dissatisfaction, is what produces revolt. If the virtue of you, Sir, cannot be sung, who will be attracted by you? (Legge 5 : 249b–250b)

For a disgruntled minister to name a set of songs Nine Elegies would suggest to every reader that his aim was ironic: to sing the virtues of a ruler who possessed none. The inconsistency of the number served only to accent the irony.

In summary, the prefaces relate unanimously (the latter three relying heavily on Wang I) the essential history of the *Ch'u Tz'u*, as given in the *Shih Chi*: Ch'ü Yüan was slandered and banished to the southern region of Ch'u, where he observed the local rituals and adapted their hymns to his political purpose 因爲作九歌之典. They are ritual hymns on the surface 上陳事神之敬 and express his personal feelings beneath the surface 下見己之寃. He uses them to criticize his ruler 託之以風諫.

The verbatim incorporation of Wang I's commentary by the *Wen Hsüan* editors and the extensive borrowing from it by Chu Hsi, along with the relatively sparse "correction" by Hung Hsing-tsu, all suggest forcefully that Wang I's explanation was generally accepted. This is one key to understanding the place of the Nine Elegies in Chinese literature. It ought also to counsel against the modern fashion of discarding many of Wang I's substantive comments out of hand, as such writers as Hawkes and Waley have done.

Moreover, the prefaces state the traditional view of the Nine Elegies: that they were the work of the paragon, Ch'ü Yüan, who was a loyal minister of King Huai of Ch'u. He was slandered by a rival before his king, and was banished. He wrote poems to express his grief and anger in the didactic tradition of Chinese letters. In order that these poems "might be spoken without giving offense," he modeled them on hymns from the aboriginal religion of southern Ch'u; in order that "the hearing of them might be sufficient to make men careful of their conduct," he expressed his reproof, "cunningly insinuated," beneath the surface of his elegies. In doing so, he placed himself squarely in the tradition of the *Shih Ching* odes, and in turn was the precursor of the *fu*, the genre which carried the principles of the *Great Preface* to their full flowering.

Tung Huang T'ai I

Metaphrastic Translation

THE MAGNIFICENT ONE OF THE EAST, GRAND MONARCH

(Preparations for the ceremony of summoning the Spirit)

1. Auspicious the day, the date propitious.
2. Reverently we are about to please the High Magnificent One.

3. I grasp the long sword with its jade hilt-ring.
4. The *ch'iu*-jewel clashes, the *lin*-jewel and the *lang*.

5. The mats are of *yao*-jewel with jade weights.
6. Why not now take up the gem-like fragrant branch?

7. The *hui*-wrapped sacrificial victim is presented on a *lan* mat.
8. The libations of cassia wine and peppery beer are set out.

9. Raise the drumsticks, strike the drum.
10. Distanced and slow the beat, quiet the song.

11. The ranks of reed organs and zithers play loudly.

12. The sorceress dances lofty and arrogant, beautifully ornamented.
13. The scent wafts fragrantly and fills the hall.

14. The Five Notes are in abundance, confusedly mixed.
15. The Lord is taking his pleasure, happy and content.

Paraphrastic Translation

(The chief minister prepares for his crucial audience with the king.)

1. I have chosen an auspicious day, a propitious date;
2. Respectfully, I am about to be in accord with my superior.

3. Grasping the ceremonial sword with its jade hilt-ring,
4. With the stones in my official girdle clashing, I enter the court.

5. I set out the jeweled mats, the jade insignia;
6. I have taken up the fragrant jeweled token of office.

7. The *hui*-wrapped ritual viands are brought in on a *lan* mat.
8. I set out the cassia wine and peppery beer.

9. I command that the drumsticks be raised, the drums be struck,
10. That the music be slow and dignified, the singing soft.

11. Suddenly, the ranks of reed organs and zithers play loudly.

12. The king enters arrogantly in his unceremonious manner.
13. His disorderly influence pervades the audience chamber.

14. The music is reduced to confusion, a disorderly melee,
15. But the king is greatly pleased with himself, content and oblivious.

Title

東	皇	太	一
ARC			
tung	g'wang	t'ad	iet

ARC	tung	g'wang	t'ad	iet
ANC	tung	γwang	t'ai	iet
MSC	tung	huang	t'ai	i
GSR	1175	708	317	394
	east	august, sovereign	great	one

META: The Magnificent One of the East, Grand Monarch

PARA: The Magnificent One of the East, Grand Monarch

The Commentaries

WANG I: no note.

FIVE MINISTERS: Hsiang says: T'ai-i is the name of a star. It is the most revered Spirit of Heaven. In the east of Ch'u it is the object of sacrifices as the companion of the Emperor of the East. Ch'i says: The themes of the sections are all Spirits of Ch'u, so they are appended after the body of each section after the custom of the *Mao Shih*. [32/15a6]

HUNG HSING-TSU: The *Han Shu* "Treatise on State Worship and Sacrifice" says: "The most highly honored Spirit in Heaven is the T'ai-i. His subordinates are called the Five Emperors 五帝. In ancient times, the Son of Heaven sacrificed to the T'ai-i at the southeastern altar." The "Treatise on Astronomy" says: "The brightest of the far stars of the polar region is where the T'ai-i dwells." *Huai Nan Tzu* says: "The constellation Great Subtlety 太微 is the T'ai-i's court. The constellation Imperial Palace 紫宮 is his dwelling. It is said that the T'ai-i is the most highly esteemed Spirit of Heaven, the Jewel of the Dipper." A note to the "*Fu* on the Great Manifestations of Astronomy" 天文大象賦 says: "The Magnificent One of Heaven, Great Emperor 天皇大帝, is a star within the constellation Imperial Palace, located in the mouth of the Angular Arranger 鉤陳. His spirit is called Illustrious Soul Treasure 曜魄寶 and holds the Spirit Plan of the Ten Thousand Affairs of State. He is lord over all the *Ling* 靈. His star is hidden and invisible. If he is seen in divination, there will be a calamity." It is also said that the T'ai-i is a star to the north of, and minister to, the Emperor of Heaven. He is in charge of the Sixteen Dragons, and of wind and rain, flood and drought, sword and shield, famine and starvation, pestilence and disease. If in divination he is unclear or in retrograde motion, there will be a disaster. [2/3b5–9]

CHU HSI: T'ai-i is the name of a Spirit, the most revered Spirit of Heaven. In the east of Ch'u it is sacrificed to as the companion of the Emperor of the East: hence, it is called Magnificent One of the East. The *Han Shu* says: "The most highly honored Spirit in Heaven is the T'ai-i. His subordinates are called the Five Emperors. The brightest of the far stars of the polar region is where the T'ai-i dwells." *Huai Nan Tzu* says: "The constellation Great Subtlety is the T'ai-i's court. The constellation Imperial Palace is his dwelling." This section describes the extreme sincerity and utmost decorum with which the Spirit is served in the hope that it will be happy and at peace, thus insuring his manifestation through the celebrant. In the same way, the minister is loyal to the utmost and conscientiously puts forth his effort to serve his prince without thought of self. This may be said to be the metaphor of the whole section. [2/2a5–7]

Notes

Tung 東 (CW 14827) "east" is the quarter of the sunrise. It designates the season of Spring, the element wood. It is the place of honor in a house or palace; thus, it designates the host. In combinations, it often retains this courtly sense: *tung-kung* 東宮 (Cd. 446b), rather than the immediate "eastern hall," means the heir-apparent or empress-regent. This is presumably due to their residence in the place of honor, the eastern quarter of the palace. Also compare *Ode* #57 (Legge 4:95).

As the quarter of the first light, east may suggest (as does *tung-huang* 東皇 "eastern brilliance") the dawn, as in *Ode* #96 (Legge 4:151), where the equation of sun and moon with king and minister prefigures a common theme of the Nine Elegies:

> The cock has crowed;
> The court is full.
> But it was not the cock that was crowing;—
> It was the sound of the blue flies.
>
> The east is bright;
> The court is crowded.
> But it was not the east that was bright;—
> It was the light of the moon coming forth.

Blue flies are emblems of the "small man" 小人 or rascal, signifying a situation in which good and evil are confused. The theme of confusion between the king and the slanderer who bested Ch'ü Yüan and controls the court is a persistent theme. Read in the tradition of the *Mao Shih*, the ode says: the rascals are making noises like men of virtue, the bad minister is beginning to influence the court. This image recurs in the Nine Elegies repeatedly.

Huang 皇 (CW 23220) means "august, magnificent." It is often prefixed to terms to add to them the connotation "imperial."

One traditional view is that the T'ai-i 太一 (CW 5963.1) is another name of the Great Emperor, August of Heaven 天皇大帝, our Polaris:

> Le nom chinois de cette étoile est significatif car, tandis que toutes les autres étoiles ont un mouvement, l'étoile polaire paraît sans mouvement, et être le point fixe autour duquel tous les autres astérismes tournent, et auxquels il semble imprimer le mouvement. Elle était donc comme le Souverain du Ciel et on lui en donne conséquemment le nom. Or, comme un Souverain terrestre est toujours accompagné de sa cour qui l'entoure et l'environne, de même les Chinois ont donné aux étoiles qui environnent l'étoile polaire, le Souverain des Cieux, des noms de ministres et de membres de la famille impériale. (Schlegel, pp. 1/523–24)

These surrounding stars, reflecting the microcosm of the court, are enclosed by the large circular constellation (Purple =) Imperial Palace 紫宮. Among them are the Angular Arranger 鉤陳, the Five Emperors 五帝, and the Dipper 北斗.

The usual interpretation of the role of the T'ai-i is that rather than being the Emperor of Heaven, he is the chief minister and companion of the Emperor of Heaven. Just as the ministrant in the primitive ceremony serves the Spirit, and the minister serves his earthly king, so the T'ai-i serves the Emperor of Heaven.

The description of the stellar macrocosm clearly reflects the court: the ministers go about their duties within a rigid system of protocol, the stars revolve around the fixed Polaris in a no less determined order. To generations of bureaucratic literati and their sympathizers, the star map represented the order of their official lives in clear equivalents. Both good and bad had their respective stars. Every human role, mirrored in the stellar arena, could be described discreetly in stellar terms.

Thus the poem presents the scene at court. By parallels to the ritual of spirit-possession, where the sorceress summons the soul of the dead, the poet describes the royal court. His song, like those of the sorceress, is an attempt to summon the spirit, the attention of his king.

1

	吉	日	兮	辰	良
ARC	kiet	niet	g'ieg	diən	liang
ANC	kiet	nziet	γiei	zien	liang
MSC	chi	jih	hsi	ch'en	liang
GSR	393	404	1241	455	735
	auspicious	day		time	good

2

	穆	將	愉	兮	上	皇
ARC	miok	tsiang	diu	g'ieg	diang	g'wang
ANC	miuk	tsiang	iu	γiei	ziang	γwang
MSC	mu	chiang	yü	hsi	shang	huang
GSR	1035	727	125	1241	726	708
	respectful	about to	to please		superior	magnificent

META: Auspicious the day, the date propitious.
Reverently we are about to please the High Magnificent One.

PARA: I have chosen an auspicious day, a propitious date;
Respectfully, I am about to be in accord with my superior.

The Commentaries

WANG I: *Jih* refers to *chia-i* 甲乙. *Ch'en* refers to *yin-mao* 寅卯. *Mu* means "reverent." *Yü* means "to please." *Shang-huang* refers to the Magnificent One of the East, Grand Monarch. One is about to prepare to sacrifice and worship, therefore one must select an auspicious day and purify oneself with great reverence in order to entertain the Spirits of Heaven. [2/2a7–9]

FIVE MINISTERS: [included under notes to the title, above].

HUNG HSING-TSU: Shen K'uo 沈括, who was called Ts'un-chung 存中, says: "When in literature the natural word order is reversed, the language becomes even more strong and active. For example: Tu Fu says 'Red bean seeds, in excess, parrots peck,/Green *wu-t'ung* branches, with old age, phoenix nests' 紅豆啄餘鸚鵡粒, 碧梧棲老鳳凰枝; and Han Yü says 'Spring, ah!, monkey sing, oh!;/Autumn crane, ah!, fly' 春與猿吟兮秋鶴與飛." *Yü* sounds like 俞 [*diu/iu*]. [2/2a7−9]

CHU HSI: *Jih* refers to *chia-i*. *Ch'en* refers to *yin-mao*. Shen K'uo, who was called Ts'un-chung, says of the first line: "When in literature the natural word order is reversed, the language becomes even more strong and active. For example: Tu Fu says 'Red bean seeds, in excess, parrots peck, / Green *wu-t'ung* branches, with old age, phoenix nests.'" *Yü* sounds like 俞. *Mu* means "reverent." *Yü* means "to please." *Shang-huang* refers to the Magnificent One of the East, Grand Monarch. [2/1b2−3]

Notes

Chi 吉 (CW 3349) and *liang* 良 (CW 31289) are synonyms in the astrological context: auspicious.

Jih 日 (CW 14048) means "day." *Ch'en* 辰 (CW 39548) may be "day," "hour of the day," or merely "time." Dictionaries (e.g., CW 39548.13) obligingly give us the equivalent 辰良 = 良辰 = 吉日. An alternate reading at CW 3349.25 gives for *liang-ch'en* 良辰 the synonym 良時.

Chia 甲 (CW 22221) and *i* 乙 (CW 165) are the first two of the Ten Celestial Stems. *Chia* represents the East, is Yang, and denotes the first day of the ten-day week. *I* represents East also, is Yang, and denotes the second day of the ten-day week. Wang I may use them *pars pro toto* to indicate the whole set of Celestial Stems, but the inappropriate analogy of the unfamiliar compound *yin-mao* 寅卯 to designate the Twelve Earthly Branches (where by parallelism we would expect the equally unfamiliar *tzu-ch'ou* 子丑) suggests an alternate interpretation is necessary.

Chia and *i* appear as a compound term (CW 22221.1). Both are Yang and represent East, the quarter of the Grand Monarch. They are Yang, reinforcing the Yang power of the poems: the minister seeking to make Yang his theme must above all choose a Yang-imbued day and hour for his presentation. Moreover, in the "Monthly Ordinances" of the *Li Chi*, they are associated with the first month of spring, the season of pardons and mercy: "In the first month of spring, the sun is in Shih 室, the star culminating at dusk being Ts'an 參, and that culminating at dawn being Wei 尾. Its days are *chia* and *i*" (*Li Chi* 1 : 249).

Yin and *mao*, as we have seen, do not appear as a compound term. They are the third and fourth of the Twelve Earthly Branches. *Yin* 寅 (CW 7353) was the name of the first month of the Hsia calendar, *mao* 卯 (CW 2895) was the second. Both, as did *chia* and *i*, signify the east, and are Yang. They also designate the hours between three and seven in the morning, when the morning audience was held at court.

To determine astrologically the auspiciousness of a day requires references to both Stem and Branch. This strongly suggests synonymic parallelism both in the text and in Wang I's note. This would expand the terse line: "The day is auspicious with regard to both Stem and Branch." The most satisfying solution is to recognize the polytropic possibilities of Chinese and state that there is reference to an auspicious date in both its signs as well as the season, the hour, and the theme of the minister's remonstrance.

Hung's reference to Shen K'uo (quoting the *Meng Chi Pi T'an* 夢溪筆談 , ch. 14, item 246) analyzes the chiasma in line 1. We would expect the more conventional 吉日兮良辰 (CW 3349.25), the form to which the modern reader automatically emends the given line to make it intelligible in Modern Standard Chinese: "an auspicious day, a propitious time." This is merely altering the text to eliminate its difficulty.

Wang I expands *mu* 穆 (CW 25832) into the four-word phrase 齋戒恭敬 "to purify oneself with great reverence." This concept, in fact these very words, are prominent in the following explanation of the gentleman's purification from the *Li Chi*, "Chi T'ung":

> When the time came for offering a sacrifice, the man wisely gave himself to the work of purification. That purification meant the production of uniformity (in all the thoughts);— it was the giving uniformity to all that was not uniform, till a uniform direction of the thoughts was realized. Hence a superior man, unless for a great occasion, and unless he were animated by a great reverence, did not attempt this purification. When he was about to attempt it, he guarded against all things of an evil nature, and suppressed all his desires. . . . He allowed no reckless movement of his hands or feet, but kept them firmly in the way of propriety. Thus the superior

man, in his purification, devotes himself to carrying to its utmost extent his refined and intelligent virtue. (*Li Chi* 2 : 239–40)

Ch'ü Yüan surely meets these standards, and the reader, aided by Wang I's note, with its overlapping terminology, would certainly have realized the grave political situation in which a gentleman would make these preparations.

Yü 愉 (CW 11194) may be read, in addition to **diu* (= to please), as **t'u* (= to be negligent). Wang I's note and the reassuringly unnecessary phonetic gloss of Hung, point the reader safely away from (= at?) this disrespectful reading. The notes may be our first encounter with the habit of the commentators of glossing the obvious to provide an alibi for the slanderous. The alternate reading **t'u* is a brocade: the king neglects his duties, contrary to the Tao.

In the political interpretation, the poem opens with the statement that the minister must be careful to choose the proper time to give counsel to his king. Astrology was no less important in the court than in the temple, and in court, careers and necks were hanging in the balance. The Chief Minister (Ch'ü Yüan) is preparing for his audience. This is the theme of the whole poem, when read in the didactic/political mode. He chooses an auspicious time in the first two lines; the balance of his detailed preparations is suggested by the remainder of the poem.

The word *hsi* 兮 (CW 1479) is a particle used in poetic composition. In the *Shih Ching* odes, it occurs medially and finally, emphasizing the preceding words. A good example is in *Ode* #55 (Legge 4 : 91):

> 瑟兮僩兮赫兮咺兮
> 有匪君子終不可諼兮
> How grave is he and dignified!
> How commanding and distinguished!
> Our elegant and accomplished prince,
> Never can he be forgotten!

The *Shuo Wen* dictionary says: "*Hsi* is that which prolongs the utterance." The *Wen Hsin Tiao Lung* adds, "The ancient poets used *hsi* as an integral part of a sentence; but in the *Ch'u Tz'u* it is used as an extra word. *Hsi*, in a sentence, assists the words by prolonging their sound" (WHTL, p. 267). It seems to be so in the *Ch'u Tz'u*, where it occurs both medially and finally, as in the *Shih Ching* odes. As it is here an empty word, of prosodical function rather than semantic content, we will not discuss it further; our attention is mainly directed toward the political/allegorical use of words, a use to which *hsi* is not put.

Hsi deserves a study of its own. One particularly challenging question is why a word said to be so characteristic of the Ch'u style does not occur anywhere in the poetic parts of the presumably genuine Ch'u Silk Manuscript (cf. Barnard, *The Ch'u Silk Manuscript*, especially pp. 211–35).

I assume, therefore, that *hsi* marks the caesura in the poetic line. Karlgren claims insufficient authorities to propose its ARC pronunciation, but T'ang and Sung rhyme books suggest the formula ARC **g'ieg*(?) / ANC *γiei* (GSR 1241). Tung Tung-ho proposes ARC **γieg*; Chou Fa-kao gives **geγ*.

3

	撫	長	劍	兮	玉	珥
ARC	p'iwo	d'iang	kliam	g'ieg	ngiuk	niəg
ANC	p'iu	d'iang	kiem	γiei	ngiwok	nzi
MSC	fu	ch'ang	chien	hsi	yü	erh
GSR	103	721	613	1241	1216	981
	to grasp	long	sword		jade	hiltguard

4

	璆	鏘	鳴	兮	琳	琅
ARC	g'liog	ts'iang	mieng	g'ieg	gliəm	lang
ANC	g'ieu	ts'iang	miweng	γiei	liəm	lang
MSC	ch'iu	ch'iang	ming	hsi	lin	lang
GSR	1069	727	827	1241	655	735
	a gem	tinkle	sound		a gem	a gem

META: I grasp the long sword with its jade hilt-ring.
The *ch'iu*-jewel clashes, the *lin*-jewel and the *lang*.

PARA: Grasping the ceremonial sword with its jade hilt-ring,
With the stones in my official girdle clashing, I enter the court.

The Commentaries

WANG I: *Fu* means "to grasp." *Yü-erh* refers to the sword's hilt-ring. The sword is
that with which one subdues evil, awes the rebellious, and protects the
virtuous. This is why he grasps it. *Ch'iu*, *lin*, and *lang* are all names of
precious stones. The *Erh Ya* says: ". . . among them are *ch'iu*, *lin*, *lang*,
and *kan* 玕. They clash and sound as pendant jewels." The *Shih Ching*
says: "The gems of her girdle pendant tinkle." This says that there is a
prescribed way of sacrificing to the Spirits. The sorceress who is to be
the agent of the Soul usually grasps a fine sword in order to ward off evil,
hangs numerous pendants from her waist, and dances in a circle. The

motion causes the five precious stones to sound like *ch'iang-ch'iang* 鏘鏘 and be harmonious and orderly. Another text has, incorrectly: 糾鏘鳴兮琳琅. Here *lin* and *lang* would be used for their sound, the sword and pendants clashing in confusion. The *Shih Wen* 釋文 text has 鎗 for 鏘. [2/2b1–5]

FIVE MINISTERS: {shows the pronunciation of 珥 with 餌 [*niəg/nzi]}

Han says: *Erh* is the sword's hilt-ring. *Ch'iu*, *lin*, and *lang* are all names of precious stones. Pendants are made from them which sound like *ch'iang*. [22/15b1–2]

HUNG HSING-TSU: *Fu* means "to follow," the hand follows the hilt of the sword. The *Po Ya* says: "The *erh* of a sword is called *t'an* 鐔." The *t'an* is the nose of the sword, or some say its mouth or ring. The *t'an* is what hangs from a sword, hence the name. *Erh* sounds like 餌. *T'an* either like 覃 [*d'əm/d'am], or like 淫 [*diəm/iəm]. *Ch'iu* is pronounced 渠幽 [*g'iog/g'ieu]. *Ch'iang* is pronounced 七羊 [*ts'iang/ts'iang]. The *Li Chi* says: "Anciently, men of rank did not fail to wear their girdle-pendants with their precious stones." When they entered, they gathered them together; when they departed, they spread them out. Thus, the stones sounded *ch'iang*. *Lin* sounds like 林 [*gliəm/liəm]. *Lang* sounds like 郎 [*lang/lang], and is usually written 瑯. The *Erh Ya* says: "On Kunlun, in the northwest, the beautiful jewels are the *ch'iu*, *lin*, *lang*, *kan*. *Ch'iu* and *lin* are the names of beautiful precious stones; *lang* and *kan* are shaped like pearls." The *Pen Ts'ao Kang Mu* says: "The *lang* and *kan* are beautiful precious stones; they have a bright lustre like the color of a pearl." This describes how they carried a sword and wore pendants of precious stones in order to sacrifice to and serve the Spirits. [2/2b1–5]

CHU HSI: *Erh* sounds like 餌. *Fu* is "to follow." *Erh* is the hilt-ring of a sword. *Ch'iu* is pronounced 渠幽. *Ch'iang* is pronounced 七羊. *Ch'iu* and *ch'iang* are the sounds of the precious stones. The *Kung Tzu Shih Chia* 孔子世家 says: "The precious stones of the girdle-pendants sound like *ch'iu*." The *Yü Ts'ao* 玉藻 says: "Anciently, men of rank did not fail to wear their girdle-pendants with their precious stones." When they entered, they gathered them together; when they departed, they spread them out. Thus, the stones sounded *ch'iang*. *Lin* and *lang* are the names of the beautiful precious stones and refer to the pendant stones. This describes how the one who manages the sacrifice purifies himself with great reverence for ten days, carries a sword, and wears pendants of precious stones in order to perform a ritual for the Spirit. [2/1b2–4]

Notes

The modern translators cannot agree on which of the words in line 4 are onomatopoeic:

Pfizmaier: Hell tönen mit der Edelstein Klang der Lin und Lang.

Harlez: L'agate, le lapis-lazuli pendant à ma ceinture, rendent un son argentin.

Biallas: The tinkling of the stones goes ding-dong.

Giles: Let our jade ornaments tinkle and clang.

Waley: My girdle pendants tinkle with a *ch'iu-ch'ang*.

Hawkes: And our girdle pendants clash and chime.

On the other hand, the commentators are practically unanimous.

Ch'iu 璆 (CW 21688) is a precious stone. The *Shuo Wen* indicates 美玉也. The *Erh Ya* agrees. In the *Shu Ching* (Legge 3 : 121) we learn that "musical gemstones" are a product of Liang-chou 梁州. Han and later texts cited in CW generally agree. The onomatopoeic use of *ch'iu* appears no earlier than the *Shih Chi*, and is limited to the descriptive *ch'iu-jan* 璆然 "like a *ch'iu*-jewel." But this is not an independent meaning; it is merely a descriptive use of the name of the jewel.

Ch'iang 鏘 (CW 41734) is the musical ringing of stone instruments. It is found in the compound *keng-ch'iang* 鏗鏘 "the sound of music" (literally: the sound of metal and stone instruments). Wang I's phrase *ch'iang-ch'iang-jan* 鏘鏘然, echoing the *Shih Chi* usage, indicates the onomatopoeic use.

According to the *Shuo Wen*, *lin* 琳 (CW 21531) and *lang* 琅 (CW 21462) are precious stones, blue-green and red respectively. The *Erh Ya* identifies *ch'iu*, *lin*, and *lang* as musical gemstones.

Wang I refers to a textual variant with an alternate interpretation: *lin-lang* is an onomatopoeic binome, not the names of two different stones.

The alliterative effect prized by modern readers, which influences their acceptance of this interpretation, is far less precise in ARC than today: ARC **gliəm-lang*, MSC *lin-lang*. This variant may be correct, but no other text until the *Wen Hsüan* uses the words in this way. It is plain that *lin* and *lang* are gemstones on a girdle-pendant. The musical effect of the words themselves is a concomitant but secondary phenomenon.

According to the political interpretation, our attention should be focused on the minister preparing for his audience. In the first two lines of the poem, he chooses an auspicious time; here, he carefully dons his insignia of office, the jeweled girdle *p'ei* 佩. Beyond this basic description, there are references to themes that reappear throughout the poem.

There is mentioned an interesting variant 糾 for 璆. *Chiu* 糾 (**kiog/ kieu*) means "in confusion," which, if it is admitted to this line, would be a striking indication of the poet's view of the court scene. Ceremonial music must be harmonious, not confused. The theme of inappropriateness is important: if the court music is disorderly, the king is unfit to rule. If his court is in disorder, his kingdom is in disorder. In this line, the variant *chiu* is rejected, but the presence of this variant in the commentaries signaled to the reader a return to this theme in the following lines.

The significance of the sounding stones goes beyond even the repeated suggestion of ceremonial pendants and their association with the court. The *Li Chi* explains: "The sounding-stones give out a tinkling sound, as a summons to the exercise of discrimination. That discrimination may lead to the encountering of death. When the ruler hears the sounding-stone, he thinks of his officers who die in defense of his frontiers. . . . When a superior man thus hears his musical instruments, he does not hear only the sounds which they emit. There are associated ideas which accompany these" (*Li Chi* 2: 120–21).

To the reader familiar with his Classics, the secondary associations would be ministers advising their king on military affairs at the frontier, and loyal officers who die for their king. These ideas are all likely to be in the mind of the minister as well, as he goes through the necesssary preparations before his royal audience, with all the risk it entails.

The picture of the court ceremonial is rich: girdle gems clashing, music; yet it hints at a court in confusion, a confusion which the poet seeks to dispel. Decorum is the essence of the court and its ceremony, yet the king's minister prepares to enter a court in disorder.

5

	瑤	席	兮	玉	瑱
ARC	diog	dziak	g'ieg	ngiuk	tien
ANC	iäu	ziäk	γiei	ngiwok	tien
MSC	yao	hsi	hsi	yü	chen
GSR	1144	797	1241	1216	375
	a gem	mat		jade	weight

6

	盍	將	把	兮	瓊	芳
ARC	g'ap	tsiang	pa	g'ieg	g'iweng	p'iwang
ANC	γap	tsiang	pa	γiei	g'iwäng	p'iwang
MSC	ho	chiang	pa	hsi	ch'iung	fang
GSR	642	727	39	1241	167	740
	why not?	about to	grasp		precious	fragrant

META: The mats are of *yao*-jewel with jade weights.
Why not now take up the gem-like fragrant branch?

PARA: I set out the jeweled mats, the jade insignia;
I have taken up the fragrant jeweled token of office.

The Commentaries

WANG I: *Yao* is a stone which is inferior to jade. The *Ode* says: "And I returned for it a beautiful *yao*-gem." For 瑱 one text has 鎮. *Ho* means "Why not?" *Pa* means "to grasp." *Ch'iung* is a jeweled branch. It says there are made adornments and purifications. Mats are made of *yao*-jewels, weights of beautiful jades. What will the sorceress grasp? Answer: she grasps a beautiful jeweled branch because it is fragrant. [2/2b6–8]

FIVE MINISTERS: Ch'i says: Why shouldn't the sorceress grasp the jeweled branch? It is of excellent fragrance and purity. [32/15b1–3]

HUNG HSING-TSU: *Yao* sounds like 遙 [*diog*/*iau*]. *Chen* means "to press down," and sounds like 鎮 [*tien/tien*]. Below, the text says: "White jade, to make the weights" ["Hsiang Fu Jen," line 27], and this is the same. In the *Chou Li* the *yü-chen* 玉鎮 was a utensil of great value so it was written with the jade radical. Tseng Ssu-nung 鄭司農 says: "瑱 should be 鎮." *Ho* sounds like 合 [*g'əp/ɣap*]. [2/2b6–8]

CHU HSI: *Yao* sounds like 遙. *Chen* sounds like 鎮. One text has 鎮, and one text gives the pronunciation 他甸 [*t'ien/t'ien*]. These are all wrong. *Yao* is a beautiful precious stone. *Chen* is the same as 鎮 and is that with which the mat of the one who stands for the Spirit is held down. *Yao* sounds like 遙. *Ho* means "Why not?" *Pa* means "to grasp." *Ch'iung-fang* is a plant branch which is as precious as a jewel. The sorceress holds it as she dances. [2/1b6–7]

Notes

Yao 瑤 (CW 21646) is a precious stone mentioned first in the *Shu Ching*, "Tribute of Yü": "Yang-chou's articles of tribute were gold, silver and copper, *yao-* and *kun*-stones" (Legge 3 : 110–11). The line from the *Shih Ching* cited by Wang I is from this stanza of *Ode* #64:

> There was presented to me a peach,
> And I returned for it a beautiful *yao*-gem;
> Not as a return for it,
> But that our friendship might be lasting.
>
> (Legge 4 : 108)

That the mats prepared for the ceremony by the minister are of *yao* is not accidental; they are the emblem of his hope for restored good relations between his king and himself.

Chen 瑱 (CW 21638), usually read *t'ien*, is a jade ear-pendant. Here, as often, it is borrowed for *tien* (CW 41662), a weight stone. From the context we infer the secondary reading with its meaning: a jade weight. Hung discreetly points us to the political context, quoting the *Chou Li*, whose complete description follows: "Le chef du magasin céleste est chargé de la conservation et de la surveillance dans les salles de l'Ancêtre, ainsi que des règlements et prescriptions qui la concernent. Il

conserve tous *les insignes en jade* et les objects de grande valeur apparten-
ant à l'Etat" (Biot, *Tcheou Li*, 1 : 480–81).

Cheng Hsüan 鄭玄 (A.D. 127–200) explains in his note: (from Biot)
"ceci désigne les belles tablettes de jade." If *yü-chen* are the national
treasures entrusted to the Chief of the Heavenly Storehouse, then the
reader would presumably know it. This may be why the commentators
are so quick to correct the normal assumption and say "No, not the jade
tokens; he means the precious weights."

Ho 盍 (CW 23501) is a cover. It is almost universally borrowed for a
homophone meaning "Why?" or, as here, "Why not?" It is written
variously 盇, 盍, 嗑, 蓋, 盇, and 闔. Written 盍, it is attested in *Lun Yü*
5 : 25; 12 : 9; and in other locations in the standard Classics.

Ch'iung-fang 瓊芳 (CW 21827.25) is "the fragrance of the *ch'iung*-
branch." All of our jewels appear in a lost passage from *Chuang Tzu*
(quoted at CW 21822.19): "Mt. Chi-shih is a thousand *li* distant; the Ho
springs from its foothills; phoenix dwell on its peak. Its tree is called
ch'iung-chih 瓊枝, it rises eight hundred feet and bears *ch'iu, lin, lang*,
and *kan*-jewels as its fruit." In medieval times *ch'iung-chih* became a
polite term of address for descendants of the Imperial House.

Ch'iung, when used alone, is best rendered (after its usual usage) as
"beautiful" when describing jewels. From his note, it is clear that Wang
I takes *ch'iung-fang* to be a tree branch, though whether it is natural or an
item of jewelry is unclear.

Just as the sorceress summoning a spirit must brandish the jeweled
branch, the minister preparing for his royal audience, attempting to
capture the attention of the king, must take up the insignia of his office
and make acceptable offerings to represent symbolically the value of his
advice, his purity, and excellent virtue.

7

	蕙	肴	蒸	兮	蘭	藉
ARC	g'iwəd	g'og	tiəng	g'ieg	glan	dz'iag
ANC	γiwei	γau	tsiəng	γiei	lan	dz'ia
MSC	hui	yao	cheng	hsi	lan	chieh
GSR	533	1167	896	1241	185	798
	a plant	viands	kindling twigs *loan*: to present		a plant	mat

8

	奠	桂	酒	兮	椒	漿
ARC	d'ien	kiweg	tsiog	g'ieg	tsiog	tsiang
ANC	d'ien	kiwei	tsiəu	γiei	tsieu	tsiang
MSC	tien	kuei	chiu	hsi	chiao	chiang
GSR	363	879	1096	1241	1031	727
	to present offerings	cassia	wine		pepper	beverage

META: The *hui*-wrapped sacrificial victim is presented on a *lan* mat.
The libations of cassia wine and peppery beer are set out.

PARA: The *hui*-wrapped ritual viands are brought in on a *lan* mat.
I set out the cassia wine and peppery beer.

The Commentaries

WANG I: *Hui-yao* is meat presented on *hui*-plants. *Chieh* is the mat upon which the food is presented. The *I Ching* says: "For a mat, use the white *mao* 茅 grass." For 蒸 one text has 烝, one text has 蒸. *Kuei-chiu* is wine with pieces of cassia cut and put into it. *Chiao-chiang* is beer with pepper in it. It means one offers service with abundant respectfulness, then presents meat wrapped in *hui* and mats woven of fragrant *lan*, brings near cassia

wine and pepper beer in order that the five flavors should be in
harmony. [2/2b8–9]

FIVE MINISTERS: Liang says: The meat is presented with *hui*, the mats for the
feast are of *lan*. Cassia is put into the wine, pepper into the beer. All are
chosen for their fragrance. *Yao* is "meat." *Hui* and *lan* are fragrant
plants. *Tien* is "to lay out for sacrifice." Cassia and pepper are both trees
with a pleasing fragrance. [32/15b6–7]

HUNG HSING-TSU: *Yao* means "the body of the sacrificial victim." *Cheng* means "to
present." It is the same as 烝 and 烝. The *Kuo Yü* says: "When a
multitude of ministers is invited to the emperor's feast, there are delicacies presented 蒸." The note says: "The disjointed ritual victim is
elevated on a platter." *Chieh* means "the straw mat upon which the
sacrifice is presented," and is pronounced 慈夜 [*dz'iag/dz'ia*]. According to the *Shuo Wen*, *tien* means "to lay out for a sacrifice." The Han
Temple Hymn says: "Set out the cassia wine, ladle out the peppery
beer." Of the four things to drink cited in the *Chou Li*, the third was
called *chiang* 漿 . [2/2b8–3a1]

CHU HSI: For *cheng*, one text has 烝, one text has 烝. *Chieh* is pronounced 慈夜.
Yao is the body of the sacrificial victim. *Cheng* means "to present." The
Kuo Yü says: "At the feast there are delicacies presented." It is the same
word. This says that they offer sacrificial meat wrapped in *hui* and also
make a mat of *lan*. *Tien* means "to lay out for a sacrifice." Cassia wine is
made by cutting pieces of cassia and putting it into the wine. Beer is one
of the four drinks mentioned in the *Chou Li*. In the same way, this has
pepper soaked in it. These four plants are all chosen for their fragrance to
be an acceptable offering to the Spirit. [2/1b7–8]

Notes

Hui 蕙 (CW 32677) is a fragrant perennial plant, sometimes erro-
neously translated as "orchid." *Hui* is often used as an abbreviated name
of *hui-lan* 蕙蘭, which is another plant altogether. This usage is well
established in later sources, but would be extremely awkward here, as
lan occurs independently in the same line. The *hui* cannot be identified
to our satisfaction; at least as it was known to the Han reader. The graph
is used in the names of so many plants now, complicated by the eager-
ness of modern Chinese botanists to accommodate Western authorities

by incorporating their errors into orthodox Chinese taxonomic vocabularies, that one is at a loss to say what the *hui* is or is not in this line. Neither do traditional sources help: the descriptions of the *hui* are so varied as to make guessing a more hazardous proposition than usual.

Yao 肴 (CW 29991) usually refers in a general way to cooked meat with bones. In the *Ch'u Tz'u* the commentators unanimously make it a ceremonial item: the disjointed sacrificial victim presented during a ritual.

Modern botanists identify *lan* 蘭 with *Eupatorium*, the thoroughwort (CMH, p. 167), also called boneset. In the West as well as in China, the leaves are used for medicinal purposes. Among other uses is the fabrication of a hair pomade, said by the Chinese to be beneficial to the scalp.

The graph 蘭 appears, either along or in combination, in the names of many plants. Often our only clues are the commentators' expanded glosses, e.g.: 蘭者, 木蘭也. For an example of the confusion surrounding *lan*, I present a list of plants, culled from CMH, the names of which contain the graph 蘭: *Agbia odorata, Bletia hyacinthina, Forsythia suspensa, Chloranthus inconspicuus, Crinum sinensis, Eupatorium* spp., *Aster* spp., *Iris tectorum, Magnolia yulan, Metaplexis stauntonii, Oecoeoclades falcada, Pogonia ophioglossoides,* and *Reineckia carnea.*

Cheng 烝 (CW 32346), over which many translators have tripped, belongs to an intertwined group of graphs which are all pronounced approximately **tiəng*: [GSR 896]

丞	to lift up
承	to lift up, present, assist
丞	to assist
丞	to assist
烝	to steam, present, elevate
拯	to lift, assist, present
脀	to present sacrificial meat
蒸	kindling twigs
騰	to ascend
丞	to lift
偁	to lift
稱	to lift
乘	to rise
升	to rise
抍	to lift

These graphs are an excellent example of how a simple word can be written many ways, and of the imprecise state of the writing system in early times. All these words are pronounced similarly enough to be essentially interchangeable. Their meanings are basically "to lift up" with the various extensions: to help up, to help, to present. Most of the words belong to the same family (GSR 896) 丞. The Chou graph shows the origin of the family: two hands helping up a kneeling man. The horizontal line under 丞 in some of the graphs is a simplified 凵 representing a pit—two hands helping a kneeling man out of a pit.

We have seen that the specific word as written in our text means kindling-twigs. This cannot fit into the context of either the sorceress or the minister. It must be a borrowing for one of the many "lift/present" cousins that were listed above. We would prefer to see in our text the more appropriate 脀, but remembering that radicals were applied haphazardly, even in Han times, we may be content with the text as received and as explained by the commentators. The basic meaning of all the words is "to lift"; the various members are merely graphical representations of the various senses in which "to lift" takes on more specific identities.

Tien 奠 (CW 6090) means "to present an offering." Even more clear is the early Chou (ca. 900 B.C.) form. It is a jar on a stand, presumably indicating an offering presented in such a jar like the wine and beer of our line. The meaning "to pour" (Harlez: "j'ai versé . . ."), as most give it, is later than the Han period and cannot be admitted here without reservation. The *Shuo Wen* note (quoted in CW) adds that the offered libations were set out on a mat *chieh* 藉 (CW 33048).

Cassia wine, *kuei-chiu* 桂酒 (CW 15064.61), is wine made with "cassia flowers" 桂花. With the aid of CMH, which cites the *Pen Ts'ao Kang Mu*, we may attempt to clear up the mystery of the cassia:

> In the *Pentsao*, at the close of the article on *Ch'ün-kuei*, it is said that there is a tree much cultivated in China, and bears the names of 巖桂 (Yen-kuei) and 木樨 (Mu-hsi). There are three varieties named according to the color of the flowers they bear; the white being called the 銀桂 (Yin-kuei), the yellow 金桂 (Chin-kuei), and the red 丹桂 (Tan-kuei). The flowers appear in the axils of the leaves, are very fragrant,

and are used for scenting tea. The common name used by the
flower gardeners, who cultivate it extensively for sale, is
桂花 (Kuei-hua, "cassia flowers"). It is the *Olea* (*Osmanthus*)
fragrans, and has none of the properties of true cinnamon.
(p. 108)

Further, "The flowers are very fragrant and are used for scenting tea and
wine . . ." (p. 296).

CW 15064.45 concurs, identifying *kuei-hua* through old citations as
the flower of the *mu-hsi* (CW 14750.227), *Osmanthus fragrans*, the
fragrant olive.

This does not undermine the commentaries since their terseness may
well be turned either way: wine with cassia bark floating in it or wine
fermented with *Osmanthus* leaves. In addition, the relative ages of the
two sources, Wang I and the *Pen Ts'ao Kang Mu* (16th century) lends
some element of risk to accepting *Osmanthus* without reservation. The
translators agree: cassia.

The translators are not so unanimous about *chiao-chiang*:

Pfizmaier:	Saft des Pfeffers
Harlez:	sirops parfumés de capsicum
Biallas:	drink with pepper
Giles:	pepper sauce
Waley:	pepper drink
Hawkes:	pepper sauces

The troublesome *chiang* 漿 (CW 18614) appears in the *Chou Li*, and
Han annotations explain it as a sour-tasting alcoholic beverage made
from millet and rice. *Shuo Wen* agrees: " 漿 is a sour alcoholic drink."
The translation "beer" is suggested by the similarity of the ingredients
and the method of preparation. In the *Pen Ts'ao Kang Mu* (after CW) one
finds the recipe: "boil millet, throw it into cold water, let it soak for five
or six days until it tastes sour and becomes white in color." Even today,
boiling, steeping, and fermenting are the basic steps of the brewing
process.

This is exactly, save the substitution of the indigenous barley for the
millet, the recipe for Tibetan beer, or *chang*. The linguistic and cultural
connection between *tsiang* and *chang* seems irrefutable. Interestingly,

the Tibetans also make *chang* with cassia bark called *shing-shun-chang*, "tree-bark beer" (Das, p. 407a). For details concerning the brewing and ingredients of these primitive millet and rice beers, see M. Hoffmann, *5000 Jahre Bier* (Nürnberg, 1956).

Chiao 椒 (CW 15343), like the English word "pepper," may indicate any of a number of plants prized for their pungent taste. Most common are the various species of *Capsicum* and *Xanthoxylum*. The distinguishing terms in modern Chinese are:

> *Capsicum* species: *la chiao* 辣椒 or *hu chiao* 胡椒
> *Xanthoxylum* species: *ch'in chiao* 秦椒 or *shan chiao* 山椒

Capsicum exists in China but gets little mention in the *Pen Ts'ao Kang Mu*. Most early notices of *chiao*, including our Five Ministers, describe it as a tree. *Capsicum* is a small shrub, not a tree in any environment. It appears as early as *Ode* #117:

> The clusters of the pepper plant,
> Large and luxuriant, would fill a pint.
> That hero there
> Is great and friendless.
>
> (Legge 4:179)

A Han note (quoted in CW) explains that *chiao* "is a tree like the 茱萸 dogwood, with pointed leaves which are hard and glossy. In the countries of Shu 蜀 and Wu 吳 they make tea, putting some of its leaves in for fragrance." This tree is probably the *Xanthoxylum piperitum*, or *shu-chiao* 蜀椒. It is a small shrub that produces small purple fruits the size of a pea, used to season cooking. Additionally, glands on the leaves contain an aromatic oil used to flavor tea (see CMH, p. 463).

Thus, "pepper" may be used in translation, but only in its loose sense. The associations of pepper, and of the *hui*, *lan*, and *kuei* as well, are of an excellent man of high virtue. (Compare the recent practice in China of labeling counterrevolutionaries "poisonous weeds.") This is the unvarying association in the *Li Sao* (lines 14, 56, 139, 160, and 163) and in these poems. The *hui* and the *chiao* are emblems of the minister. It was understood that the poet would crowd into his description of the ceremony as many emblems of his virtue as possible in order to give more weight to his remonstrance.

Wang I's note also furnishes the continuing thread of harmony. The offerings are to be an embodiment of the universe, the court. The minister tries to harmonize the five flavors of his offerings in order to exert a harmonious influence on the cosmos. The minister, in his preparations, hopes through his example of harmonious dress, music, and offerings, as well as the numerous symbols of his virtue, to rectify his king. The commentators are clearly pointing in this direction. The choice of words makes it certain.

9

	揚	枹	兮	拊	鼓
ARC	diang	b'iog	g'ieg	p'iu	ko
ANC	iang	b'iəu	γiei	piu	kuo
MSC	yang	fou	hsi	fu	ku
GSR	720	1113	1241	136	50
	to lift	drumstick		to strike	drum

10

	疏	緩	節	兮	安	歌
ARC	sio	g'wan	tsiet	g'ieg	an	ka
ANC	siwo	γuan	tsiet	γiei	an	ka
MSC	shu	huan	chieh	hsi	an	ko
GSR	90	255	399	1241	146	1
	widely spaced	slack, negligent	regular divisions		peaceful	song

META: Raise the drumsticks, strike the drum.
Distanced and slow the beat, quiet the song.

PARA: I command that the drumsticks be raised, the drums be struck,
That the music be slow and dignified, the singing soft.

The Commentaries

WANG I: *Yang* means "to raise." *Fou* means "to strike." For *fou* one text has 桴. *Shu* means "sparse." It describes how once the sacrificial meat and delicacies and the wine and the beer are prepared, one does not dare place them silently nearby. One raises the drumsticks and strikes the drums and causes the sorceress to dance to a slow beat and sing slowly along with it in order to please the Spirit. [2/3a3–4]

FIVE MINISTERS: Hsien says: *Yang* means "to raise." *Fou* is a drumstick. Cause the music to be slow and softly sing a quiet song. [32/15b9–10]

HUNG HSING-TSU: *Fou* is pronounced 房尤 [*b'iug/b'iəu*], and is a mallet for striking a drum. *Shu* is the same as 疎. [2/3a3–5]

CHU HSI: For *fou*, one text has 桴. It is pronounced 房尤. *Shu* is pronounced in the even tone. *Yang* means "to raise." *Shu* means "sparse." They raise the drumsticks and strike the drums and cause the sorceress to dance a slow dance and sing slowly along with it in order to please the Spirit. [2/1b11–2a1]

Notes

The rhyme scheme of the poem indicates a probable lost line between the present lines 9 and 10. The rhyme *-*iang*/*-*ang* is very regular. Yet all editions that divide the text into couplets do so as follows: 1 + 2, 3 + 4, 5 + 6, 7 + 8, 9 + 10, 11, 12 + 13, 14 + 15. The editors could read Chinese, and knew of the deficient rhyme scheme. They ignored it in dividing their texts. It is for this reason that the missing rhyme is mentioned here, but the text is divided according to the native custom: 9 + 10, then 11, rather than the more regular 9 + (10?), then 10(11) + 11(12).

Hung's gloss 房尤 for *fou* 枹 (or 桴) illustrates a common phenomenon. The combination yields, in ANC *b'iəu*, exactly as 枹 itself: *b'iəu*. The gloss was therefore correct in Sung Chinese, though why this relatively common word required the note is not evident. In ARC, however, much closer to the time of the literary polishing of the text and the dialect into which it fits perfectly, the phonetic combination of 房尤 gives **b'iug* and 枹 is read **b'iog*. (Tung: **b'iwəg* vs. **b'iog*; Chou: *bjwəɣ vs. *bjəw.) These do not rhyme in the ARC rhyme system of the *Ch'u Tz'u*, though they may be close enough to be borrowed for each other. Thus, as will occur frequently, the Sung ear demanded a gloss that was originally unnecessary from the phonetic point of view. These glosses are commonly used to identify to the reader which of two or more possible readings (and therefore meanings) the commentator feels is intended in a particular passage. This method often yields much specific information about the later understanding of the text.

Shu 疏 (CW 22505) means "far apart." In the musical context, as here, it means slow. Compare *shu-chi* 疏擊 (CW 22505.171) which means "to beat a drum slowly."

Shu-huan 疏緩 (CW 22505.153), however, is not a musical term at all. It means "lazy and negligent." With this in mind, one would recall *I Ching* hexagram #60, *Chieh* 節 "Limitation," and the text: "Galling limitation must not be persevered in" (Wilhelm, p. 231), to read the line in a political way: "I sing quietly 安歌 despite being limited by this galling negligent treatment 疏緩節," a brocade. This statement of personal feeling is a counterpoint to the continuing theme of disharmonious sensation representing disharmonious government.

Chieh 節 (CW 26874) does not appear in any other old text meaning "rhythm." The *Erh Ya* lists a rhythm instrument called *chieh*, and this may be the present use. The basic meaning "joint" is easily extended and whether "rhythm" or "rhythm instrument" is intended in the surface narrative is not a critical question. The sense of the line is clear: raise the sticks, beat the drums; let the rhythm be slow, the song soft. This serves equally well in the political context of the minister preparing the ceremony before the arrival of the king. The differing contexts provide the different interpretations.

The minister wishes the music to be slow and quiet so that decorum may be preserved, as befits a royal ceremony. He wishes the inappropriate and disharmonious behavior of the king to change. To accomplish this, he orders that the ceremonial music conform to the model of the stately music of the ancient kings, such as that mentioned by the sage Yü in the *Shu Ching*, "Tribute of Yü," which was quoted earlier: "When the nine services thus indicated have been orderly accomplished, let that accomplishment be celebrated by songs. Caution the people with gentle words; correct them with the majesty of law; stimulate them with the songs on those nine subjects" (Legge 3:56).

We see the chief minister continuing his preparations for the audience, ensuring as the poem progresses that each element of the service will be in harmony with the Tao of the ancient kings. He models his music, the Nine Elegies, after the Nine Songs of Yü to gain the same benefit: that his accomplishments be celebrated, and that the king be cautioned, corrected, and stimulated to return to the Tao of the ancient kings.

11

陳	竽	瑟	兮	浩	倡
ARC	d'ien	giwo	siet	g'ieg	g'og	t'iang
ANC	d'ien	jiu	siet	γiei	γau	ts'iang
MSC	ch'en	yü	se	hsi	hao	ch'ang
GSR	373	97	411	1241	1039	724
	to arrange	reed organ	zither		vast	to sing

META: The ranks of reed organs and zithers play loudly.

PARA: Suddenly, the ranks of reed organs and zithers play loudly.

The Commentaries

WANG I: *Ch'en* means "arranged in order." *Hao* is "big." It describes how the reed organs and zithers are arranged in ranks, play loudly, and make music to the extent of their strength. [2/3a5]

FIVE MINISTERS: Hsien says: They make music in order to bring their emotions to a peak. [32/15b11]

HUNG HSING-TSU: The *Li Chi* says: "Bells and sounding-stones, accompany them with reed organs and zithers." The *yü* is of the class of reed-pipe instruments, with thirty-six metal reeds. The *se* 瑟 is of the class of stringed instruments and has twenty-five strings. [2/3a5–6]

CHU HSI: *Ch'ang* sounds like 昌 [*t'iang/ts'iang*]. *Ch'en* means "arranged in order." *Hao* is "big." The *yü* is of the class of reed-pipe instruments, with thirty-six metal reeds. The *se* is of the class of stringed instruments and has twenty-five strings. [2/2a1–2]

Notes

Yü 竽 and *se* 瑟 stand *a minore ad maius* for wind and string instruments collectively.

Aside from the themes of the minister's preparations, this line presents a fascinating brocade. In addition to being a musical instrument, *yü* (CW 26433) also means "the chief bandit," as in *Tao Te Ching* 53:

> When the court is arrayed in splendor,
> The fields are full of weeds,
> And the granaries are empty.
>
> Some wear fine clothes,
> Carry sharp swords,
> And indulge themselves with food and drink;
>
> They have more possessions than they can use.
> They are the chief bandits [芋].
> This is not the Tao.
>
> (after Gia-fu Feng)

Huai Nan Tzu, in the chapter "Explaining *Lao Tzu*," clarifies:

> When the big bandits act, the little bandits follow. When the big bandits sing, the little bandits must harmonize. The *yü* is the leader of the five notes. Thus, the *yü* leads and the *se* and bells follow. The *yü* plays and the musicians all harmonize. Nowadays there are big bandits acting and their underlings sing along. When their underlings sing along, the petty robbers must harmonize. Thus it says "They dress in fine clothes. . . ." (Text from CW, my trans.)

Hao 浩 (CW 17932) means "vast water," and by extension "vast," or "large." *Hao-ch'ang* 浩倡 is unique to this line. *Hao* may also mean "haughty," interchanging with 傲. *Ch'ang* (CW 793), read in the level tone as Chu Hsi suggests, does not mean "sing." The *Shuo Wen* says: "*Ch'ang* is a musician." The word is a noun and is used for musicians of either sex. Our mention of it here is based on Chu Hsi. If we ignore his suggestion and read *ch'ang* in its secondary meaning **t'iang* (ANC going tone) we may translate it "sing." The question is, why does Chu Hsi specifically exclude the reading?

He may understand the line to say: "Arranged, the *yü* and *se*; (vast =) numerous the musicians." He forecloses this possibility with his own equation of *hao* = large 大. *Hao* may also mean "rashly wild." This would permit us to enlarge the brocade of the bandit leader: "Blatant, the bandit leader and his minions; haughty and wild." The brocade may be construed either to refer to the king or the slanderer, either way it is an unflattering comment.

The commentators are in agreement in their explication of *hao-ch'ang* in the ritual of the sorceress: sing loudly. We unearth the political sense as a result of the almost pathological glossing of the self-evident terms in this line by the commentators.

In contraposition to the prepared ceremony with its dignified music, the king enters to a loud and raucous fanfare. The careful plan of the minister is disrupted. The (musicians =) court is no longer under his control. The discordant influence of the king and his associate is too powerful.

12

	靈	偃	蹇	兮	姣	服
ARC	lieng	ian	kian	g'ieg	kog	b'iuk
ANC	lieng	ien	kien	γiei	kao	b'iuk
MSC	ling	yen	chien	hsi	chiao	fu
GSR	836	253	143	1241	1166	934
	sorcerer	stiff +	lame		beautiful	clothes
		binome: haughty				
		and arrogant				

13

	芳	菲	菲	兮	滿	堂
ARC	p'iwang	p'iwər	p'iwər	g'ieg	mwan	d'ang
ANC	p'iwang	p'jwei	p'jwei	γiei	muan	d'ang
MSC	fang	fei	fei	hsi	man	t'ang
GSR	740	579	579	1241	183	725
	fragrant	fragrant +	fragrant		to fill	hall
		binome: fragrant				

META: The sorceress dances lofty and arrogant, beautifully ornamented.
The scent wafts fragrantly and fills the hall.

PARA: The king enters arrogantly in his unceremonious manner.
His disorderly influence pervades the audience chamber.

The Commentaries

WANG I: *Ling* refers to the sorceress. *Yen-chien* is used to depict dancing. *Chiao* is "beautiful." *Fu* means "an ornament." For *fu* one text has 服. For *chiao*, one text has 妖. *Fei-fei* is characteristic of a fragrance. It says that they then cause the beautiful sorceress to wear beautifully ornamented clothes, raise her feet and spread her sleeves and dance *yen-chien*. The pleasing fragrance fills the hall. [2/3a6—9]

FIVE MINISTERS: Hsiang says: *Fei-fei* is the fragrant air. [32/16a2]

HUNG HSING-TSU: In former times sorceresses made Spirits descend. *Ling-yen-chien* refers to the descent of the Spirit and its possession of the sorceress. Another note says: "*Yen-chien* means 'sinuous'." One says it means "like a multitude." The *Fang Yen* says: "*Hao* 好, some call it *chiao* 姣." The note says: "It means 'beautiful'." *Chiao* and *yao* 妖 both sound like 狡 [*kog/kau*]. *Fu* is the same as 服. [2/3a6–8]

CHU HSI: For *chiao-fu*, one text has *yao-fu* 妖服. Formerly the two words were used interchangeably. *Ling* refers to the Spirit descending into the body of the sorceress. *Yen-chien* means "beautiful." *Chiao* means "pleasant." *Fu* is an ornament. In former times sorceresses made Spirits descend. The Spirits descended and possessed the sorceress. Thus, as for seeing its beautiful appearance and fine adornment, the body is of the sorceress but the mind is that of the Spirit. *Fei-fei* is the characteristic of a fragrance. [2/1b11–2a3]

Notes

Ling 靈 (CW 43483), one of the key words of the Nine Elegies, is equated by the commentators with *wu* 巫 "magician," "sorceress." The archaic graph is composed of the symbol for rain with two or three mouths below it. It appears to mean "incantator for rain" (GSR 836). The superfluous 巫 added in the fuller form is perhaps a later addition, a product of the Ch'in-Han script reform.

Wu 巫 (CW 8927) appears on many bronzes, in numerous variants. The *Shuo Wen* defines: "A woman who is able to serve the formless ones; by dancing she induces the Spirits to descend." The idea of possession, clearly indicated by Chu Hsi, is critical to our rendering, and the relationship of the text to shamanism.

Shaman is a specialized term, possibly adopted from the Tunguz word *saman*. What does a Chinese *wu* have in common with a Siberian shaman? There have been attempts, including some using these poems, to prove that the people of Ch'u were the product of a mass southern migration of Tungusic peoples from the north. Aside from the irrelevance of this notion to our discussion, there is good reason to dismiss it on more factual grounds.

In the present context, the *wu* exhibits only some of the features of orthodox shamanism. From Eliade, *Chamanisme*: "Depuis les temps les plus anciens, le moyen classique d'aboutir à l'extase fut la danse. Comme partout ailleurs, l'extase permettait aussi bien le 'vol magique' du chaman que le descente d'un 'esprit'" (p. 352).

Yet, Eliade dismisses this spirit possession, the descent of a "spirit," as an inferior form of shamanism. Shamanistic ecstasy is more than mere possession: "On ne peut donc pas considérer n'importe quel extatique comme un chaman; celui-ci est le spécialiste d'une transe, pendant laquelle son âme est censée quitter le corps pour entreprendre des ascencions célestes ou des descentes infernales" (p. 23).

This is the criterion by which a shaman is to be tested. Spirit-possession is, in fact, an anti-criterion: "Lorsqu'on ne réussit pas à maîtriser les 'esprit' on finit par être 'possédé' par eux, et la technique magique de l'extase devient, en ce cas, un simple autonomisme médiumnistique" (p. 351).

This "mediumnistic automatism" describes well the phenomenon we seek to understand in our line. If we accept this standard, we must insist that the *wu* may not be a shaman at all. Shamanologists, however, cannot even agree among themselves. A student of the Tunguz shamans asserts: "In all Tungus languages this term refers to persons of both sexes who have mastered Spirits, who at their will can introduce these Spirits into themselves and use their power over the Spirits in their own interests" (Shirokogoroff, p. 269).

This exchange of dicta portrays clearly the fundamental problem. "Shamanism" is a highly charged and overused word. Not even the shamanologists are able to settle on an unambiguous definition for others to use. Thus, it seems best to follow Eliade and render *wu* with the noncontroversial "sorceress" (Kalgren at GSR 836 has "sorcerer," but in a neutral sense) and leave the discussion of shamanism's finer points to the specialists. As to assertions that these poems are shamanist hymns exclusively, with no allegorical or political importance, we leave it to the commentators and the simple facts of Chinese literary history to reject them.

Yen 偃 (CW 877) means "to lie down stiffly." *Chien* 蹇 (CW 38590) means "lame" or in the *I Ching*, as the name of hexagram #39, "obstruction."

Together (CW 877.61) they are an onomatopoeic binome which may describe loftiness, haughtiness, arrogance, abundance, beauty, dancing, dangerous and high rocks, lying idly around, crookedness, sinuousity, or thwarted ambition. Quite a flexible word!

In this line, the commentators say the binome describes dancing (Wang I, Hung) or beauty (Chu Hsi). If either of these is correct, the line would represent the only such use known in either CW or DK (as they appear in the list above from the notes we are reading in our commentaries). The most common senses of the word, as attested by legions of citations in the dictionaries, are "lofty," and "arrogant." Our translators surround the phrase, but only Pfizmaier has hit the mark:

Pfizmaier:	Der Gottheit her und hoch
Harlez:	Les danses se déroulent
Biallas:	The wonderful (priestess) moves slowly
Giles:	The medium will begin to dance
Waley:	The Spirit moves proudly
Hawkes:	Now the priestesses come

While Waley has the idea, Pfizmaier has found an uncanny equivalent: an onomatopoeic binome of the same sense. English can offer only the déclassé "hoity-toity." The haughtiness of the Spirit is evident in the fact that he requires the most sensuous and concerted coaxing to descend even for the briefest of visits among mortals.

Chiao 姣 (CW 6354), besides "beautiful," means "lewd" when read either in the ANC going tone or even tone: *g'og/γau*. Hung points to exactly this sense by saying that *chiao* sounds like *hsiao* 狡, which carries the ANC going tone, and means "perverse." Further support is found in the notes to the *Shuo Wen* which note that *chiao* may mean the same thing as *hsiao*, even when read in the rising tone!

Why do the commentators say "beautiful" and then misread the pronunciation to make it "lewd"? The answer may be a brocade in the court context. Instead of comporting himself in a solemn and ritualistic manner, the king is swaggering arrogantly in his (lewd =) ostentatiously decorated robes, contrary to the rules of ceremonial behavior. His behavior, as always, is the mirror of his government. The big bandit plays, and the little bandits harmonize. The good minister cannot oppose such a pervasive influence.

Fang 芳 (CW 31393) "fragrance" may also stand for such an influence, as it frequently takes exactly this meaning in Chinese: "influence," "reputation."

The solemn and dignified ceremony, intended to display the minister's sincerity and represent his good advice through the symbolic associations of the offerings, music, and the like, has been disrupted by the loud and haughty entrance of the king and his crowd of "little bandits." Ch'ü Yüan has been forced out of the role he had envisioned for himself: preparer of ceremonies, supreme advisor. The disharmonious influence of the king has pervaded the court.

14

	五	音	紛	兮	繁	會
ARC	ngo	iəm	p'iwən	g'ieg	b'iwan	g'wad
ANC	nguo	iəm	p'iuən	ɣiei	b'iwan	ɣwai
MSC	wu	yin	fen	hsi	fan	hui
GSR	58	653	471	1241	265	321
	five	sound	confused, mixed		numerous	to combine

15

	君	欣	欣	兮	樂	康
ARC	kiwən	χiən	χiən	g'ieg	glak	k'ang
ANC	kiuən	χiən	χiən	ɣiei	lak	k'ang
MSC	chün	hsin	hsin	hsi	lo	k'ang
GSR	459	443	443	1241	1125	746
	lord	to rejoice + to rejoice binome: to rejoice			happy	at ease

META: The Five Notes are in abundance, confusedly mixed.
        The Lord is taking his pleasure, happy and content.

PARA: The music is reduced to confusion, a disorderly melee,
        But the king is greatly pleased with himself, content and oblivious.

The Commentaries

WANG I: The Five Notes are *kung* 宮, *shang* 商, *chiao* 角, *chih* 徵, and *yü* 羽. *Fen* depicts abundance. *Fan* means "multitudinous." *Hsin-hsin* depicts happiness. *K'ang* means "content." It says that the movements and music mixed with the five tones in profusion are beautiful. The Spirit is pleased, satisfied, and happy. Thus the people receive from the Spirit blessing and protection, the families much good fortune. Ch'ü Yüan believed that the Spirit, as a formless silent being, was difficult to serve and easy to pique. Thus, people exerted their effort and exhausted themselves in sacrifice and then the Spirit only sometimes accepted their sacrifices and was gracious to them with blessings. In the same way, the minister may distress himself in observing faithful and loyal conduct in order to be of service to his king. The king, however, may not employ him in good faith, instead banish him, casting him out into danger. [2/3a9–3b3]

FIVE MINISTERS: Han says: *Fan-hui* means they are confusedly mixed. *Chün* refers to the Magnificent One of the East. *Hsin-hsin* depicts happiness. It says that if one prepares purified wine and food and displays much drumming and music, then the Spirit will be pleased with the sacrifice and send down his blessings. One distresses oneself in loyal and faithful service to a superior and does not receive loyal behavior in return; instead, one suffers banishment and encounters danger and misery. [32/16a5–6]

HUNG HSING-TSU: This piece uses the August One as a metaphor for the king. It says that if ministers display virtue and proper conduct and serve their superior with rites and music, their superiors will be happily content and without vexation. [2/3a9–3b3]

CHU HSI: *Lo* sounds like 洛 [*glak/lak*]. The Five Notes are *kung, shang, chiao, chih,* and *yü*. *Fen* depicts abundance. *Fan* means "multitudinous." *Chün* refers to the Spirit. *Hsin-hsin* depicts happiness. *K'ang* means "content." This describes how music is prepared to please the Spirit, because they desire his happiness and contentment. [2/2a1; 2a3–4]

Notes

The five notes of the scale share the political associations commonly connected to other sets of five:

宮	*kung*	君	lord
商	*shang*	臣	minister
角	*chiao*	民	people
徵	*chih*	事	affairs
羽	*yü*	物	things

(Ssu-ma Ch'ien, 3.240–41)

The efforts of the commentators to equate *fen* 紛 (CW 27919) with abundance may have its origin in these associations. The basic meaning of *fen* is "mixed," "confused." This leaves the immediately perceived sense of the first line: "The Five Notes are in disorder." Presented with such a phrase, the classically literate Chinese, knowing the correspondence between the Five Notes and the five basic constituents of existence (*wu-hsing*), would read a clear statement of political import: the cosmos is in confusion. If the cosmos is in confusion, the government is *ipso facto* incompetent.

The kinship of music with politics is ancient:

> The Emperor said, "Kuei, I appoint you to be Director of Music, and to teach our sons, so that the straightforward may yet be mild, the gentle may yet be dignified, the strong not tyrannical, and the impetuous not arrogant. Poetry is the expression of earnest thought; singing is the prolonged utterance of that expression. The notes accompany that utterance; and they are harmonized themselves by the pitch pipes. In this way the eight kinds of instruments can all be adjusted so that one shall not take from or interfere with another, and spirits and men will thereby be brought into harmony." (*Shu Ching*; Legge 3:47–48)

> Even the acute ear of the music master K'uang, without the pitch-tubes, could not determine correctly the five notes. The principles of Yao and Shun, without a benevolent government, could not secure the tranquil order of the kingdom. (*Mencius* 4A:1.1; Legge 3:288)

> If there be no disorder or irregularity in these five notes, there will be no want of harmony in the state.... If the five notes are all irregular, and injuriously interfere with one another, they indicate a state of insolent disorder; and the state where this is the case will at no distant day meet with extinction and ruin. (*Li Chi*, 2:94)

Innumerable examples may be adduced (e.g., cf. also Han Ying, *Han Shih Wai Chuan* 1/16; Hightower, pp. 24–25). The statement that the Five Notes are in disorder is the clearest of indications that the author is flagrantly criticizing the king. We may recognize the commentators' desire to soften or provide an alibi for this bald statement. They equate *fen* tenuously with *sheng* 盛 "abundant" and *fan* 繁 (CW 28487) properly with "multitudinous." This yields the dubitable formula: "The Five Notes are abundant, multitudinously assembled."

Yet even this sanitized image suggests a cacophony rather than the orderly music mandated by the *Li Chi*. The Five Ministers assent obliquely: *fen-hui* means "confusedly mixed" 錯雜. In all these equations recur the derogatory terms 紛, 亂, 雜, 錯; never the essential 和 "harmony."

The hierarchical associations of numbered sets, such as the Five Notes, appear throughout the commentaries to the *Ch'u Tz'u*. Often, they represent the court and its political intrigues through their reference to things which, in common ordered sets, represent the actors or events of the drama. Thus if music is disordered, the court is disordered; all determined phenomena are disordered. The accession of an evil king to the throne was routinely accompanied by earthquakes and storms. No doubt at such times the music was licentious and out of tune.

Hsin-hsin 欣欣 (CW 16375.10) is the appearance of happiness. If the king is happy, can the kingdom be in disorder? Most assuredly so. The continuation of the *Mencius* passage quoted previously follows:

> Now, your Majesty is having music here.—The people hear the noise of your bells and drums, and the notes of your fifes and pipes, and they all, with aching heads, knit their brows, and say to one another, "That's how our king likes his music! But why does he reduce us to this extremity of distress?"—Fathers and sons cannot see one another. Elder brothers and younger brothers, wives and children, are separated and scattered abroad.... Their feeling thus is from no other reason but that you do not allow the people to have pleasure as well as yourself. (*Mencius* 1B:1.6; Legge 2:151–52)

There is nothing incongruous about the image of a king who takes his pleasure while his subjects are distressed. To point it out is an indictment of the king and therefore reinforces the political context rather than contradicting it. In the political context we may read: "The government is in disorder and confusion, yet the king takes his pleasure and is content."

The poem has depicted the carefully detailed preparation of the chief minister for an audience with the king. Emphasizing harmony in all elements of the ceremony, the minister hopes to provide examples to teach the king that his government was out of harmony with the Tao. Disrupting the quiet music prepared by the minister, the king enters to a loud raucous fanfare and then takes his ease to the accompaniment of his out-of-tune music, hilariously pleased at the clever way he has asserted his power, ruining the preparations of his minister for the audience.

If we accept this political interpretation, which did not escape the critical view of the Chinese commentators and readers, we may infer the sequence of thoughts left unuttered but clearly intended by the author of the poem: with the audience hopelessly disrupted, the minister has lost his chance to present his advice, to restore his position in the king's favor, and to influence the course of affairs which are pressing on to a bad end. Ch'ü Yüan has described his fall from grace.

Yün Chung Chün

Metaphrastic Translation

(The sorceress invites the Cloud Spirit Feng Lung to descend)

1. I have bathed in *lan*-scented water, washed my hair in *angelica*.
2. My garment is five-colored and glorious with *pollia* blossoms.

3. The Spirit moves sinuously, he is already here.
4. The fiery luminescence shines brightly, still increasing.

5. Lo! The Spirit will soon be at peace in the House of Long Life;
6. His luminosity rivals that of sun and moon.

7. In a dragon-drawn cart and polychrome robes
8. For a while the Spirit wanders here and there, roaming.

9. He is magnificent, having descended;
10. Then suddenly he rises far and high into the clouds.

11. He looks out over Chi-chou and beyond.
12. He traverses the Four Seas, knowing no limit.

13. Thinking of the lord, I heave a great sigh.
14. My heart toils to its utmost, but I am grieved and distressed.

Paraphrastic Translation

THE LORD BECLOUDED

(The king acts contrary to the Tao)

1. I have ritually purified myself, head and body.
2. My Great Officer's robe displays my excellent virtue.

3. The king's arrogant behavior shows he is completely possessed.
4. He injures us through his ignorance, the worst is yet to come.

5. I am obstructed at the palace, to the point of burning with grief,
6. Because he dares to match power with the king and his minister.

7. He has harnessed the king and taken his power.
8. Meanwhile, I am trying to dissipate my grief at failing to prevent this calamity.

9. The Efficacious One is unhappy at having been brought low;
10. The slanderer ascends into his element.

11. He has gained control of the capital, and even more.
12. He outrages the whole world and impoverishes the people.

13. I think of the king and heave a great sigh;
14. Concerned to the utmost, I am vexed and disappointed.

Title

	雲	中	君
ARC	giwən	tiong	kiwən
ANC	jiuən	tiung	kiuən
MSC	yün	chung	chün
GSR	460	1007	459
	cloud	in, middle	Lord

META: The Lord in the Clouds

PARA: The Lord Beclouded

The Commentaries

WANG I: no note.

FIVE MINISTERS: no note.

HUNG HSING-TSU: This is the Cloud Spirit Feng Lung 豐隆. One says it is P'ing I 屏翳. See the *Li Sao*. The Lord in the Clouds is mentioned in the *Han Shu*, "Treatise on State Worship and Sacrifice." [2/5a6]

CHU HSI: This is the Cloud Spirit. Also see the *Han Shu*, "Treatise on State Worship and Sacrifice." This section says that the Spirit descended and was detained a long time in close contact with the people. Then it departed and when the people thought of it they were unable to forget it. Here the subtle idea of the minister's respect for his Lord is plain to see. [2/2b8—9]

Notes

The Lord in the Clouds is known only in this title. The commentators take it to be an epithet of the cloud-spirit Feng Lung, or of P'ing I. Feng Lung (CW 37149.145) is also known as Master of Thunder 雷師. The *Han Fei Tzu* includes him in a list of stars: ". . . Feng Lung, Wu Hsing 五行, T'ai I 太一, Wang Hsiang 王相, She T'i 攝提." He is mentioned in the *Li Sao*, line 112, where Hung Hsing-tsu adds a voluminous note detailing the intense confusion surrounding the names Feng Lung, P'ing I, and others with regard to the meteorological division of labor. In the absence of consensus, he declares this the most likely arrangement:

Feng Lung　豐隆 = Master of Clouds
Fei Lien　　飛廉 = Master of Wind
P'ing I　　　屏翳 = Master of Rain

We need not quarrel with this, but it is by no means universal. P'ing I, for example, may have any of the phenomena assigned to him, depending only upon the source consulted.

The earliest reference to this spirit, mentioned by all commentators from Hung to Waley, is one line in the *Han Shu*, itself a quotation from the *Shih Chi*, which mentions not the Lord in the Clouds, but the similar name "One in the Clouds" 雲中: "The Chin sorcerers sacrifice to the Five Emperors, the Lord of the East, the One in the Clouds, the Arbiter of Fate. . . ." The passage reads almost as a table of contents of the Nine Elegies! Unlike T'ai I, whose cult may be traced with modest success, the Lord in the Clouds eludes us as a full-fledged Spirit. We must be content with the epithet.

In the political interpretation, clouds may represent sexual tension ("The Lord Distracted by Affairs") or the nefarious excessive Yin influence of an evil minister. Most likely is some interpretation related to the idea of the relationship between the dragon (= king) and the clouds (= ministers).

The relationship between a king and his ministers, the interplay of charisma and influence, is best described in a short essay by Han Yü (A.D. 768–824), paraphrased from Bischoff, pp. 391–92 (wherever the original has "dragon" 龍 or "clouds" 雲, I have substituted "king" or "ministers"):

> The king, by a manifestation of his will empowers the ministers. The charisma of a minister is, of course, not comparable to the king's. Indeed, the king is master of his own will which reaches to the limits of the world, humbles sun and moon, subdues light and shade, stirs up earthquakes and lightning, masterminds change, falls like water on dry earth and drenches hills and valleys. And it is obvious that the ministers are wondrously participating in the king's charisma. A minister is charismatic only when the king can employ him. As for the king's charisma, he is *not* charismatic

when a minister can use him. But if the king does not obtain ministers, he would lack that which makes his charisma effective. He would lose support on which to rest. Isn't this incredible? Strange! The support on which he rests is his own nature. The *I Ching* says: "The clouds obey the dragon." Thus we may conclude: the king is the one whom the ministers obey.

This may turn the title several ways. It may mean "The functioning king is one of the ministers, not the legitimate king." It may mean "The king is reduced to the low status of one of his retainers." It may mean "The king is surrounded by Yin." The polytropic nature of the Classical Chinese sentence is even more pronounced in a title, where rules of grammar are of even less avail than in more regular composition.

In light of the symbolism of clouds and the dragon, we are at least safe in assuming that the reader attached immediate political significance to the title. Nor was he limited to holding only a single interpretation to be relevant.

Chu Hsi refers the reader to the theme of the whole piece: the minister's respect for his king. In fact, the poet often bewails the king's lack of understanding. With so powerful an enemy at court, Ch'ü Yüan is powerless to plead his case other than through a poetical allegory of the preparations made by a minister for an audience with his king.

Chu Hsi may be indulging in alibi-making. The poet respects the king as king, respect demanded of him by the Chinese orthodoxy, but makes plain his disgust for the king's behavior in opposition to that orthodoxy.

Compare Mencius' explanation of the killing of Chou, last king of the Yin Dynasty, by King Wu, founder of the Chou dynasty:

> The king Hsüan of Ch'i asked, saying, "Was it so, that T'ang banished Chieh, and that king Wu smote Chou?" Mencius replied, "It is so in the records." The king said, "May a minister then put his sovereign to death?" Mencius said, "He who outrages the benevolence proper to his nature, is called a robber; he who outrages righteousness is called a ruffian. The robber and ruffian we call a mere fellow. I have heard of the cutting off of the fellow Chou, but I have not heard of the putting a sovereign to death, in his case. (*Mencius* 1A:8; Legge 2:167)

1

	浴	蘭	湯	兮	沐	芳
ARC	giuk	glan	t'ang	g'ieg	muk	p'iwang
ANC	iwok	lan	t'ang	γiei	muk	p'iwang
MSC	yü	lan	t'ang	hsi	mu	fang
GSR	1202	185	720	1241	1212	740
	to wash the body	a plant	warm water		to wash the hair	fragrant

2

	華	采	衣	兮	若	英
ARC	g'wa	ts'əg	iər	g'ieg	niak	iang
ANC	γwa	ts'ai	jei	γiei	nziak	ieng
MSC	hua	ts'ai	i	hsi	jo	ying
GSR	44	942	550	1241	777	718
	flower	color	clothes		a plant	blossom

META: I have bathed in *lan*-scented water, washed my hair in *angelica*.
My garment is five-colored and glorious with *pollia* blossoms.

PARA: I have ritually purified myself, head and body.
My Great Officer's robe displays my excellent virtue.

The Commentaries

WANG I: *Lan* is a fragrant plant. *Hua-ts'ai* means "pentachromatic." *Jo* is *tu-jo* 杜若. It says that when one is about to prepare for the sacrifice to the Spirit of the Clouds, one must first cause the sorceress to bathe in *lan*-water, wash her hair in fragrant *chih* 芷. Then dress her in a five-colored garment ornamented with *tu-jo* flowers in order that she will be purified. [2/4a1−4]

FIVE MINISTERS: Liang says: *Lan* and *jo* are fragrant plants. [32/16b2]

HUNG HSING-TSU: The *Pen Ts'ao Kang Mu* says that *pai-chih* 白芷 is also called the fragrant perfume. There is a *yüeh-fu* song called "Mu Yü Tzu" 沐浴子. Liu Tz'u-chuang 劉次莊 says: "The *Ch'u Tz'u* says that a person who has just washed his hair must dust off his cap, and that a person who has just washed his body must dust off his robe." The other lines "Together we wash our hair in Heaven's Pool," and "Dry your hair on the sun-side of the hill" are also references to purification. Li Po also used this phrase: "Wash hair in *fang*, don't shake your cap. Wash body in *lan*, don't shake your robe. In the world, eschew great purifications. Among people, honor the hidden glory." He used it however to contradict Ch'ü Yüan.

Hsün Tzu's *fu* on clouds says: "Prepare the five colors and make a multicolored garment." *Hua-ts'ai* garments are like this.

The *Pen Ts'ao Kang Mu* says that *tu-jo* is also called *tu-heng* 杜蘅. The leaves are like ginger, but lined. The taste is acrid and aromatic. The *tu-heng* we have now is not the same. In the *Erh Ya*, *tu-heng* is called *tu-t'u-lu* 杜土鹵. In the *K'uang Ya*, *tu-jo* is called *ch'u-heng* 楚衡. These varieties are different but the ancient ones confused them many times.

The *Erh Ya* says: "That which flowers but does not set fruit is called *ying* 英." [2/4a1–5]

CHU HSI: *Hua* is pronounced 户花 [*g'wa/γwa]. *Ying* is pronounced for the rhyme 於姜 [*iang/iang]. *Fang* means *chih* 芷. *Hua-ts'ai* means a pentachromatic plant. That which flowers and does not set fruit is called *ying*.

It says one must first cause the sorceress to wash in *lan*-water and *chih*-perfume, then put on a colored gown like the flowers of plants and trees in order to purify herself. [2/2a9–10]

Notes

Yü 浴 (CW 17930) is to wash the body, *mu* 沐 (CW 17552) is to wash the hair. Taken together, 沐浴 (CW 17552.16), they denote the ritual purification undertaken by a minister before entering court. For example:

> Confucius bathed, went to court, and informed the duke Ai, saying "Ch'en Heng has slain his Lord. I beg that you will undertake to punish him." (*Lun Yü* 14:22.2)

> [Legge's note]: 沐浴 implies all the fasting and all the solemn preparation, as for a sacrifice or other great occasion. (*Lun Yü* 14:22.2; Legge 2:284)

> Though a man be wicked, yet if he adjusts his thoughts, fast and bathe, he may sacrifice to God. (*Mencius* 4B:25.2; Legge 2:330)

Legge notes that it was the sole imperial prerogative to sacrifice to *shang-ti* 上帝, thus the ruler must also purify himself in this way. The hair was washed with rice-water, *fan* 潘 (CW 18737), for which term *mu* has become a synonym. Here it means only to wash the hair. The body was washed with hot water, *t'ang* 湯 (CW 18246). *T'ang* may also be boiling water, as in *Lun Yü* 16:11.1: "Contemplating good, and pursuing it as if they could not reach it; contemplating evil, and shrinking from it, as they would from thrusting the hand into boiling water:—I have seen such men ..." (Legge 1:314.) In the political context of the court, the minister is expected to purify himself, not scald his hands: we may be content with "warm water" and the clear association with the minister's pre-audience ritual. For *lan*, see above at "Tung Huang T'ai I," line 7.

Fang 芳 (CW 31393), "fragrance," stands metaphorically for a good reputation, for virtue, for one's influence. Additionally, the commentaries give the formula *fang* = *fang-hsiang* 芳香 (CW 31393.53) = *pai-chih* 白芷 (CW 23191.359). These interlocking identities are confirmed by the *Pen Ts'ao Kang Mu* and other references cited by CW *in loco*. The dictionaries provide the Latin *Heracleum lanatum* for *pai-chih*, but CMH (p. 41) identifies it as *Angelica anomala*, an aromatic herb, the roots of which were anciently worn in the girdle for their fragrance. (In medieval Europe, *Angelica* was steeped in water to make a perfume. See OED s.v. *angel-water*.)

The juxtaposition of *lan* and *chih* (CW 33297.100) stands metaphorically for an excellent and virtuous person. CW gives examples from the *Ta Tai Li Chi*, *Shih Chi*, *Wen Tzu* 文子, and this from *Li Sao*, line 155: "Orchid [*lan*] and iris have lost all their fragrance" (Hawkes). I.e., men of virtue have lost all their influence. Wang I's note to that line of the *Li Sao* says of this transformation: "This means the king has become a rascal, and the loyal ministers have become deceitful slanderers." Hung's additional note ends: "At this time, of course, only one man in Ch'u was constant in his loyalty, even to the point of death: this was Ch'ü Yüan."

The modern translators have unanimously ignored the commentators' identification of *fang* with *pai-chih*:

Pfizmaier:	Sie ölt sich mit der duft'gen Plfanze
Harlez:	la tête parfumée
Giles:	washed with perfumes
Waley:	bathed in sweet scents
Hawkes:	washed our hair with perfumes

As a brocade, to illustrate yet another possible way in which the political interpretation may have been perceived by readers still familiar with the tradition: the first line has a near Han-time homophone: **giuk-klan-diang* 欲諫揚 "I wish to raise my voice in remonstration."

The phrase *hua-ts'ai-i* 華采衣 (CW 31910.119) originates in this line. Dictionaries quote Wang I's note by way of definition. Such circularity is often insoluble, but *hua-ts'ai* and *wu-ts'ai* 五采 are not associated merely in the fertile mind of Wang I. The *Han Shu*, "Treatise on the Five Elements" (quoted from CW 31910.III) says: "*Hua* means 'colorful'." The *Li Chi*, "T'an Kung," says (1:128): "How beautifully colored and bright! Is it not the (bed-)mat of a Great Officer?" To which Cheng Hsüan's 鄭玄 note says: "All things decorated with the five colors must be splendid."

The five-colored garment is directly associated with the Emperor and his court in *Chou Li*, *Hsün Tzu*, and the *Shu Ching* in its spurious (but until recently generally accepted) chapter "I and Chieh":

> The Emperor said, "My ministers constitute my legs and arms, my ears and eyes. I wish to help and support my people;—you give effect to my wishes. I wish to spread the influence of my government through the four quarters;— you are my agents. I wish to see the emblematic figures of the ancients, the sun, the moon, the stars, the mountain, the dragon, and the flowery fowl..., the temple-cup, the aquatic grass, the flames, the grains of rice, the hatchet and the symbol of distinction, which are embroidered on the robes. I wish to see all these displayed with the five colors, so as to form the official robes. (Legge 3:79–80)

Jo-ying 若英 (CW 14796.151), over which all the modern translators have tripped (e.g., Waley: "like a flower"), is expanded by the commentaries to mean the flower of the *tu-jo* 杜若. The *tu-jo* is described in *Pen Ts'ao Kang Mu* and identified by CMH (p. 338) with the *Pollia japonica*. The experts warn of confusion between the *Pollia* and *tu-heng* 杜衡, *Asarum forbesii*, and *kao-chiang* 高薑, *Alpina officinarum*. The roots of *Pollia* are often used as a restorative or tonic.

Ying 英 (CW 31525) the commentaries define with a quotation from the *Erh Ya* (echoed in the *Shuo Wen*): "That which flowers but does not set fruit is called *ying*." The term also denotes a man of exceptional talent, virtue, or wisdom, as in *Mencius* 7A : 20.4: [Among those things in which the gentleman delights is] "that he can get from the whole kingdom the most talented individuals 天下英才 and teach and nourish them" (Legge 2 : 459).

Talented individuals are more properly the inhabitants of the royal court than are *Pollia* blooms; perhaps an alternate reading of the couplet might be: "Ritually purified, head and body, dressed in five-colored robe, he looks like a man of excellence (but really is not)." It is possible.

Against the background imagery of the voluptuous ritual of the sorceress, the associations are again clearly those of the royal court. The minister purifies himself and dons his official court robes before the great occasion when his counsel is to be heard. His outward rituals and adornments are emblematic of his inner excellence and virtue and loyalty, as in the previous poem.

3

	靈	連	蜷	兮	既	留
ARC	lieng	lian	g'iwan	g'ieg	kiəd	liog
ANC	lieng	liän	g'iwän	γiei	kjei	liəu
MSC	ling	lien	ch'üan	hsi	chi	liu
GSR	836	213	226	1241	515	1114
	sorceress	connected + wiggly			already	to detain
		binome: sinuous				

4

	爛	昭	昭	兮	未	央
ARC	glan	t'iog	t'iog	g'ieg	miwəd	iang
ANC	lan	tsiäu	tsiäu	γiei	mjwei	iang
MSC	lan	chao	chao	hsi	wei	yang
GSR	185	1131	1131	1241	531	718
	brilliant	bright +	bright		not yet	complete
		binome: brilliant				

META: The Spirit moves sinuously, he is already here.
The fiery luminescence shines brightly, still increasing.

PARA: The king's arrogant behavior shows he is completely possessed.
He injures us through his ignorance, the worst is yet to come.

The Commentaries

WANG I: *Ling* is the sorceress. The Ch'u people call the sorceress *ling-tzu* 靈子. *Lien-ch'üan* depicts the sorceress welcoming the Spirit. *Chi* means "already." *Liu* means "to stop." One edition has 子 below *ling*. *Lan* depicts brightness. *Chao-chao* is "bright." *Yang* is "finished."

It says that the sorceress appears sinuously with a respectful and welcoming facial expression and with a precise and dignified posture. Then the Spirit is pleased and induced to remain. See how his face shines brilliantly without limit. [2/4a5−8]

FIVE MINISTERS: Liang says: *Ling* is the sorceress. *Lien-ch'üan* depicts welcoming the Spirit. *Chi* means "complete." The Lord in the Clouds is caused to remain. The essence of his Spirit is bright and brilliant without limit. The Lord in the Clouds is P'ing I, Master of the Clouds. [32/16b2–3]

HHUNG HSING-TSU: *Ch'üan* sounds like 拳 [*g'iwan/g'iwän*]. The "*Fu* of the Southern Capital" says: "Eyebrows are *ch'üan*." The note says: "They appear long and sinuous." [2/4a5–7]

CHU HSI: *Ch'üan* sounds like 拳. *Ling* is that which causes the Spirit to descend. The Ch'u people call the sorceress *ling-tzu* or *shen-tzu* 神子. *Lien-ch'üan* means "long and crooked." Once the Spirit has stopped his progress he is pleased with the pure clothes and ornaments of the sorceress, he descends, possessing her body, and is detained there a long while. The Han Temple Hymn 漢歌 says: "The Soul is detained at peace." This also describes the Spirit. *Lan* depicts brightness. *Chao-chao* means "brilliant." [2/2a10–2b1]

Notes

Ling 靈 indicates the sorceress possessed by the Spirit. For details, see above at "Tung Huang T'ai I," line 12.

Lien-ch'üan 連蜷 (CW 39743.193) appears several times in the *Ch'u Tz'u*, but not elsewhere. For the definition in CW and all other dictionaries: "long and sinuous," there is only the note of Wang I to thank. Yet the onomatopoeic binome may yield some clue to its semantic content by means of analysis of its separate elements.

Lien 連 (CW 39743) originally meant "to pull a cart," with the supplementary image of "connected," perhaps from the way draft humans or animals were harnessed to carts. The word is also glossed "long-appearing" in a Han gloss to *Chuang Tzu* (quoted in CW), but this is an isolated instance and the passage is not clear enough to allow one to be certain whether or not the gloss is likely to be correct.

Ch'üan 蜷 (CW 33952) is not in the *Shuo Wen*. The binome appears only in the *Ch'u Tz'u*. Perhaps because of its lack of formalization in official word lists, the second element in the binome is written variously 蜷, 婘, 卷, or 拳. The family of words (at GSR 226) proceeds from *kiwan 卷 "to roll" and *g'iwan (same graph) "curved." Thus the written element of the word suggests sinuosity. The definition may be confirmed reasonably well in the light of the analysis of the elements of the binome.

"Sinuous" thus describes the movement of the sorceress' body which indicates that she is being possessed. An interesting comparison can be made to the Tibetan State Oracle of *gnas-chung* (pronounced Nechung), who exhibits sinuous, dance-like movements to show that he has been invested with the Spirit of *pe-har*, the Spirit who speaks through the oracle (cf. Lama Govinda, pp. 181–83).

Thus, expanding the text: "The Spirit manifests himself by the sinuous movements of the sorceress: this shows that he is already possessing her."

The *Shuo Wen* defines *lan* 爛 (CW 21139) as "cooked on a fire." The meaning is extended by Classical usage to "overcooked," "wounded by fire," and "to destroy," as in the most famous occurrence: "King Hui of Liang, for the matter of territory, tore and destroyed his people, leading them to battle. Sustaining a great defeat, he would engage again, and afraid lest they should not be able to secure the victory, urged his son whom he loved till he sacrificed him with them" (*Mencius* 7A : 1.2; Legge 2 : 478).

The commentators, in defining it "brilliant," are following Mao's interpretation of *Ode* #82, which begins with a wife awakening her husband to warn him that he may be late for the morning audience:

> Says the wife, "It is cock-crow";
> Says the husband, "It is grey dawn."
> "Rise sir, and look at the night,—
> If the morning star be not shining."
>
> (Legge 4 : 134)

Yet, even this simple text, perhaps more likely to be remembered by the classically trained reader, provides a reference to the royal court. Along with Mao Ch'ang's gloss goes his interpretation, described in Legge's note: "Mao understands the people of Cheng wishing to retain the good men who were dissatisfied with Duke Ch'uang and leaving the public service." The reluctance of the husband in our lines is explained: "Do not hate me for trying thus to detain you; it is because Duke Ch'uang is not swift to pursue the way of our former ruler that I do so."

Whether it is "to injure" as in *Mencius*, or "brilliant" as in the political ode, the associations of the word are not flattering to the ruler.

The similarity of context between the two Classical sources and the traditional Ch'ü Yüan story is inescapable: an unwise ruler has squandered his people in an unwise war; men of virtue can no longer serve him.

Chao-chao 昭昭 (CW 14172.91) means "bright" in both the senses of bright light and enlightened thinking. The second sense is most obvious in a Mencian formula using this compound no less than three times: "The sage enlightens others by means of his own enlightenment. Nowadays, however, men try to enlighten others by means of their own igorance!" (*Mencius* 7B:20). If a king who is himself ignorant tries to enlighten others, the result is bound to be the injury 爛 of the people.

None of the commentators bothers to mention the compound *wei-yang* 未央 (CW 14753.15). *Yang* (CW 5975) means either "middle" or "complete," as Wang I states. The compound seems to have no additional lexical significance beyond the simple connection of the words: "not yet complete." It later became the name of a Han Palace, the Wei-yang Kung 未央宮. Prior to the Han, it occurs only in this line, and once in *Ode* #182:

> How goes the night?
> It is not yet midnight.
>
> (Legge 4:294)

This ode, like the two which follow it, is said to be a criticism of King Hsüan of Chou. The grounds for the remonstrance are noted by Legge under the title of *Ode* #183: "Allusive, bewailing the disorder of the times, and the general indifference to it, and tracing it to the slanderers encouraged by the men in authority." If the reader sought an association for the term, this would be a most likely candidate, especially considering the quite striking relationship between the slanderers in the ode with Ch'ü Yüan's own personal situation.

In the descriptive context of the possession of the sorceress by the Spirit, we may postulate some kind of luminescence issuing from the body of the sorceress, giving us a paraphrase:

> 3. The Spirit manifests himself by the sinuous movements of the sorceress; this is evidence that he is already possessing her.
> 4. The fiery luminescence is brilliantly shining; it is still increasing.

In the context of the royal court and its intrigues we may also paraphrase:

3. The king is completely possessed, his arrogant behavior is a sign of it.
4. Through his ignorance, he injures us more and more; the worst is yet to come.

5

寒	將	憺	兮	壽	宮
ARC					
kian	tsiang	d'am	g'ieg	diog	kiong
kiän	tsiang	d'am	γiei	ziəu	kiung
chien	chiang	tan	hsi	shou	kung
143	727	619	1241	1090	1006
an	about to	to calm		long life	palace
exclamation					

Row labels: ARC, ANC, MSC, GSR.

6

與	日	月	兮	齊	光
zio	niet	ngiwat	g'ieg	dz'iər	kwang
iwo	nziet	ngiwet	γiei	dz'iei	kwang
yü	jih	yüeh	hsi	ch'i	kuang
89	404	306	1241	593	706
with	sun	moon		equal	bright

Row labels: ARC, ANC, MSC, GSR.

META: Lo! The Spirit will soon be at peace in the House of Long Life;
His luminosity rivals that of sun and moon.

PARA: I am obstructed at the palace, to the point of burning with grief.
Because he dares to match power with the king and his minister.

The Commentaries

WANG I: *Chien* is an exclamation. *Tan* is "peaceful." *Shou-kung* is the place where
the Spirit is worshipped. Since the aim of all sacrifices and worship is to
attain long life, they call it the House of Long Life. This says that the
Spirit of the Clouds has already arrived at the House of Long Life, has
received with pleasure the offered wine and food, and is calmly and
happily contented with no thought of departure. *Ch'i* is "to be equal."
Kuang is "brightness." It says that Feng Lung 豐隆, the Spirit of the

Clouds, has been accorded the place of highest rank and respect, and thus is of equal brightness with the sun and moon. When the clouds rise, the sun and moon are darkened; when the clouds are hidden, the sun and moon are bright. This is why it says "his luminosity rivals . . ." For 齊, one has 爭. [2/4a8–4b2]

FIVE MINISTERS: Hsien says: *Chien* is an exclamation. *Shou-kung* is the place where the Spirit is worshipped. The Spirit is happy and also his *Te* 德 is shining brightly. Thus he is equal to the sun and moon. [32/16b6–7]

HUNG HSING-TSU: *Tan* is pronounced 徒濫 [*d'am/d'am*]. The Emperor Wu of the Han established the House of Long Life for the Spirit Lord. Minister Ts'an in his note [to the *Han Shu*] says: "The House of Long Life is where the Spirit is served." [2/4a8]

CHU HSI: *Tan* is pronounced 徒濫. *Kung* is pronounced for the rhyme 古荒 [*kwang/kwang*]. For 齊 one text has 爭. *Chien* is an exclamation. *Tan* means "peaceful." *Shou-kung* is the place where the Spirit is served. In the time of Emperor Wu of the Han there was established the House of Long Life for the Spirit Lord. This is the same. It says the Spirit has arrived and is calmly and happily contented, with no thought of departure. [2/2b1–2]

Notes

Chien 蹇 (CW 98590) appeared above in line 2 of "Tung Huang T'ai I" as the second syllable of the onomatopoeic binome *yen-chien* 偃蹇. Here, when the graph is used alone, the commentators all offer the laconic equivalence 蹇, 詞也. The lexical meaning is "lame," "crooked," and in the *I Ching*, "obstruction."

In the *Ch'u Tz'u*, the word is used either as an initial exclamatory particle like the English "Lo!" (as here), or to mean "obstruction" (e.g., *Ai Shih Ming*, line 19: "*Helpless* I hover, unable to go on"). It is also used in the sense of "abundance" (e.g., *Chiu Pien*, line 92: "*Full* of impatient thoughts . . ."). It is occasionally borrowed for its homophone cousin 謇 "honest speech."

The translators, when presented with the initial exclamation in our line, are defeated. Pfizmaier ("sprechend") and Harlez ("invoquons-le") must misread 蹇 for 謇. Waley transliterates. The rest completely omit

it. Within the context of the sorceress and her Spirit, the proper rendering is clearly "Lo!" or an equivalent.

Tan 憺 (CW 11592) is one of a family of graphs that mean "peaceful"
or "bland" and all are read *d'am*: 倓, 惔, 淡, 憺, and 澹. Those based on
炎, especially 惔 (CW 10990), may also mean "burning with grief"
extended from the basic lexical meaning of 炎 "burning." "Peaceful" is
much more common, although none of the forms, save 惔, appears in
indisputably pre-Ch'in writing. The exception, 惔, occurs twice in the
Shih Ching, most noticably in *Ode* #191. This ode, "Chieh Nan Shan"
節南山, is among the most open and direct of those written to criticize a
king. Legge introduces the ode: "A lamentation over the miserable state
of the kingdom, denouncing the injustice and carelessness of the Grand
Master Yin as the cause of it, and blaming also the conduct of the King.
This piece is assigned to the reign of King Yu. Yu was son to King Hsüan
but was worse than his father in the days of his decline. His compara-
tively short reign ended in his violent death and immediately after, there
took place the removal of the royal residence to the eastern capital." The
first stanza:

> Lofty is that southern hill,
> With its masses of rocks!
> Awe-inspiring are you, O Grand-Master Yin,
> And the people all look to you!
> A fire burns in their grieving hearts;
> They do not dare to speak of you even in jest.
> The kingdom is verging to extinction;—
> How is it that you do not consider the state of things?
>
> (Legge 4 : 309–10)

The similarity of the events of that took place under the Chou kings to
the events of the royal succession in Ch'u during the lifetime of Ch'ü
Yüan is remarkable and would not have escaped the attention of the
educated reader of Han or T'ang times.

The use of *d'am* in this ode, being the most prominent prior to
our poem, points to the sense of the line so far, paraphrased:
"Helpless/obstructed, to the point of burning with grief . . ."

Shou 壽 (CW 5798) means "long life" or "old age" and is one of the
most auspicious and most frequently encountered words in Chinese.
There can be no doubt about its sense. The commentators base their

interpretation of *shou-kung* (CW5789.91) on the *Han Shu*, which in turn quotes *Shih Chi* in describing the creation of the House of Long Life by Emperor Wu. The only other appearance of this phrase in a pre-Han text is in the *Lu Shih Ch'un Ch'iu* 呂氏春秋 (quoted in CW) which uses it in the sense of "bedroom." This seems to be derived from the concept of the restorative power of sexual intercourse and its seminal contribution to longevity. In a political context, it may be that the House of Long Life is the king's palace, but there is no obvious connection that can be verified by a quotation from the Classics. If the Cloud Spirit is the slanderer, then the place where he is worshipped could refer to the ministries, or to the royal chamber where he is held in such high regard.

As an aside, at this point recall Waley's explanation of *shou-kung*, in the context of his assertion that the Nine Elegies may be the partial libretto of a shamanist song performance: "To what sort of performances do the Songs belong? References to a hall (*t'ang*) seem to show that they were carried out near or perhaps inside a formal building, and as in Song II the Spirit halts at an Abode of Life (*Shou-kung*), a sort of chapel for the worship of spirits, attached to palaces, it seems they took place at the Court of some great personage, possibly the King of Ch'u" (Waley, p. 15).

To match brightness with the sun and moon requires an unnatural source of light. No star may hope to do so. The concept of unnatural competition with legitimate power is central to the political interpretation. In sources as old as the "Kuo Feng," the oldest odes of the *Shih Ching*, the sun represents the king, the moon his minister. The prime example is *Ode #29*:

> O sun; O moon,
> Which enlighten this lower earth!
> Here is this man,
> Who treats me not according to the ancient rule.
> How can he get his mind settled?
> Would he then not regard me?

> O sun; O moon,
> Which overshadow this lower earth!
> Here is this man,
> Who will not be friendly with me.
> How can he get his mind settled?
> Would he then not respond to me?

O sun, O moon,
Which come forth from the east!
Here is this man,
With virtuous words, but really not good.
How can he get his mind settled?
Will be then allow me to be forgotten?

O sun, O moon,
From the east which come forth!
O father, O mother,
There is no sequel to your nourishing of me.
How can he get his mind settled?
Would he then respond to me, contrary to all reason?

(Legge 4:44—46)

The traditional interpretation: the king treats his minister badly, not with the ancient rule of loyalty nor with friendship. He neither regards nor responds to his minister. The king's reputation is therefore suffering. This is exactly the predicament known to have troubled Ch'ü Yüan. The traditional reader, along with the ode quoted above, would have also remembered *Ode #26*, which contains the lines:

There are the sun and the moon,—
How is it that the former has become small, and not the
latter?

Legge's note is clear: "The meaning seems to be:—The sun is always bright and full, while the moon goes through regular changes, now full and now absent from the heavens. In Wei the ruler was at this time obscured by the unworthy officers who abused his confidence and directed the government. The sun had become small and the moon had taken its place" (Legge 4:40).

Whether we read the unnatural light as a third source competing with the king and minister, or as a secondary light which has obscured the primary, the political context is well defined. Ch'ü Yüan indicts the slanderer who exerts power proper only to the king. The culpability extends also to the king: "The virtue of the prince is as illustrious as the sun and moon and he may thus see all under Heaven and traverse the six

Cardinal Points. King Huai, however, is unable to do these things, hence the heart of the poet is sad" (Hung's note to line 13, below).

If the king's virtue were all it should be, this unnatural situation could never have come to pass. Thus the minister who abuses his king is no less a subject for remonstrance than his tolerant and weak king.

7

	龍	駕	兮	帝	服
ARC	liung	ka	g'ieg	tieg	b'iuk
ANC	liwong	ka	γiei	tiei	b'iuk
MSC	lung	chia	hsi	ti	fu
GSR	1193	15	1241	877	934
	dragon	yoke		emperor	clothes

8

	聊	翱	遊	兮	周	章
ARC	liog	ngog	diog	g'ieg	tiog	tiang
ANC	lieu	ngau	iəu	γiei	tsiəu	tsiang
MSC	liao	au	yu	hsi	chou	chang
GSR	1114	1040	1080	1241	1083	723
	meanwhile	wander + wander			complete + splendid	
		binome: to wander			binome: unsettled	

META: In a dragon-drawn cart and polychrome robes
       For a while the Spirit wanders here and there, roaming.

PARA: He has harnessed the king and taken his power.
       Meanwhile, I am trying to dissipate my grief at failing to prevent this
          calamity.

The Commentaries

WANG I: *Lung-chia* describes the Cloud Spirit's harnessed dragons. It is as in the *I
         Ching*: "Clouds follow the dragon." *Ti* refers to the Emperors of the Five
         Directions. It says that Heaven's esteemed Cloud Spirit is mounted on a
         dragon and his robes are of the five colors of the robes of the Emperors of
         the Five Directions. *Liao* is "meanwhile." *Chou-chang* is like 周流, to
         float about with no fixed route. It says that the Cloud Spirit does not

dwell at a fixed place. He moves and then flies and floats around, coming and going and playing at his leisure. [2/4b2–4]

FIVE MINISTERS: Hsiang says: The Spirit harnesses the Cloud Dragons to his cart. He wears the robe of the Emperors of the Five Directions. *Au-yu chou-chang* 翱遊周章 depicts swift coming and going. [32/16b9]

HUNG HSING-TSU: no note.

CHU HSI: *Lung-chia* means "having the cart pulled by dragons." *Ti* refers to the Supreme God. *Liao* is "meanwhile." *Chou-chang* is like 周流. [2/2b2–3]

Notes

Lung 龍 (CW 48912), the dragon, is described by the *Shuo Wen*: "The *lung* is a long scaly serpent. It can be hidden or visible, minute or huge, long or short. It can ascend to heaven in spring; in fall it plunges into the watery depths." The word may also indicate a prize horse or the emperor. The identification of the emperor with the dragon and the clouds with his ministers is an ancient one that plays an important role in metaphor throughout Chinese literature. An example was adduced earlier (under the title of this poem) from Han Yü's "The Dragon and the Clouds."

For the Cloud Spirit, which in this poem represents the minister who engineered the downfall of Ch'ü Yüan, to harness a dragon to his cart is a most obscene political image: the minister has reduced the king to the status of his advisor's cart horse! "Clouds follow the dragon," not the other way around. Wang I's quotation from the *I Ching* (quotations of any sort are extremely rare in his commentary) supports this interpretation.

In the surface narrative, *lung-chia* may either be a cart decorated with figures of dragons, as the phrase is invariably glossed in the *Shih Ching*, or a cart drawn by dragons, as occasionally in the *Ch'u Tz'u*. In almost every chapter of the *Ch'u Tz'u* the image of a flying cart drawn by flying dragons appears, usually with similar words involved.

According to Wang I and the T'ang commentators, *ti-fu* 帝服 means "wearing a garment of the colors of the Five Emperors." The Five Emperors (CW 262.529) represent the five directions. Their colors are

East	blue/green
South	red
Center	yellow
West	white
North	black

This seems plausible, but not compelling, as it requires the reader to ignore (or, in the frequent habit of the commentators, pay specific attention to?) the natural and obvious sense of the phrase: royal garment. One may also follow Hawkes, who translates the line "He yokes to his dragon car the steeds of God," taking *ti* to mean *shang-ti* and *fu* to mean "horse," for which he claims *Yüan Yü*, line 54, as model.

Fu occurs twenty-nine times in the *Ch'u Tz'u* in several senses, clothing and horse among them, yet none may claim precedence by greater number. One may read *fu* as yoke horse and preserve the syntactic parallelism with *chia*, but *fu* must then be parallel with *lung*. Perfect parallelism of this type would produce a line read: (dragon =) king + cart horse, emperor + yoke horse. This is a most inauspicious (and politically daring) formula.

Parallelism of the adjective + noun type would yield "dragon cart" and "imperial clothes/yoke horse." This type is preferred by the commentators.

The reading of "horse" for *fu* that Hawkes derives from Wang I's note to the *Yüan Yu* line cited above is not convincing here for the simple reason that the authority he cites for "horse" in one place contradicts him here in this line. One must believe either that Wang I knows the meaning of *fu* or that he does not. One cannot have it both ways. To compound the confusion, *fu* when read **b'iug* means "carriage box," which adds yet another possible version: "Dragon yoke horse, imperial carriage."

The surface narrative is clearly explained by the commentators: dragons are yoked to pull the Cloud Spirit's cart; his robes are five-colored. The political interpretation is also clear: the minister has subdued his king and dresses in his clothes (= illegitimately exercises royal power).

A brocade is furnished by the well-known reading of *fu* to mean "defeated, forced to surrender": "the king is harnessed, the ancestor is brought to submission."

Liao 聊 (CW 29689) means "ringing in the ears." It is borrowed for homophonous words meaning "to rely on," "to wish to," "for a while," and a particle. The commentaries provide the laconic 聊, 且也, as at similar occurrences in the *Li Sao*, lines 99, 124, et al.

The only common sense of *liao* and *ch'ieh* 且 is that of "for a while." Hawkes, perhaps following the *Shih Ching* usage of *liao* as a mild desiderative particle, often translates it "I wanted to . . ." Most of the translators avoid the problem by not translating the word at all.

Ao-yu 翱遊 (CW 29454.2) and *chou-chang* 周章 (CW 3597.487) are onomatopoeic binomes of the alliterative type: **ngog-diog* and **tiog-tiang*.

For *ao-yu*, "to roam here and there," CW gives the variant 敖遊, which we find in *Ode* #26, in which "an officer of worth bewails the neglect and contempt with which he was treated." This ode was also mentioned earlier in connection with the equation sun = king and moon = minister.

> It floats about, that boat of cypress wood;
> Yea, it floats about on the current.
> Disturbed am I, and sleepless,
> As if suffering from a painful wound.
> It is not because I have no wine,
> And that I might not wander and saunter about.
>
> (Legge 4:38)

The metaphor of a drifting boat for a government without a true king at its head is known from the *Odes* all the way to the Grand *Fu* of the Sung (e.g., Su Shih's "First Fu on the Red Cliff," cf. Bischoff, pp. 221–22).

The minister of the ode, according to Legge's note, is suffering from his inability to aid his country in its time of peril, not because he lacks wine for solace or that "I could not dissipate my grief by wandering about." The notion of wandering about as a means to dissipate one's grief is carried into the last stanza of the same ode:

> There are the sun and the moon,—
> How is it that the former has become small, and not the
>   latter?
> The sorrow cleaves to my heart,
> Like an unwashed dress.
> Silently I think of my case,
> But I cannot spread my wings and fly away.
>
> (Legge 4:40)

If he could fly (cf. 翺翔) he could escape his sorrow. Similarly in *Ode* #82 (Legge 4:134) the protagonist is urged to "move about" to lighten his grief.

The second binome, *chou-chang*, equated by the commentaries with *chou-liu* 周流 "to wander about" in our line, is defined in most other places in the *Ch'u Tz'u* by synonyms such as 惶懷 "to look about in fear" and 不定 "unsettled."

Yet, the consensus of the commentators leaves us with the repetitious and insipid "For a while I roam here and there, I wander about."

Chou-chang is also written with the graphs 惆悵 (CW 11042.2), which take the more specific meaning of "disappointment at failure in one's ambition." This fits the contexts of both the sorceress and the Spirit, as well as the minister and his king, and we may accept it as a valid interpretation of the broad category of onomatopoeic binomes *tiog-tiang* meaning "fearful" or "disappointed."

The political reading is continued with the image of the king harnessed and supplanted (in effect) by his slanderous minister; and the poet, helpless to come to the aid of the king who has banished him, wanders about aimlessly to dissipate his disappointment at having failed to prevent this calamity.

9

	靈	皇	皇	兮	既	降
ARC	lieng	g'wang	g'wang	g'ieg	kiəd	kong
ANC	lieng	ɣwang	ɣwang	ɣiei	kjei	kang
MSC	ling	huang	huang	hsi	chi	chiang
GSR	836	708	708	1241	515	1015
	sorceress	magni- ficent	magni- ficent		already	to descend

+

binome: magnificent

10

	猋	遠	舉	兮	雲	中
ARC	piog	giwan	kio	g'ieg	giwən	tiong
ANC	piäu	jiwən	kiwo	ɣiei	jiuən	tiung
MSC	piao	yüan	chü	hsi	yün	chung
GSR	1155	256	75	1241	460	1007
	violent	far	to lift		cloud	in, middle

META: He is magnificent, having descended;
         Then suddenly he rises far and high into the clouds.

PARA: The Efficacious One is unhappy at having been brought low,
         The slanderer ascends into his element.

The Commentaries

WANG I: *Ling* refers to the Cloud Spirit. *Huang-huang* depicts beauty. *Chiang* means "to descend." It says the Cloud Spirit comes and descends, his appearance is beautiful and bright. *Piao* is the appearance of going quickly. *Yün-chung* is the dwelling of the Cloud Spirit. It says that the Cloud Spirit comes and goes quickly, drinks and eats until sated. Then in an instant he rises far into the sky and returns to his place. [2/4b4–6]

FIVE MINISTERS: {shows pronunciation of *piao* 必遙 [*piog/piäu]}
Han says: *Yün-chung* is the Spirit's dwelling place. [32/17a1]

HUNG HSING-TSU: *Piao* is pronounced 卑遙 [*piog/piäu]. It depicts a mass of dogs running. The "Great Man *Fu*" says: "The violent wind flows like a flood and the clouds float." Li Shan took this meaning when he miswrote the character 焱, following 火. [2/4b4–6]

CHU HSI: {writes 焱 for 猋}
Chiang is pronounced for the rhyme 胡攻 [*g'ong/γuong]. *Piao* is pronounced 卑遙. It is written with three fires. *Huang-huang* depicts beauty. *Chiang* means "to descend and possess the sorceress." *Yün-chung* is the dwelling place of the Spirit. It says the Spirit drinks and eats until sated. Then in an instant he rises far into the sky and returns to his place. [2/2b5–6]

Notes

Ling, as above, is the Spirit manifested through the sorceress.

Huang 皇 (CW 23220) is one of a large group of graphs used to write words pronounced *g'wang, some of which are reduplicated to form descriptive binomes. The basic groups are shown below. Those which are customarily construed doubly are underlined.

$$\text{Magnificent} = \begin{cases} \text{Bright} = \underline{\text{光皇}} \text{煌熿} \\ \text{Vast} = \underline{\text{皇光}} \text{侊潢廣橫曠} \\ \text{Fearful} = \underline{\text{皇惶}} \text{遑徨偟怳} \end{cases}$$

[v. GSR 706–8]

The multiple varia within each group are generally interchangeable. Adding to the confusion is the obvious appearance of several graphs in more than one category. Thus *huang* 皇 can be written for any of the various *g'wang words.

The binome appears in the *Shih Ching* (*Odes* #249, 299, 300) with the sense of "vast, great", the idea of brightness is reserved for the variant writing 煌 (*Odes* #140, 163, 226). As radicals were added or omitted with impunity during Chou and even Han times, one may nevertheless allow "bright" in this line as the commentators suggest. "Magnificent" occupies an ambiguous middle ground.

In the political context, however, it is not enough that the Lord be magnificent. We must find another association of *huang-huang* that fits the political context better. The most promising of the **g'wang* family is "anxious," especially in this context:

> Chou Hsiao asked Mencius, saying: "Did superior men of old time take office?" Mencius replied: "They did. The Record says 'If Confucius was three months without being employed by some ruler, he looked anxious and unhappy [皇皇如也]'. The loss of his place to an officer is like the loss of his State to a prince" (*Mencius* 3B:3; Legge 2:266).

This is an excerpt from a long discourse on the gentleman out of office, exactly the status of our supposed author. Early readers may have made this connection: the poet is anxious and unhappy at having been put out of office.

This requires the reading of 降 in a causative sense, a reading reinforced by the gloss of Chu Hsi, which clearly indicates the ANC pronunciation *yuong*. In ANC, "to descend" was read *kang* (going tone) = MSC *chiang*. "To be brought low" was read *yang* (even tone) = MSC *hsiang*. Chu Hsi's *yuong* is a much nearer homophone of *yang* than *kang*. Because the couplet rhymed perfectly well in ARC, his gloss is superfluous to our analysis of the original text. Yet, it indicates something of the requirements of Chu Hsi's ear in making sense of the line.

The confusion in the commentaries between *piao* 猋 (CW 20981) written with three "dogs," and *piao* 焱 (CW 19586) written with three "fires," must be resolved in favor of the three-dog *piao*. Three-fire "*piao*" is properly read **diam*, having the same pronunciation and meaning as *yen* 炎 : "blazing bright." Tuan's note to the *Shuo Wen* dictionary explains: "When something is abundant it is tripled." There are numerous examples: 驫 *piao*, written with three horses, means "many horses running together;" 轟 *hung*, written with three carts, means "the rumbling of carts," and by extension, describes the sound of thunder.

Our word *piao* 猋 means "a pack of dogs," and hence their running; by extension, it suggests rapid and violent motion. The sound **piau* or *biau is frequently descriptive of the motion of wind and may be written with any of a host of graphs (from GSR):颮 猋 飈 颮 飆 飊 飄 飀 颮 飃. All these words mean roughly the same thing and are pronounced similarly. The common miswriting of 焱 for 猋 persists in several additional varia: 熛, 飈, and 焱.

All the translators save Pfizmaier, who reads 焱 and translates "feuer-flackern," correctly give variations on "suddenly."

Yüan-chü 遠舉 (CW 39908.322) may mean either "to make an example of some ancient event (and yet be afflicted with the same error they were)" as in *Hsün Tzu*, "Fei Hsiang": 遠舉則病繆, or "to fly up high," which is merely a parroting of the commentaries to the line we are already reading. The only occurrence in the aeronautical sense is in this line.

The Spirit may "like a sudden wind fly far and high," but the evil minister is not so talented. The image of a sudden and violent wind is the emblem of the slanderer at court, originating in the *Shih Ching*. An example is *Ode* #199, according to the *Little Prefaces*: "Some noble suffering from slander and suspecting that the slanderer was an old friend, intimates the grounds of his suspicion, and laments his case, while he would welcome the restoration of their former relations" (Legge 4 : 343). Since this ode is so much to the point, and is an excellent example of the minister's complaint in plain language, filled with the common associations connected with such a situation at court, it is quoted here in full:

> What man was that?
> His mind is full of dangerous devices.
> Why did he approach my dam,
> Without entering my gate?
> Of whom is he a follower?
> I venture to say,—of Pao.
>
> Those two who follow each other in their goings;—
> Which of them wrought me this calamity?
> Why came he to my dam,
> Without entering to condole with me?
> Our former relations were different from the present,
> When he will have nothing to do with me.

What man was it?
Why came he to the path inside my gate?
I heard his voice,
But did not see his person.
He is not ashamed before men;
He does not stand in awe of Heaven.

What man was it?
He is like a violent [飄 *p'iao*] wind.
Why came he not from the north?
Or why not from the south?
Why did he approach my dam,
Doing nothing but perturb my mind?

You go along slowly,
And you have not leisure to stop!
You go along rapidly,
And yet you have leisure to grease your wheels!
If you would come to me but once!—
Why am I kept in a state of expectation?

If on your return you entered my house,
My heart would be relieved.
When on your return you do not enter it,
It is hard to understand your denial.
If you would come to me but once,
It would set me at rest.

The elder of us blew the porcelain whistle,
And the younger blew the bamboo flute;
I was as if strung on the same string with you.
If indeed you do not understand me,
Here are the three creatures (for sacrifice),
And I will take an oath to you.

If you were an imp or a water-bow,
You could not be got at.
But when one with face and eyes stands opposite to another,
The man can be seen through and through.
I have made this good song,
To probe to the utmost your veerings and turnings.

(Legge 4:343–46)

In this ode we find several themes that are common in the *Ch'u Tz'u*: close relations turned sour through slander, unrighteous behavior and shamelessness, the slanderer like a violent wind, the excuse for cancelling an agreed meeting, and the sinuous veerings and turnings of an evasive superior. In Legge's note to this poem he says: "Violent wind, as in [*Ode* #149; Legge 4:218–19] expresses the uncertainty of the person's movements, characteristic of a slanderer." The unfavorable connotation of the phrase "violent wind" was undoubtedly known to every slandered minister and disappointed scholar-official from the late Chou down almost to the present day.

Yün-chung 雲中 "in the clouds" was mentioned under the notes to the title of the poem. There however, the political context concerned in part the Lord whose court was in the clouds (Yin = under negative influence). Here we are describing the man who slandered Ch'ü Yüan, his rival. If *he* is "in the clouds," if he has beclouded the court (中), he is at home in his Yin element, surrounded by his emblematic violent winds: the fountainhead of nefarious Yin.

11

	覽	冀	州	兮	有	餘
ARC	ɡlam	kier	tiog	g'ieg	giug	dio
ANC	lam	kji	tsiəu	ɣiei	jiəu	iwo
MSC	lan	chi	chou	hsi	yu	yü
GSR	609	603	1086	1241	995	82
	to see	a place	district		with	surplus

12

	橫	四	海	兮	焉	窮
ARC	g'wang	siəd	χməg	g'ieg	ian	g'iong
ANC	ɣwəng	si	χai	ɣiei	iän	g'iung
MSC	heng	ssu	hai	hsi	yen	ch'iung
GSR	707	518	947	1241	200	1006
	transverse	four	sea		how?	extreme

META: He looks out over Chi-chou and beyond.
He traverses the Four Seas, knowing no limit.

PARA: He has gained control of the capital, and even more.
He outrages the whole world and impoverishes the people.

The Commentaries

WANG I: *Lan* is "to look out upon something." The area between the two rivers is called *Chi-chou* 冀州. *Yü* is the same as 他 ["other"]. It says the Cloud Spirit is at a place which is high and far off. He looks down upon Chi-chou and can see still other places. *Ch'iung* is "extremity." It says that the Cloud Spirit's comings and goings are so rapid that in the space of an instant he traverses the Four Seas. How can there be a limit to him? [2/4b6–9]

FIVE MINISTERS: Chi says: It says the Spirit's dwelling place is high and isolated. Below, he sees Chi-chou; to the sides, he sees the Four Seas. His vision is unobstructed in all directions. Chi-chou is that which was controlled by

Yao. Since the poet longs for a king who possesses the Tao of being a king, he looks at Chi-chou. [32/17a3–4]

HUNG HSING-TSU: *Huai Nan Tzu* says: "In the center is Chi-chou which is called the Central Land 中土." The note says that *chi* means "large." The *Master of the Four Quarters* 四方師 says: "Kill the black dragon in order to cross Chi-chou." The note says that Chi is the central of the Nine Chou, that which we now call "within the four seas." The *Li Chi* says: "Therewith to be complete in all the world." The note says: "*Heng* means 'to be complete'." [2/4b6–5a1]

CHU HSI: *Yen* is pronounced 於虔 [*ian/iän]. *Lan* means "to look out upon something." Between the two rivers is called Chi-chou. *Yu-yü* means that he can see so far that his vision is not limited to one *chou* 州. *Ch'iung* is "extremity." It says that the Cloud Spirit's comings and goings are so rapid that in the space of an instant he traverses the four seas. How can there be a limit to him? [2/2b5–7]

Notes

Lan 覽 (CW 35804) means "to see." More specifically, it is often used in the sense of "to look at something far away." This is how the commentators read it here. This is in fact evident from the context of the sorceress' narrative.

An exact homophone, for which *lan* is often written, is 攬 (CW 13356) meaning "to grasp" and by extension "to control." It is also written 擥 and 擸. The word is not found in the standard literary collections or the Classics, making its use here in the political context uncertain; however, the preponderance of *glam words meaning "hold," "control," and the like, make it a probable choice. The variant does occur in the *Li Sao*, lines 8 ("In the evening, I *plucked* the sedges of the islets," Hawkes) and 36 ("I *pulled up* roots to bind the valerian . . . ," Hawkes). The notes to line 36 prefer "grasp."

The similarity of usage between 覽 and 攬 stems from their parent graph 監 (GSR 609a) "to look at" and by extension "to superintend." Thus we may read either "He sees (= controls) . . ." or "He takes control of . . ."

Locating Chi-chou is relatively simple if one limits oneself to the

Classics, especially the *Shu Ching*. According to Legge's translation and notes (Legge 3 : 94–95) we may place it in about the modern provinces of Hopei and Shansi. This is far from the borders of Ch'u, in fact comprising approximately the state of Chao 趙 in Ch'ü Yüan's time.

This area is not "between the rivers" Ho and Kiang, as some scholars have suggested, but rather between the two arms of the Ho: the southward-flowing section which marks the eastern boundary of the Ordos, and the eastward-flowing section which passes through northern Honan.

Thus, strictly speaking, Chi-chou is in northeastern China, and not a part of Ch'u. The term has acquired a more general sense implying all of China, but this is a later development arising from the traditional location of the ancient capital of China in that region. The antecedent of this usage is found in the *Shu Ching* (Legge 3 : 159–60) in the chapter called "The Songs of the Five Sons," to which I have made reference previously:

> The third said: "There was the prince of T'ao and T'ang,
> Who possessed this country of Chi.
> Now we have fallen from his ways,
> And thrown into confusion his rules and laws;
> And the consequence is extinction and ruin."

Legge's note: "Yao of course possessed the whole empire; but it was in Chi-chou that he had his capital." Thus the phrase is a synechdoche: to own the capital is to own the kingdom.

The fact that this is from one of the chapters that were forged in the fourth century A.D. does not discredit our citation. We are more interested in the use of the phrase and its associations than in the relative dates of the two texts. Also, the stories told in the *Shu Ching* are ancient, and it is entirely possible that a phrase can antedate the book in which one finds it.

Thus we paraphrase the line so far. "He has got control of the capital and even more (i.e., the whole kingdom)."

Heng 橫 (CW 15897) normally means "crosswise." It is read **g'wang* in this sense. Here, however, an alternate reading may be intended: *kwang with the meaning "completely," "entirely." If so, the couplet would be read "Looking out upon Chi-chou and beyond/To the entirety of the

Four Seas, limitless (his vision)," following the commentators in their explication of the surface narrative.

The commentators, save Hung, contort themselves to justify *heng* as "laterally" by construing *lan* as a downward vision (contradicted by all sources) to counterbalance *heng* as a lateral motion. Hung's discreet quotation from the *Li Chi* indicates his disagreement. Still another *Li Chi* passage in support of Hung is found in the "Yüeh Chi" (*Li Chi* 2 : 120: "The bells give out a clanging sound as a signal. The signal is recognised by all, and that recognition produces a martial enthusiasm. When the ruler hears the sound of the bell, he thinks of his officers of war."

The reading "completely," which Legge translated "by all" in the passage above, is more prudent in another way. The phrase *heng-hsing* 橫行 (CW 15897.39), by which Chu and Wang explain *heng* to mean "to go laterally," is by universal convention extended to mean "perversity," and a very specific kind of perverse behavior: "actions not in accord with the Tao."

This is a crucial concept, central to the universal theme of the disaffected minister. In the context of political intrigue and the Ch'ü Yüan legend, the reader would certainly recall the appearance of *heng-hsing* in: "There was one man pursuing a violent and disorderly course in the kingdom, and King Wu was ashamed of it. This was the valor of King Wu. He also, by one display of his anger, gave repose to all the people of the kingdom" (*Mencius* 1B : 3.7; Legge 2 : 157).

Our king, however, urged on by his new advisor, continues his "violent and disorderly course" (*heng-hsing*), he is the antithesis of King Wu, for not only does he not display his anger and remove the slanderer from office, he follows the latter's advice! What ought a good man to do when his king behaves in such a disorderly way? When the king treats his good ministers in such a mean fashion?

> Here is a man, who treats me in a perverse and unreasonable manner. The superior man in such a case will turn round upon himself—"I must have been wanting in benevolence; I must have been wanting in propriety;—how should this have happened to me?" He examines himself, and is especially benevolent. He turns round upon himself, and is specially observant of propriety. The perversity and unrea-

sonableness of the other, however, are still the same. The superior man will *again* turn round on himself—"I must have been failing to do my utmost." He turns round upon himself, and proceeds to do his utmost, but still the perversity and unreasonableness of the other are repeated. On this the superior man says, "This is a man utterly lost indeed! Since he conducts himself so, what is there to choose between him and a brute? Why should I go to contend with a brute?" (*Mencius* 4B:28; Legge 2:333–34)

The answer is that a minister ought to cease to serve such a man:

Po I would not allow his eyes to look on a bad sight, nor his ears to listen to a bad sound. He would not serve a prince whom he did not approve, nor command a people whom he did not esteem. In a time of good government he took office, and on the occurence of confusion he retired. He could not bear to dwell either in a court from which a lawless government emanated, or among lawless people. He considered his being in the same place with a villager, as if he were to sit amid mud and coals with his court robes and court cap. In the time of Chou he dwelt on the shores of the North sea, waiting the purification of the kingdom. Therefore when men now hear the character of Po I, the corrupt become pure, and the weak acquire determination. (*Mencius* 5B:1.1; Legge 2:369)

In fact, Ch'ü Yüan has largely replaced Po I as the personification of this role. The basic idea of the Mencian description is that kings are prone to outrageous behavior. If this occurs, the virtuous minister tries his best to correct his ruler, and if he is unsuccessful, withdraws and remains untainted.

It is more than a little confusing that the third century compilers of *Mencius* do not mention Ch'ü Yüan in any of the numerous similar passages they include in the book. One should not argue solely *ex silentio*, but one may hazard a guess that Mencius had never heard of Ch'ü Yüan because of their being roughly contemporaries. The truth of the matter is that there was copious communication between the feudal states, as well as an exchange of wandering persuaders and advisors. We may not conclude that our poet is a fiction solely on these grounds, but his total absence from any pre-Han writing is curious.

In the context of the discussion of what a good minister ought to do about a bad king, the later reader would have recalled *Han Shih Wai Chuan* 1/27 (Hightower, p. 35): "One who thinks his prince is impure should not walk in his territory." If we assume the late Warring States context of the political interpretation, as later readers did, we must note the fact that an advisor was not limited to one king. As is evident in the *Chan Kuo Ts'e*, common practice was for these wandering persuaders to change princes frequently at the slightest provocation, to travel from court to court seeking a hearing. Ch'ü Yüan, by not "following custom" (cf. "Hsiang Chün," lines 15–16), demonstrated a rare loyalty to his country and king, in spite of having been banished in disgrace. This is one reason for the great respect in which he has been held since. Generations of mandarins forced to choose between exile and serving the frequent non-Chinese invader dynasties, such as Ch'in, Northern Wei, T'ang (originally Turks), Yüan, Liao, Hsia, and Ch'ing, must have felt a sharp kinship with the poet of these lines.

Wang I, and imitating him Chu Hsi, explains *yen-ch'iung* 焉窮 by the extended paraphrase 安有窮極也 "How can there be any limit (to it)?" This allows us to read it **ian* "how?" The phrase may also mean "How have we come to this extreme of poverty?" (CW 26910.175).

Yen (CW 19510), besides an interrogative particle, is used as a synonym of *tse* 則 "then," "thus," and is then read **gian*. Either reading allows us to continue the court paraphrase:

(*yen* = how?)

       He outrages the world, can there be an end?

(*yen* = then)

       He outrages the world, thereby driving us to extremity.

The picture of a king influenced by an evil minister is supplanted here by that of a king who rules his entire realm perversely and acts against the Tao. Is there any wonder that his people are driven to such an extreme and desperate state?

13

	思	夫	君	兮	太	息
ARC	siəg	piwo	kiwən	g'ieg	t'ad	siək
ANC	si	piu	kiuən	γiei	t'ai	siək
MSC	ssu	fu	chün	hsi	t'ai	hsi
GSR	973	101	459	1241	317	925
	to think	man	lord		great	to sigh

14

	極	勞	心	兮	憧	憧
ARC	g'iək	log	siəm	g'ieg	d'ong	d'ong
ANC	g'iək	lau	siəm	γiei	d'uong	d'uong
MSC	chi	lao	hsin	hsi	ch'ung	ch'ung
GSR	910	1135	663	1241	1009	1009
	extreme	to toil	heart		grief +	grief
						binome: grief

META: Thinking of the lord, I heave a great sigh.
        My heart toils to its utmost, but I am grieved and distressed.

PARA: I think of the king and heave a great sigh;
        Concerned to the utmost, I am vexed and disappointed.

The Commentaries

WANG I: *Chün* refers to the Cloud Spirit. *T'ung-t'ung* depicts a grieving heart. Ch'ü Yüan saw the clouds move a thousand miles effortlessly, going all around the Four Seas and his thoughts followed them. To look into the four quarters in order to forget one's grieving thoughts is an impossibility. So he heaved a great sigh and was distressed in his heart. Some say that *chün* refers to King Huai, that Ch'ü Yüan plainly sets forth the significance of the Cloud Spirit. In the main, it is sufficient as a lament, and to that extent he is sadly pondering King Huai's inability to distinguish good from evil. Thus the poet sighs over and over with a distressed heart but is ultimately powerless. For 憧 one text has 忡. [2/5a1–4]

FIVE MINISTERS: {Replacing 憽 with 忡 in the text and notes}
> Liang says: *Fu-chün* refers to the Soul Spirit as a metaphor for the lord. It says that the place where the lord dwells is high and far and from it he regulates the kingdom below him. "I think of my lord but cannot see him; thus, I heave a sigh and am sick at heart." [32/17a6–7]

HUNG HSING-TSU: The *Li Chi* says: "This man 夫人 is he who studies the Rites." *Fu* sounds like 扶 [*b'iwo/b'iu*]. *T'ung* is pronounced 敕中 [*t'iong/t'iung*]. The *Shuo Wen* says that *ch'ung* 忡 means sorrow, quoting the *Shih Ching*: "A sorrowing heart is *ch'ung-ch'ung*." In the *Ch'u Tz'u* 忡 is written 憽. This section uses the Cloud Spirit as a metaphor for the king. It says the virtue of the prince is as illustrious as the sun and moon and he may thus see all under heaven and traverse the six Cardinal Points. King Huai, however, is unable to do these things; hence the heart of the poet is sorry. [2/5a2–5]

CHU HSI: *Fu* sounds like 扶. *Ch'ung* is pronounced 敕中. One edition has 忡. *Fu-chün* refers to the Spirit. The *Li Chi* says: "This man is one who studies Rites." This is the same. *Ch'ung-ch'ung* depicts a heart affected by some emotion. [2/2b5–7]

Notes

Ssu 思 (CW 10734) means "to think of" especially in an affectionate, concerned, or mournful way.

Fu 夫 (CW 5962) may be read *piwo* meaning "man," or *b'iwo* meaning "this one," or an initial particle. Hung clearly takes *fu* here in the second sense: "This lord," evident from his reference to the *Li Chi* formula *fu-jen* 夫人 "this man." Moreover, he explicitly indicates the reading to be *b'iwo* in his gloss. Chu Hsi incorporates Hung's note verbatim, from which we assume his concurrence in the indicated reading of *b'iwo* in Hung's note.

In the Classics, *fu-chün* 夫君 (CW 5962.22) means "husband," and is a respectful term of address used by wives. Only in our line is it said to be a term for "the lord." Yet, the parallelism in the various relationships (i.e., king-minister, husband-wife) allows one to stand for the other in this context.

T'ai-hsi 太息 (CW 5965.312) means "a great loud sigh." It is an expression of grief, as in the *Shih Chi*, "Basic Annals of Kao Tsu" (quoted in CW): "Sighing a great sigh, he said 'Alas! That such a remarkable man should act like this!'" The correspondence of husband-wife with king-minister (from the Five Relations) allows an additional reading: "I think of my relationship with the king, and it makes me sigh."

The line is clear in either context. The sorceress sighs after her departed Spirit-lover. The minister mourns the sad state of his relation-ship with the king.

Lao-hsin 勞心 "to trouble the heart" appears prominently in the refrain of *Ode* #102. This ode shares not only its theme, but also much of its vocabulary with our concluding couplet. Legge introduces the ode: "Metaphorical. THE FOLLY OF PURSUING OBJECTS BEYOND ONE'S STRENGTH. . . . The Preface refers the piece to duke Hsiang, possessed by a vaulting ambition which over-leapt itself. It may be applied to the insane course which he pursued to acquire the foremost place among the States." The ode itself follows:

> Do not try to cultivate fields too large;—
> The weeds will only grow luxuriantly.
> Do not think of winning people far away;—
> Your toiling heart will be grieved.
>
> Do not try to cultivate fields too large;—
> The weeds will only grow proudly.
> Do not think of winning people far away;—
> Your toiling heart will be distressed.
>
> How young and tender
> Is the child with his two tufts of hair!
> When you see him after not a long time,
> Lo! He is wearing the cap!
>
> (Legge 4:157–58)

In the background of the ode we may also see parallels with Ch'ü Yüan's situation. The king is being ruined by his ambition, fueled by the advice of an evil minister (= a proudly growing weed). Soon his incom-petent son will be on the throne. But the king is beyond the poet's influence; thinking of him only troubles the poet's heart to no avail.

Lao-hsin is also found in the oft-quoted political aphorism of *Mencius* 3A:4.6 (Legge 4:249–50): "Those who *labor with their minds* govern others, those who labor with their strength are governed by others."

T'ung 恫 (CW 11793) and 恫 (CW 10793) are varia of 恫 (CW 10608). Doubled, with the sound *d'ong-d'ong*, they and several other graphs have the meaning "the appearance of being grieved and distressed":

恫	*t'iong	恫	*d'ong
恫	*d'ong	恫	*t'ung
痛	*t'ung	憧	*tiung
衝	*t'iung	慟	*d'ung

Thus we have on either level: "My heart toils to its utmost but I am still grieved and distressed." Their relationship is no longer that prescribed by the Ancient Kings for king and minister. His king has departed from the model and is heading for disaster. The poet, throughout the poem, has expressed his disgust for the king's course and for the complicity of his own rival. He is now far from court, unable to influence affairs, and can only mourn the sad state to which events have led them.

Hsiang Chün

Metaphrastic Translation

THE PRINCESS OF THE HSIANG

(The ministrant attempts to induce the appearance of the river Spirit and laments his failure.)

1. The lady does not move, she hesitates;
2. Who awaits her in the middle of the island?

3. Beautiful and adorned,
4. I mount the flow in my cinnamon boat.

5. Let the Yüan and Hsiang rivers be without waves!
6. Make the waters of the Great River flow quietly!

7. I watch for the lady, she has not come.
8. I blow on my pipes; of whom do I think?

9. I yoke the flying dragon and go north,
10. Sinuous my way over Lake Tung-t'ing.

11. Mat-walls of fig creeper, bound round with iris;
12. Oars of sweet flag, pennon of thoroughwort.

13. I look off toward Ch'en-yang on the far shore,
14. Crossing the Great River, I display my sincerity.

15. I display my sincerity, but to no avail.
16. My sister dissuades me, sighing for me a great sigh.

17. Copiously flow my tears, without ceasing;
18. From my rude exile, I think of the lady.

Paraphrastic Translation

MINISTER AND RULER

(The banished minister describes the events that led to his banishment and laments his failure to dissuade the king from his unwise course of action.)

1. The king cannot act, he is indecisive.
2. Who is left at the center of the government?

3. The virtuous one who could set all aright,
4. I was expelled by a miscreant king, and sailed into exile.

5. Let there be an end to the great unrest in the south of Ch'u,
6. Put a stop to the great disorder in the north.

7. I mourn for my king, for his future.
8. Idle, I play my pipes: of whom do I think?

9. The king is controlled, unwise policies prevail in the north.
10. I am obstructed down here in my southern exile.

11. My king is tied up and helpless, I am in bonds;
12. I receive no proper summons, the palace doors are shut.

13. I look off toward the capital, across the Kiang.
14. Defying the flow of events, I made known my virtue.

15. I made known my virtue, but it did no good.

16. My king was led like a cow on a tether; it makes me heave a great sigh.

17. Copiously flow my tears, without ceasing;
18. I conceal my thoughts of the king, who is no fit match for Yao.

19. Cinnamon oar, thoroughwort sweep;
20. I chop the ice and pile up the snow.

21. I pluck the fig creeper in the water,
22. Pick the lotus from a tree branch.

23. When hearts are not one, the matchmaker must toil;
24. When affection is shallow, it is easily broken off.

25. The rocky rapids flow rapidly;
26. The flying dragon flits and flutters.

27. Our relationship was insincere, bad feelings increased;
28. At the trysting time you were faithless and said you were busy.

29. At dawn I gallop along the marshes of the Great River.
30. At dusk I stop to rest at the Northern Island.

31. Birds nest on my roof.
32. Water swirls beneath my house.

33. I throw my jade semicircle into the Great River.
34. I abandon my girdle on the banks of the Li.

35. I pluck ginger on the fragrant island,
36. Which I shall pass on to the ones who follow.

37. This opportunity cannot be had twice;
38. So for a while I will take my ease, aimlessly wandering.

19. Nothing I did was of any use;
20. I was reviled and ignored, I made no progress.

21. Everything is topsy-turvy:
22. The evil rule, the worthy are banished!

23. When intentions differ, the mediator must toil;
24. When royal favor is shallow, it is easily lost.

25. My unassailable virtue incited the slanderers;
26. The king was beset by fawning sycophants.

27. They served him without sincerity, my enmity grew;
28. At the appointed time, he broke our agreement, deigning to inform
    me: "Urgent affairs of state."

29. When I was in power, I exerted myself in the king's service.
30. Now, while others are in control, I must rot in a southern exile.

31. Evil portents indict the king!
32. Evil influences pervade the ministries!

33. I throw my symbol of dismissal into the Kiang.
34. I abandon my insignia of office on the bank of the Li.

35. I have chosen these examples of my virtue:
36. I bequeath them to posterity, to the worthies who will follow.

37. My opportunity is lost, it will never come again,
38. But I will endure this decline in dignified idleness.

Title

湘	君
ARC	siang	kiwən
ANC	siang	kiuən
MSC	hsiang	chün
GSR	731	459
	a river	lord

META: The Princess of the Hsiang

PARA: Minister and Ruler

The Commentaries

WANG I: no note.

FIVE MINISTERS: no note.

HUNG HSING-TSU: Liu Hsiang's *Lieh Nü Chuan* 列女傳 says: "Shun died at Ts'ang-wu 蒼梧. His two consorts died between the Kiang 江 and the Hsiang 湘. They are customarily referred to as the princesses of the Hsiang." The *Li Chi* says: "Shun was buried at Ts'ang-wu. His two consorts did not follow him at that time." The [Han] note says: "The Lady of the Hsiang 湘夫人 sung of in the *Li Sao Ching* is the consort of Shun." Han Yü's "Inscription for the Huang-ling Temple" says: "On the bank of the Hsiang there is a temple called Huang-ling Temple 黃陵廟. It was established in antiquity for the worship of Yao's two daughters, the two consorts of Shun." The Ch'in *po-shih* 博士 said to the first Ch'in Emperor: "The ladies of the Hsiang are Yao's daughters, Shun's consorts." Liu Hsiang and Cheng Hsüan also both regarded the two consorts to be the princesses of the Hsiang. [2/8b6—9a3]

CHU HSI: For the significance of the lines, see within the notes to the poem. This section is probably the words of a male sorcerer, master of ceremonies to the Yin spirits. Thus his emotions are intricate and manifold. The purpose of it all is to allude by hidden references to the idea of loyalty to the ruler, but the old explanations were lost, complicating the matter. Now I have set it all aright. [2/4a11—4b1]

Notes

The Hsiang Chün 湘君 (CW 18223.30) is the guardian spirit of the Hsiang River and the greater area that is the watershed of the great rivers which collect in Lake Tung-t'ing, then enter the Kiang. She is often called the Hsiang Fei 湘妃, which means "the Hsiang consort."

Tradition combined the legends of the Hsiang spirit with that of the death of the two wives of Shun, Yao's daughters, O-huang 娥皇 and Nü-ying 女英. The medieval cults of the Hsiang spirits took the "Hsiang Chün" of this poem to be the elder O-huang, "Hsiang Fu Jen" of the fourth Elegy to be the younger Nü-ying.

Edward Schafer, in his *Divine Woman*, gives a thorough survey of the legends and cults associated with the Hsiang goddess(es). I refer the reader there, and here omit a detailed pedigree of the Hsiang ladies.

The Hsiang River is described in the context of line 5, below.

The political associations of the phrase *hsiang-chün* may be either of the following. The name may recall to the reader the story of Yao and Shun, how Yao ceded the throne to the worthy Shun in preference to his natural heir. Ch'ü Yüan may be comparing himself to Shun, as he certainly does later in the poem.

Much more compelling a clue is the perfect homophonous nature of 湘 and 相 *siang*. Hsiang-chün 相君, "minister and ruler," calls up a host of concepts central to the political principles which dominate the Nine Elegies: the ruler rules, the ministers minister, any deviation is heresy. The relationships between ruler and minister are set down in Confucian orthodoxy for all literati to remember.

In fact, the poet simply announces his theme: "Minister and Ruler."

1

	君	不	行	兮	夷	猶
ARC	kiwən	piug	g'ang	g'ieg	diər	ziog
ANC	kiuən	piəu	γəng	γiei	i	iəu
MSC	chün	pu	hsing	hsi	i	yu
GSR	459	999	748	1241	551	1096
	lord	not	to act, move		level + binome:	suspicious hesitant

2

	蹇	誰	留	兮	中	州
ARC	kian	diwər	liog	g'ieg	tiong	tiog
ANC	kiän	zwi	liəu	γiei	tiung	tsiəu
MSC	chien	shui	liu	hsi	chung	chou
GSR	143	575	1114	1241	1007	1086
	an exclamation	who?	to detain		in, middle	island

META: The lady does not move, she hesitates;
Who awaits her in the middle of the island?

PARA: The king cannot act, he is indecisive.
Who is left at the center of the government?

The Commentaries

WANG I: *Chün* refers to the Hsiang Chün. *I-yu* is "indecisive." This line says that the Hsiang Chün is located to the left of the Yüan and Hsiang rivers and to the right of the Kiang. The area between embraces the waves of Tung-t'ing, some hundreds of *li* square. Many birds nest there; fish and turtles are plentiful. The land is rich and abundant. It also has dangerous places. Thus, its spirits must often be pacified, as they dare not be allowed to wander unsettled. So there are rites and sacrifices where a sorceress invites them and calls out to them once more to be at peace. *Chien* is an interjection. *Liu* means "detained." *Chung-chou* 中州 means "in the middle of the island" 州中. A place in the water where one may stay is called a *chou* 州. This line says that the Hsiang Chün is *chien*-like, moving with difficulty. Who waits in the island in the river? Yao gave his two daughters to marry Shun. The Miao tribe was rebellious. Shun went to quell them. The two daughters also went, but didn't return, dying en route between the Yüan and Hsiang rivers. Thus, they are called Hsiang Fu Jen. "Who is waiting" probably refers to these two daughters of Yao. [2/5a7–5b1]

FIVE MINISTERS: Hsien says: *Chün* is the Spirit of the Hsiang River. *Chien* is an interjection. The couplet says the spirit is happy, its dwelling is peaceful. It does not descend. Who is waiting in the river's island? One who wishes for the Spirit's speedy arrival. [32/17b2–3]

HUNG HSING-TSU: Wang I believes the Hsiang Chün was the Hsiang River spirit and referred to the ones awaiting the Hsiang Chün in the island as the two wives of Shun. Because of this, Han Yü believed the Hsiang Chün was O-huang 娥皇 and the Hsiang Fu Jen was Nü-ying 女英. *Liu* means "to stop." [2/5a7–5b2]

CHU HSI: *Chun* refers to the Hsiang Chün, Yao's elder daughter O-huang, who was Shun's proper wife. Shun died at Ts'ang-wu, his two wives between the Yüan and Hsiang rivers. They are customarily referred to as Hsiang Chün. By the Hsiang at Huang-ling 黃陵 there is a temple to them. *I-yu* is "indecisive." *Chung-chou* is "in the island." A place in the water where one may dwell is called *chou*. The couplet says that the Spirit has not come, one knows not by what person it may be detained. [2/3a2–4]

Notes

Pu-hsing 不行 (CW 24.262) means "does not move." In the context of the surface narrative, "The Hsiang Chün does not move"; in the political context, "The king cannot act." In MSC, it means "unacceptable."

This is continued in the phrase *i-yu* 夷猶 (CW 5977.103). There is a large family of graphs to represent the words *$diər$-$ziog$ and *$ziog$-zio meaning "hesitant," "indecisive," "suspicious":

GRAPH	ARC
猶預	*ziog-dio
猶與	*ziog-zio
猶豫	*ziog-dio
夷猶	*diər-ziog
夷由	*diər-diog
夷尤	*diər-giug

Wang I gives the equivalence 夷猶 = 猶豫. The citations of these various binomes generally expand the terms, e.g.: 夷由不能決也 "夷由 means 'unable to decide'." Thus, the translation "indecisive."

This term occurs in a section of the *Li Chi* which describes divination and the role of the king:

> Divination by the shell is called *pu* 卜; by the stalks, *shih* 筮. The two were the methods by which the ancient sage-kings made the people believe in seasons and days, revere spiritual beings, stand in awe of their laws and orders; by which they made the people determine their perplexities and settle their misgivings.
>
> Hence it is said "If you doubted, and have consulted the stalks, you need not think that you will do wrong. If the day for action is at hand, you need not hesitate." (*Li Chi* 1:94)

Of the things a king should *not* be, "indecisive" is surely one. In fact, the king is he who ought to rectify the indecision of his people.

Chien 蹇 (CW 38590) means "lame," and by extension "to hinder" and also "crooked," "heterodox." As the name of hexagram #39 of the *I Ching*, "Obstruction," it carries profound associations with political danger: "The hexagram pictures a dangerous abyss lying before us and a steep, inaccessible mountain rising behind us. We are surrounded by obstacles. . . . In such a situation, it is wise to pause in view of the danger and to retreat" (Wilhelm, p. 151).

The commentators assert that *chien* 蹇 is just a 語詞, meaning that it is an exclamatory particle.

Liu 留 (CW 22317) means "to stop," and by extension, "to obstruct," "detain." The connection of *chien* with obstruction in the first word is clearly paralleled in *liu*.

The construction 中州 may have perplexed even Wang I, whose

suggestion 中州 = 州中 "in the middle of island" is not completely satisfying. This has nevertheless been accepted by the other commentators and Western translators as well. We may therefore ignore our discomfort and accept it into the surface narrative as they have indicated.

Another interpretation is this: the line is asking a question, so we supply the answer—the popular duck-and-drake rule (cf. Smith, p. 170). The answer lies in the opening lines of *Ode* #1:

> Q: Who is waiting on the middle island?
>
> A: *Kuan-kuan* go the ospreys,
>   On the islet in the river.
>
>   The modest, retiring, virtuous, young lady:—
>   For our prince a good mate she.
>
> (Legge 4:1)

(This type of "linguistic diversion" remains immensely popular in China even today, under the name *hsieh-hou yü* 歇後語.)

Ode #1 is a song of welcome for the virtuous young lady, fit to be the mate of a prince. Based on the traditional interpretation of the ode, we may answer the question in our text: "A virtuous minister, worthy to be the support of his king." The parallelism of the initial exlamations may be effective in reinforcing the association.

The additional Yin flavor of the line ("surrounded by water") intensifies the image of the worthy one, come to be a fit counselor for his king, waiting unnoticed, surrounded by the general Yin influence of the court in its present disorder. In this spectacular brocade, the poet decries the irresoluteness of his king and complains about his own obstruction and idleness. The notion that a king who alienates worthy advisors is doomed is well known from *Han Shih Wai Chuan* 1/26 (Hightower, p. 34): "The loss of a state . . . is not caused by a lack of saints and sages, but it is the result of not using them" (cf. also 1/5, 5/3–4, 5/18, 6/13, 6/23, 8/36, and 10/14 for other examples).

The sense in which the line was read in context was probably less complex than the brocade, associating the "center" with the royal place, and the common aural pun 州 [*tiog*] = 周 [*tiog*]. One would then see the line as a less blunt, but nonetheless transparent criticism: "Who is still there, at the center of the government?"

3

	美	要	眇	兮	宜	修
ARC	miər	iog	miog	g'ieg	ngia	siog
ANC	mji	iäu	miäu	γiei	ngjie	siəu
MSC	mei	yao	miao	hsi	i	hsiu
GSR	568	1142	1158	1241	21	1077
	beautiful	waist +	tiny		proper	to adorn
		binome: beautiful				

4

	沛	吾	乘	兮	桂	舟
ARC	p'wad	ngo	d'iəng	g'ieg	kiweg	tiog
ANC	p'wai	nguo	dz'iəng	γiei	kiwei	tsiəu
MSC	p'ei	wu	ch'eng	hsi	kuei	chou
GSR	501	58	895	1241	879	1084
	amply	I	to mount		cassia	boat
	flowing					

META: Beautiful and adorned,
I mount the flow in my cinnamon boat.

PARA: The virtuous one who could set all aright,
I was expelled by a miscreant king, and sailed into exile.

The Commentaries

WANG I: *Yao-miao* depicts beauty. *Hsiu* is "an ornament." This line says the appearance of the two women is beautiful and they are also agreeably ornamented. For 眇 one text has 妙. One edition adds 又 above 宜.

P'ei depicts motion. *Chou* is "a boat." *Wu* is Ch'ü Yüan referring to himself. This line says that although he is in the midst of lakes and marshes, he still mounts his cassia-wood boat and travels on the flow among the fragrances. [2/5b2–5]

FIVE MINISTERS: {Glosses 眇 with 妙, [*miog/miau*]. 沛 is spelled 普賴 [*p'ad/p'ai*]}.

Hsiang says: One thinks of the beautiful appearance and agreeable ornamentation of the Spirit. "Once more I mount my cassia boat in order to meet the Spirit." Cassia wood is chosen for the boat because of the purity of its fragrance. For 乘 one text has 椉. [32/17b5]

HUNG HSING-TSU: *Yao* is pronounced 於笑 [*iog/iäu*]. *Miao* is the same as 妙. The *Han Shu* says that 幼眇 sounds like 要妙. This line describes the beauty and virtuous manner of O-huang 娥皇 in order to allude to the worthy minister 賢臣.

Mencius says "water goes rushing downwards 沛然, who can control it?" *P'ei* is pronounced 普賴. A cassia boat is the boat for welcoming the Spirit. Ch'ü Yüan uses this to refer metaphorically to himself. [2/5b2–5]

CHU HSI: The *Han Shu* says *yao* is 幼, pronounced 於笑. *Miao* is the same as 沙. One edition adds 又 above 宜. *Yao-miao* depicts beauty. *Hsiu* "ornament." *P'ei* depicts motion. *Wu* is the Master of Ceremonies referring to himself. He wants to mount his cassia boat in order to meet the Spirit. Cassia is chosen for the idea of the purity of its fragrance. [2/3a1–4]

Notes

Mei 美 (CW 29063) is "good," "beautiful," "excellent." Depending on the context, it may describe beauty or the "excellence of a good reputation" 美德, as in the formula *mei-jen* 美人 "the excellent one," an epithet of rulers in poems by their ministers (see especially "Shao Ssu Ming," the sixth elegy of this collection).

Yao-miao 要眇 (CW 35593.51) is a member of another large family of graphs representing a binome. There are two words, each pronounced *iog-miog* or *iog-tiog*. One word means "remote," the other "beautiful." There are literally dozens of pairs of graphs applied to these words. A representative list:

> *iog   窈窅夭妖要
> *miog   眇渺妙眇
> *tiog   窕窱瞗冶窱

The permutations are almost endless and there is no set pattern of distribution between "remote" and "beautiful" as would be usual in cases of this type. One must fall back upon considerations of context to discriminate between the two. Yet, even the reading "beautiful" may be read in a political way; for example, in *Ode* #1, cited above, the attribute of beauty renders the lady (= minister) a fit mate (= worthy advisor) for the prince. Hung confirms the metaphor in his comment.

I 宜 (CW 7263) means "reasonable," "proper," and by extension, "to put in order." Almost all words pronounced **ngia* share this basic idea of "rightness": 義 儀 議 宜 誼.

For example, in *Ode* #249, where it means "to put in order," one finds:

> Of (our) admirable, amiable, sovereign
> Most illustrious is the excellent virtue.
> He orders rightly the people, orders rightly the officers,
> And receives his dignity from heaven. . . .
>
> (Legge 4:481)

In this stanza, *mei* and *i* appear together as royal virtues. They are by extension the virtues of the minister as well, and linked this way are a clear indication of the political tone of our couplet.

Hsiu 修 (CW 805) means "to put in order" as well as "ornament," its usual reading in this line. The original graph shows a man and a hand holding a baton. A man holding a baton is an official holding his regalia, symbolic of his orderly government.

Hung provides a direct reference to the political context in his note to this line, saying that the beauty and virtue of the Hsiang Chün allude to the excellence of the worthy minister, echoing the allusion to *Ode* #1, which carries the political sense from line 2 through into line 3.

Hung identifies *p'ei* 沛 (CW 17541) by quoting a fragment of *Mencius*. Knowing the commentator's habit of providing hints by giving a partial quote, we may look up (or if we were a Chinese literatus, remember) the complete sentence (echoed in *Han Shih Wai Chuan* 3/23, Hightower, pp. 105–6): "Now among the shepherds of men throughout the nation, there is not one who does not find pleasure in killing men. If there were one . . . all the people in the nation would look toward him with outstretched necks. Such being indeed the case, the people would flock to him as water flows downwards with a rush, which no one can repress" (*Mencius* 1A:6.6, Legge 2:137).

Hung's seemingly innocent gloss is a direct pointer to this passage, in which Mencius chastises a king for exactly the kind of malfeasance that Ch'ü Yüan decries in his own King Huai.

In addition to the meanings "flowing rapidly" and "vast," the graph 沛 is also used for a homophone (**pwad*) meaning "to fall down" 顛沛 or "to be uprooted." This is commonly encountered in the binome (CW 44615.10) well known from *Lun Yü* 4:5.3: "The superior man does not, even for the space of a single meal, act contrary to virtue [仁]. In moments of haste, he cleaves to it. In seasons of danger [顛沛], he cleaves to it" (Legge 1:166).

Legge, in his note, correctly asserts that 顛 and 沛 both mean "to fall down," the only difference being that one falls prone or supine, respectively. Taken together, as in the Five Ministers' note to Pan Ku's "Reply to a Visiting Actor" 答賓戲 (*Wen Hsüan*, ch. 45), the two words allude to "danger and disorder."

This supplementary context is reinforced by the preponderance of similar meanings among the close homophones of 沛:

GRAPH	ARC	MEANING
友	*b'wat	expelled
罰	*b'iwat	to punish
敗	*pwad	defeated
跋	*b'wat	trampled

One may not rule out aural association, especially for the sound family **pwad*, which is very sparsely represented in ARC. The written substitution between 跋 and 沛 is verified in Tuan's note to the *Shuo Wen*, under 跋: "In the Classics and Commentaries, the graph 沛 is often borrowed for it."

Ch'eng 乘 means "to mount" in the most general sense. The archaic graph shows a man in a tree. It is extended by the common device of alteration of even tone (verb) to going tone (object) into a large class of nouns as well: "chariot" and the like.

In combination with *chou* 舟 (CW 31039), it recalls *Ode* #44:

> The two youths got into their boats,
> Whose shadows floated about (on the water).
> I think longingly of them,
> And my heart is tossed about in uncertainty.

> The two youths got into their boats,
> Which floated away (on the stream).
> I think longingly of them;—
> Did they not come to harm?

(Legge 4:71)

This ode is customarily taken to describe the deaths of the sons Chi-tzu 急子 and Shou-tzu 壽子 of Duke Hsüan of Wei 衛宣公. They died as a result of their father's treachery. Especially prized is the nobility of Chi-tzu, who stepped willingly into his boat knowing of the treachery, and of Shou-tzu, who went to his death in another brother's place (v. *Tso Chuan*, Duke Huan year 16; Legge 4:16–17).

This is not the only Classical association one may posit for *ch'eng-chou*. The *Li Chi* "Yüeh Ling" suggests that *ch'eng-chou* is also the act of the Son of Heaven: 天子始乘舟. [In the last month of Spring] "the Son of Heaven mounts his boat for the first time."

For a pedigree of *kuei* 桂 (CW 15064) see T'ai-i, line 8. The notion that a boat may be made from *Cassia* (or *Osmanthus*) wood is not credible. The tree was favored for its oil, leaves, bark, and buds. Moreover, its short trunk and shrub-like branches do not produce the straight limbs necessary for the production of lumber. *Kuei* as a prefixed term is common in poetic imagery: we find that doors 户, carts 車, rooms 室 or 堂, palaces 宮, goblets 尊, rafters 棟 or 樣, and especially oars 棹 or 楫 or 橈 or 櫂 are all made of "cassia." It seems likely that this use is universally figurative (i.e., nonliteral), lending a quality of exoticism and excellence to the items so described.

Kuei (**kiweg*) has few homophones: only 規 (**kiweg*) "rule," "drafting tool," and 攜 (**g'iweg*) "to be alienated," "dissent," "depart," along with the phonetic part of our word 圭 (**kiweg*) "jade insignia." There is not a clear indication of any aural element in this line, even if the multitalented 攜 would be a welcome addition to our political interpretation.

In combination with *chou* 舟 (CW 31039) "boat" we obtain the obvious "cassia boat." This the commentators gloss (and gloss over) "a boat made of cassia." Such a thing would not be expected to exist in the world of realities, so one must accept the figurative sense for 桂. What of *chou*?

Chou 舟 is frequently loaned for 周 in old texts in the sense of "Chou" the royal house, and in its lexical meaning "central," as in *Ode* #203, Legge 4:355 [mistranslated].

Similarly, it may represent the prince, as in 舟水之喻 (CW 31039.12) where the boat may float upon the water (i.e., be supported by it), or—more ominously—sink beneath it (i.e., be borne under by its weight): an allusion to the position of the prince vis-à-vis his ministers and subjects. It may also represent the minister, as in "boats and oars" 舟楫 (CW 31039.49:2), alluding to the minister who comes to the aid of his prince and saves his country from some peril (cf. *Shu Ching*, "Yueh Ming"; Legge 3:252). The allusive meanings of "boats and oars" will be important as well in lines 19 and 30.

Thus there are several interpretations of *kuei-chou*. One tempting choice is to read them for their homophones and frequent loans 攜周 **g'iweg-tiog* "to be alienated from Chou," giving us the paraphrase: "Expelled, punished, defeated, I depart. I mount the boat that carries me away from the center of government." Another is 規周 *kiweg-tiog* "(drafting-rule =) rectifier of the government."

These fit the Ch'ü Yüan legend and the statements by the commentators that the author refers to himself in these lines. One may further add the Mencian sense of *p'ei* to the interpretation, to include a direct inflammatory reference to the king in the line as well. The result is a couplet which extols the virtue and ability of the poet, bewails his defeat at court, decries the malfeasance of the king, and laments the poet's exile.

5

	令	沅	湘	兮	無	波
ARC	lieng	ngiwan?	siang	g'ieg	miwo	pwa
ANC	liäng	ngiwən?	siang	γiei	miu	pua
MSC	ling	yüan	hsiang	hsi	wu	po
GSR	823	257	731	1241	103	25
	to command	a river	a river		without	wave

6

	使	江	水	兮	安	流
ARC	sliəg	kung	siwər	g'ieg	an	liog
ANC	si	kang	swi	γiei	an	liəu
MSC	shih	chiang	shui	hsi	an	liu
GSR	975	1172	576	1241	146	1104
	to cause	a river	water		peaceful	to flow

META: Let the Yüan and Hsiang rivers be without waves!
Make the waters of the Great River flow quietly!

PARA: Let there be an end to the great unrest in the south of Ch'u.
Put a stop to the great disorder in the north.

The Commentaries

WANG I: *Yüan* and *Hsiang* are rivers. It says that while riding a boat, one is often afraid of danger and death. Thus the poet wishes the Hsiang Chün to cause the Yüan and Hsiang to be without waves and to cause the waters of the Kiang to flow straight and slow. Then all will be peaceful. [2/5b6–7]

FIVE MINISTERS: Han says: He wishes the Spirit to cause the waves to flow peacefully so that he will not be in danger of death. Yüan and Hsiang are rivers. [32/17b7]

HUNG HSING-TSU: For Yüan and Hsiang see the *Li Sao*. The *Water Classic* and the

Record of Ching-chou 荊州記 say that the Kiang has its source as Min-shan 岷山 and it is like the mouth of a jar, barely able to overflow a goblet. It travels secretly underground some *li* until it reaches the capital of Ch'u where it is ten *li* across. There it is called the Southern Kiang. Beginning at Chien-wei 犍為 with the Ch'ing-i 青衣 River and the Wen 汶 River it unites and arrives from the northeast at the capital of Pa 巴. There it unites with the Fu 涪 River, the Han 漢 River, and the Pai 白 River. It flows to the area of Ch'ang-sha, where it is joined by the Li 澧, the Yüan 沅, and the Hsiang 湘 rivers. At Kiang-hsia 江夏 it is joined by the Mien 沔 River. When it gets to Hsin-yang 潯陽, it divides into nine courses. They rejoin at P'eng-tse 彭澤 and go on to Wu-hu 蕪湖. This is called the Middle Kiang. From the northwest it flows south to Hsü-chou 徐州 and enters the sea. This is called the Northern Kiang. [2/5b7–9] [Hung's note from *Li Sao*, line 73]: The *Water Classic* says: "The Hsiang River rises at Shun's grave and flows east into the lower reach of Lake Tung-t'ing. The Yüan River rises west of T'an City 鐔城 in Hsiang Commandery 象郡. It flows east into Lake Tung-t'ing." The *Hou Han Shu*, "Treatise on Geography," says: "There is a Lin-yüan 臨沅 County in Wu-ling Commandery which looks south onto the Yüan River. Tsang-ko-ch'ieh-lan 牂牁且蘭 county is where it rises. When it reaches the border of Lin-yüan County it divides into five creeks." It also says: "At Yang-shou Mountain 陽朔山 in Ling-ling 零陵 District, the Hsiang River rises." The *Water Classic* says: "The Yüan River descends to flow into Lake Tung-t'ing at the same time as it joins the Kiang." The *Hsiang Chung Chi* 湘中記 says: "When the Hsiang River rises in Yang-shou then a goblet would look like a boat on it. When it flows into the Lake Tung-t'ing, the sun and moon seem to rise and set in its water." [1/16b1–3]

CHU HSI: He fears that there may be some danger of death in traveling, so he wants the Hsiang Chün to make the water to be without waves and to flow peacefully. [2/3a4–5]

Notes

The commentators are very straightforward in their remarks. The rivers are identified in detail. The lines are quite easily read.

The political interpretation presents no difficulty either. The wild storm is a metaphor for and signal of the crisis of government. The notion that natural calamities reflect political conditions and are subject to political remedy is ancient in China. Han Yü memorialized the God of the Flood to alleviate suffering in his district. From the Classics, one may select the following story, which illustrates both the political value of weather and the vindication of a righteous minister by Heaven. Some years ago, King Wu had fallen gravely ill. His minister and brother, the duke of Chou, prayed to Heaven to spare the king, and offered himself to die in the king's place. The prayer was sealed in a metal box, after which the king recovered. Now, a few years after King Wu's death (traditionally assigned to the year 1114 B.C.) enemies of the duke of Chou have slandered him to the new king, Ch'eng, who is sixteen. Heaven responds:

> In the autumn, when the grain was abundant and ripe, but before it was reaped, Heaven sent a great storm of thunder and lightning, along with wind, by which the grain was all beaten down, and great trees torn up. The people were greatly terrified; and the king and great officers, all in their caps of state, proceeded to open the metal-bound coffer, and examine the writings, when they found the words of the Duke of Chou when he took on himself the business of taking the place of King Wu. The king and the two dukes asked the grand historian and all the other officers about the thing. They replied, "Ah! it was really thus; but the duke charged us that we should not presume to speak about it." The king held the writing, and wept, saying, "We need not now go on reverently to divine. Formerly the duke was thus earnest for the royal House, but I, being a child, did not know it. Now Heaven has moved its terrors to display the virtue of the Duke of Chou. That I meet him a new man, is what the rules of propriety of our empire require." The king then went out to the borders, when Heaven sent down rain; and by virtue of a contrary wind, the grain all rose up. The two dukes gave orders to the people to take all the large trees which had fallen, and replace them. The year then turned out very fruitful. (*Shu Ching*, "Chin T'eng"; Legge 3:359–60)

Heaven had sent the storm to comment on human political affairs, and by elevating the duke of Chou to a place of honor, the meteorological remedy was provided by Heaven in elevating the grain to its original state.

Again in the *Tso Chuan*, Duke Chuang year 11, a ruler explains the cause of a flood: "I am as an orphan and must confess my want of reverence for which Heaven has sent down this plague" (Legge 5:88).

In the *Tso Chuan*, Duke Hsi year 21, a minister lectures his king on the way to reverse the bad effects of a drought: "Put in good repair your walls, inner and outer; lessen your food; be sparing in all your expenditure. Be in earnest to be economical, and encourage people to help one another" (Legge 5:180).

Wu-p'o 無波 (CW 19580.190) is, by contrast, an explicit and well-known metaphor for peaceful government.

Heaven has always commented on political conditions by means of storms and disasters. This has been true from the time of the Ancient Kings down to our own time: in 1976, a terrible earthquake at Tangshan preceded the death of Mao Tse-t'ung, the arrest of the "Gang of Four," and the succession of the moderates led by Teng Hsiao-p'ing.

The region around Lake Tung-t'ing is well identified by reference to the rivers, exhaustively catalogued by Hung. The Kiang, which flows by the Ch'u capital of Ying in the center of Ch'u, and the Yüan and Hsiang, which define the southern reaches of the great lake, stand *pars pro toto* for Ch'u in its geographical extent.

The sense of the couplet is aggregative rather than expository. The government of Ch'u, in its capital Ying, is in turmoil. This turmoil, as the simile of the rivers suggests, spreads throughout the kingdom. The poet wishes it were otherwise and believes his recall to office would be the remedy. The boat (metaphor and homophone of *chou* 舟 = 州 = 周, the kingdom) is riding on rough waves of political chaos. The Ship of State seems to be a universal image.

7

	望	夫	君	兮	未	來
ARC	miwang	piwo	kiwən	g'ieg	miwəd	ləg
ANC	miwang	piu	kiuən	γiei	mjwei	lai
MSC	wang	fu	chün	hsi	wei	lai
GSR	742	101	459	1241	531	944
	to look afar	man	lord		not yet	to come

8

	吹	參	差	兮	誰	思
ARC	t'wia	ts'iəm	ts'ia	g'ieg	diwər	siəg
ANC	ts'wie	ts'iəm	ts'ie	γiei	zwi	si
MSC	ch'ui	ts'en	tz'u	hsi	shui	ssu
GSR	30	647	5	1241	575	973
	to blow	uneven +	graduated		who(m)?	to think
		binome: panpipes				

META: I watch for the lady, she has not come.
        I blow on my pipes; of whom do I think?

PARA: I mourn for my king, for his future.
        Idle, I play my pipes: of whom do I think?

The Commentaries

WANG I: *Chün* refers to the Hsiang Chün. For *wei*, one has *kuei* 歸. The *ts'en-tz'u* is a flute. It says that one prepares thoroughly for the ritual of sacrifice and looks up longingly for the *chün* but she is not yet willing to come. Then one blows the flute to make music, sincerely wishing to please the *chün*. Of whom ought one to think? [2/5b9–6a1]

FIVE MINISTERS: Liang says: *Ta-chün* 大 [sic] 君 is the Spirit. It refers to the willingness of the Spirit to come. I make music with the sound of the *ts'en-tz'u*. Of whom ought I to think? It means one ought to think earnestly of the Spirit. For 參差 one has 篸篸. [32/17b9]

HUNG HSING-TSU: The *Feng Su T'ung* says: "Shun made a flute; its form was uneven and graduated *ts'en-tz'u* like a roc's wing." *Ts'en-tz'u* depicts incompleteness. It is pronounced 初簪又宜 [*ts'iəm-ts'ia/ts'iəm-ts'ie*]. It says that because one blows the flute one thinks of Shun. The *Flute Fu* says: "Blow the *ts'en-tz'u* and enter the Tao and its Power 入道德." This flute is one open at the bottom. 篸篸 depicts bamboo. [2/6a2]

CHU HSI: *Lai* is pronounced for the rhyme as 力之 [*liəg/li*]. One text has 歸, this is wrong. For 參差 one has 篸篸. The first sound is pronounced 初簪 [*ts'iəm/ts'iəm*]. The second sound is pronounced 初宜 [*ts'ia/ts'ie*]. *Ssu* 思 is pronounced for the rhyme 新齋 [*siər/siei*].

 Ts'en-tz'u is a flute. The *Feng Su T'ung* says: "Shun made a flute; its form was uneven and graduated like a roc's wing." He watches for the Hsiang Chün, but she has not yet come. Therefore, he blows the flute to lament it. [2/3a1–2; 2/3a5]

Notes

 Wang 望 (CW 14697) means "to look afar" and "to hope for." *Fu-chün* 夫君 (CW 5962.22) means "husband and wife" (as in "Yün Chung Chün," line 13 above). In this context, the commentators agree: "I watch for the Hsiang Chün," reading *fu-chün* 夫君 as an honorific epithet of the Spirit.

 Wei-lai 未來 (CW 14753.42) means "the future" taken as a binome, and "not yet come" as a verbal phrase. So, they derive the line: "I watch for the lord/Spirit, who has not yet come."

 Fu-chün as an epithet for one's superior is established in this line, but tradition is uniform: it does not mean husband and wife here. *Wei-lai* as a set expression is unknown to CW or DK in the sense of "has not yet come." Neither dictionary is usually averse to glossing obvious phrases, so the *argumentum ex nihilo* may not be excluded out of hand.

 The translators are under the wing of Wang I:

Pfizmaier:	Sie naht noch nicht
Harlez:	Mais je ne le vois point venir
Waley:	But she does not come
Hawkes:	But she comes not yet
Liu:	But he stays behind

One might also suppose that the echo of *wei-lai* 未來 gives: "I think of (= mourn) my king, oh! his future (alas!)." The reading "mourn" for *ssu* 思 is common; there is no difference in the pronunciation.

The second half of the line is one of the bald riddles that help make the balance of the political interpretation possible: "I am playing the pipes; of whom am I thinking?" The surface narrative suggests the answer: "I am thinking of the Hsiang Chün, who has not yet come." This is the explanation of Wang I and the Five Ministers. A second possibility is given quite openly by Hung, and Chu Hsi predictably in his wake: I am thinking of the sage Shun.

The *Feng Su T'ung*, origin of the story quoted by Hung, is a late Han compilation. The term 參差 "pipes" does not occur in the standard Classics in the sense of a musical instrument. It is scarcely visible at all, save in *Ode* #1 (our old friend), where it means "uneven." Nevertheless, the legends in the *Feng Su T'ung* are certainly older than the text, and the invention of the flute may have been attributed to Shun during the early Han or before. It was certainly so *after* the Han, when the text became a favorite of allusion-hunting ministers.

The allusion to flute-playing may suggest a longing for the Golden Age of good government, and thus be a criticism of the king by the device of an unfavorable comparison. Yao, after all, raised Shun up from rude surroundings "among the common people" to be his successor (cf. *Shu Ching*; Legge 3:26; and below, line 18). It may thus refer to the common plaint of the wandering persuaders of the late Chou period: "If this king won't hear my advice and treat me well, there are plenty more kings (more Yao-like) who will listen to me."

The third, and perhaps most obvious, association of a banished minister sailing away on Lake Tung-t'ing playing a flute is with the story of Wu Tzu-hsü 伍子胥 (v. *Shih Chi*, ch. 66).

Wu Tzu-hsü, a native of Ch'u, was a minister to the king of Wu, Fu Ch'ai 夫差. Wu defeated Yüeh in a battle and the king of Yüeh, Kou

Chien 句踐, sued for peace. Wu Tzu-hsü warned the king of Wu that Kou Chien had a treacherous nature. Wu Tzu-hsü was slandered at court by a rival and ordered by the king to commit suicide. Before doing so he proclaimed: "I wish my eyes to be gouged out and hung on the eastern gate of the capital so that I may see Yüeh enter to destroy Wu." Nine years later, it came about as he had foretold. A popular legend arose that his punishment had been rather to be dismissed and reduced to begging in marketplaces and wandering on lakes and rivers, playing his flute for a living.

Either way, a flute-playing minister is one who is in disgrace because he rightly reprimanded a foolish ruler and was dismissed for his trouble. Wu Tzu-hsü and Ch'ü Yüan are the archetypes; later literati officials in similar situations at court must have felt a keen identification with them (e.g., Su Shih in his "First Fu on the Red Cliff"; v. Bischoff, pp. 252–54).

If one accepts this solution to the riddle, as seems the natural choice, then one must guess that Hung's purpose here in introducing the alibi Shun is to say: "Yes, it is Wu Tzu-hsü, but it is safer for the minister to think of Shun." He points out another obscure context to defuse the libelous obvious image.

Yet, even the chaste Shun may point the finger at the king of Ch'u:

> Playing the pipes, of whom do I think?
> Compared to Yao, our king is not up to the standard of the
> great Yü.

9

	駕	飛	龍	兮	北	征
ARC	ka	piwər	liung	g'ieg	pək	tieng
SNC	ka	pjwei	liwong	γiei	pək	tsiäng
MSC	chia	fei	lung	hsi	pei	cheng
GSR	15	580	1193	1241	909	833
	to yoke	to fly	dragon		north	to attack

10

	邅	吾	道	兮	洞	庭
ARC	d'ian	ngo	d'og	g'ieg	d'ung	d'ieng
ANC	d'ian	nguo	d'au	γiei	d'ung	d'ieng
MSC	chan	wu	tao	hsi	tung	t'ing
GSR	148	58	1048	1241	1176	835
	sinuous	I, my	way		rapids, +	courtyard
					cavern	

binome: a lake

META: I yoke the flying dragon and go north,
Sinuous my way over Lake Tung-t'ing.

PARA: The king is controlled; unwise policies prevail in the north.
I am obstructed down here in my southern exile.

The Commentaries

WANG I: *Cheng* is "to go." Ch'ü Yüan is thinking of the Spirit; the result is a thought of the kingdom of Ch'u. He wishes he could mount a flying dragon and return north to his old home. *Chan* is "to turn." *Tung-t'ing* is the Great Lake. The lines say he wants to ride a flying dragon and return, but he dares not follow the main route. Going by the sinuous route along the lake shore, he wants to arrive quickly. [2/6a3–5]

FIVE MINISTERS: {邅 glossed 陟連 [*tian/tiän*]}
Liang says: Ch'ü Yüan says that he wants to return to Ch'u, to yoke the

flying dragon and go north by turning his route over Lake Tung-t'ing and return directly. [32/18a1−2]

HUNG HSING-TSU: *Chan* is pronounced 池戰 [**dian/diän*]. The *Wen Hsüan* gives 陟連 [**tian/tiän*]. Ch'ü Yüan wants to go, and turns his route to the Lake Tung-t'ing because the Hsiang Chün is there. The *Shan Hai Ching* says: "Shun's two daughters live in the mountain in Tung-t'ing. They often roam in the winds which blow over the depths of the Kiang 江, the Li 澧, the Yüan 沅. They come and go in the abyss of the Hsiao 瀟 and the Hsiang 湘 with much rushing wind and violent rain." The note to that passage says: "It means that the two women are able to wander and sport in the depths of the Kiang and can rouse the Three Kiang, command the Breath 氣 of the winds and waves and travel through them at will." It also says: "The Hsiang River rises at Shun's grave, flows east and enters the lower reaches of Tung-t'ing." The note to that passage says: "Tung-t'ing is a cave near Ch'ang-sha in Pa-ling 巴陵長沙." The *River Classic* says: "The four rivers flow together into Tung-t'ing and then north-wards to join the Great Kiang. This is called the Five Islands 五渚. When the *Chan Kuo Ts'e* says: 'Ch'in fought a battle in Ching 荊 and defeated them soundly, taking Tung-t'ing and its Five Islands,' it refers to this."

The water of the lake is wide and 500 *li* around. The sun and moon appear to rise from and set into the midst of it. In the lake is Chün-shan 君山, which is secretly connected by a land route which runs laterally through the dark and hidden place. Also note: in Wu, the Great Lake 太湖 is also called Tung-t'ing, and in Pa-ling, Tung-t'ing is also called Great Lake. Wang I said that 太湖 probably indicates the Tung-t'ing in Pa-ling. [2/6a5−9]

CHU HSI: *Chan* is pronounced 池戰, also 陟連. *Chia-lung* means to use a dragon-wing boat. *Chan* is "to turn." *Tung-t'ing* is the Great Lake, at Ch'ang-sha. It is wide, 500 or more *li* around. The sun and moon seem to rise from and set into its midst. In the lake is Chün-shan. [2/3a7−9]

Notes

The surface narrative begins clearly: "Yoke the flying dragon, oh!, travel north." We saw the yoked dragon earlier in "Yün Chung Chün," line 7. *Cheng* 征 (CW 10296) usually means "to attack" but 正 and 征 are frequently interchanged in old texts, both meaning either "to correct (= attack)" or "to go." The commentators authorize "to go," and the fact that the graphs are homophonous and interchangeable supports this choice.

"Flying Dragon" is a common metaphor for a wise ruler. This originates in the *I Ching*: "Flying dragon in the heavens, it furthers one to see the great man" (Wilhelm, p. 9). "Flying dragon in the heavens, this is the supreme Way 道 of ruling" (Wilhelm, p. 382). "A flying dragon mounts the clouds" is another such phrase (CW 44974.276, ex. *Han Fei Tzu*) which describes a worthy hero who takes advantage of circumstances and is victorious. Compare also Han Yü's "Dragon and Cloud," quoted above under the title of "Yün Chung Chün." Similarly, *pei-cheng* 北征 (CW 2615.143) "a northward attack," from *Kuo Yü*: "After Fu-ch'ai, King of Wu, had caused the death of Wu Tzu-hsü, he didn't harvest the crops; instead he raised his army and attacked northward." Such a memorably inauspicious attack, following the fall of the previously mentioned Wu Tzu-hsü, is striking. Not even pausing to harvest the crops! What is a king's main duty to the ancestors but to ensure the harvest?

This suggests a second paraphrase of the line: "The king is (yoked to a cart =) under control, a scandalous policy is pursued." Our relative ignorance of the details of the political situation at the Ch'u court hampers this interpretation, but we do know that in the orthodox hagiography of Ch'ü Yüan, he was at the head of a faction which opposed an alliance with Ch'in, which lay to the west of Ch'u, and favored an alliance with Ch'i 齊, which lay to the north of Ch'u (in the present-day provinces of Shantung, Shansi, and Hopei). To "attack to the north" (i.e., Ch'i) is the antithesis of Ch'ü Yüan's policy. No good can come of an alliance with "rapacious Ch'in" against Ch'i. Ch'in will merely conquer Ch'i and then turn on Ch'u. Ch'ü Yüan feels that Ch'u and Ch'i must stand against Ch'in. Thus his dismay at the policy of appeasing Ch'in that was promoted by the king and his new advisors.

Still another possibility is that the poet intends to go to Ying, the Ch'u capital. Ying lay some two hundred kilometers northwest of the lake region. The poet will go north to correct (征 = 行正, cf. CW 10296:1) his king and his rivals at court.

Chan 邅 (CW 4028) read *tian means "obstructed"; read *d'ian means "to turn." The origin of the reading "obstructed" is in the *I Ching*, hexagram #3: "In difficulty and hindered, cart and horse turn around; if the bandit weren't there, the wooer would come." 屯如邅如乘馬班 如匪寇婚媾 (Wilhelm, pp. 18, 398–404). The parallel with our context is clear, giving us: "I am obstructed down here at Tung-t'ing (if the bandit weren't in power, I could make progress)." This reminds us of *Chuang Tzu* (ch. 28): "One may be on the rivers and sea in body, but his mind remains at the palace gate" 形在江海之上心存魏闕之下.

Whichever alternative we prefer for the surface narrative, the political interpretation is clear: the king is beguiled; Ch'ü Yüan's policies are not being followed. He longs to return to Ying and power, but he is obstructed by the bandit/slanderer and languishes in the South, unable to return.

11

	薜	荔	柏	兮	蕙	綢
ARC	b'ieg	lieg?	pak	g'ieg	g'iwəd	d'iog
ANC	b'iei	liei	pək	γiei	γiwei	d'iəu
MSC	pi	li	po	hsi	hui	ch'ou
GSR	853	1241	782	1241	533	1083
	a plant +	a plant	cypress		a plant	to bind up
		binome: a plant				

12

	蓀	橈	兮	蘭	旌
ARC	swən	niog	g'ieg	glan	tsieng
ANC	suən	nziäu	γiei	lan	tsiäng
MSC	sun	jao	hsi	lan	ching
GSR	434	1164	1241	185	812
	a plant	oar		a plant	pennon

META: Mat-walls of fig creeper, bound round with iris;
Oars of sweet flag, pennon of thoroughwort.

PARA: My king is tied up and helpless, I am in bonds;
I receive no proper summons, the palace doors are shut.

The Commentaries

WANG I: *Pi-li* is a fragrant plant. *Po* is "a wall-curtain." *Chou* is "to bind up." The *Ode* says: "Round and round the thorns are bound." It is the same meaning. For 柏 one text has 拍. For 欂, one text has 搏.

Sun is a fragrant plant. *Jao* is a small oar of a boat. Ch'ü Yüan says that his dwelling place will be decorated by *pi-li* thatch on the four walls. *Hui* plants will bind up the room. When he is on his boat, the oars will be of *sun* and the pennons of *lan*. In his going he will be ornamented with fragrant purity. For 蓀, one text has 荃. For 旌, one text has 旍. [2/6a9–6b2]

FIVE MINISTERS: {The text adds 承 at the beginning of line 12. 薜 is glossed 薄閉 [*b'ieg/b'iei]. 荔 is glossed 麗 [*lieg/lei]. A note says: "The Five Ministers have 采 instead of 承." The text has 荃 instead of 蓀, and glosses it 七全 [*ts'iwan/ts'iwän]. 橈 is glossed 而遙 [*niog/nziäu]. A note says: "The Five Ministers have 旗 for 旌."}

Hsien says: 薜, 荔, 蕙, 荃, and 蘭 are all fragrant plants. Ch'ü Yüan is saying that the place where he lives is wrapped with fragrant plants in order to thatch the four walls. Because their fragrance is pure like these, the oars and pennons are made of them. [32/18a2–5]

HUNG HSING-TSU: 柏 and 拍 both sound like 博 [*pak/pak]. 綢 can sound like 儔 [*d'iog/d'iəu] or like 叼 [*t'og/t'ao]. For 蓀 and 荃, see the *Li Sao. Jao* is pronounced 而遙. The *Fang Yen* says: "An oar is called *jao*, some call it 櫂." The *Chou Li* says: "One splits wings to make a *ching*." The *Erh Ya* says: "Put a feather streamer on top, it is called a *ching*." 旌 and 旌 are the same. Some editions have 乘荃橈. For 乘, some have 承. Some texts have 采荃橈兮蘭旌 for the line. All later writers who emend it or transmit it thus are in error. [2/6a9–6b3]

[Excerpts from notes to *Li Sao*, line 20]:

Wang I: *Ch'üan* is a fragrant plant. It alludes to the *chün*. The lords of
            men wear clothes which are fragrant; hence one uses fra-
            grant plants to proclaim that the numerous evils are re-
            proved and that the revered one ought to change. This is
            ch'üan.

Hung Hsing-tsu: *Ch'üan* is the same as *sun* 蓀. *Chuang Tzu* says: "Once
            one has the fish, one may forget the *ch'üan*." The *Yin I*
            commentary to *Chuang Tzu* says: "It is pronounced 七全
            [*ts'iwan/ts'iwän]. *Sun* is a fragrant plant that one may use
            for fish bait." The *Shu* 疏 commentary says: " 蓀 is 荃."

CHU HSI: For *po*, one text has 拍; both sound like 博. *Chou* sounds like 儔 or like
            叼. For *sun*, one text has *ch'üan. Jao* is pronounced 而遙. For *ching*, one
            text has 旌, they are the same. Above this line, some texts have the word
            乘, or 承, or 采. For *ching*, some texts have 旗, all these are wrong. *Po*
            means "wall-curtain." *Chou* is "to bind up." *Sun* is a fragrant plant. *Jao*
            is the small oar of a boat. [2/3a7–10]

Notes

Modern sources identify *pi-li* 薜荔 to be the vine *Ficus pumila* (CMH, p. 175), a creeping fig. However, the earliest descriptions, such as Wang I's, indicate an aromatic plant 香草, on which grounds the specific identification of the creeping fig may certainly be disqualified, at least in a text as old as ours. Wang I elsewhere (*Li Sao*, line 36) describes the *pi-li* as an epiphyte 緣木而生, which the creeping fig is not. This poem is the earliest occurrence of *pi-li* and later notices are mainly in imitative passages, such as in Yang Hsiung's *Sweet Spring Fu* 甘泉賦: "He weaves the *pi-li* into mats" 席 (cf. Knechtges' *Han Rhapsody*, p. 49, line 70, where the word is translated "castor plants"—which are *Ricinus communis*, CMH, p. 378, the castor oil bean). This anonymous epiphyte, for the sake of a smooth text, is called fig creeper in the translation, but the reader should be advised of the tentative nature of the identification.

The ARC reading of 荔 is not derivable from the phonetic part. Karlgren has reconstructed the ANC *liei*, for which several ARC sounds may serve as antecedent. Tung reconstructs this compound **bieg-liab*, Chou has **bey-lear*, either of which could serve as well. For assonance, the form **lieg* is posited to match **b'ieg*. The element 力 is pronounced **liək/liək* (GSR 928).

The problem in this line is the checkered history of the word 柏. *Po* 柏 (CW 14998) is a coniferous tree, identified in modern times to be the *Chamaecyparis*, often incorrectly called cypress. Thus, without emendation or contortion, the phrase *pi-li po* means "*Chamaecyparis* with climbing vines growing on it"—the image of the upright worthy one being strangled by lowly climbing vines.

One recalls *Ode #217*, which criticizes King Yu for dissipating himself in the face of a crisis, especially the lines:

> The mistletoe and the dodder
> Are growing on the pine and the *Chamaecyparis*.
> I cannot see my Lord,
> My sorrowful heart is unsettled.

The reader may face another duck-and-drake quotation: given the opening "Epiphyte on the *Chamaecyparis*" we immediately recall our odes: "I cannot see my Lord, and my sorrowful heart is unsettled." The literati of traditional China memorized the *Shih Ching* and were thoroughly familar with the scholastic tradition surrounding it. These associations were automatically noted. The author of a satire of castigation could turn this to his advantage, and the reader could be trusted to catch the nuance.

The commentators, predictably, steer us away to alibi: 柏 means 榑壁 "wall-curtain." *Fu* 榑 (CW 15611) **b'iwo* means "to strike," but is often loaned for the exact homophone 薄 (CW 32808) "thicket" or "trellis." The trellis was an instrument of privacy, usually blocking a doorway. Since the surface narrative begins with a description of a boat, perhaps Wang I's phrase 榑壁 should be read "wall-curtains (for the boat's makeshift cabin)." This could accord with the Five Ministers: "The place where he lives (= on the boat?) is wrapped with fragrant plants in order to thatch the four walls." In this context, trellis-work indicates merely a lattice, not a frame for training climbing plants. Yet, the trellis-hut is not unknown in English literature either (cf. OED s.v. *trellis*).

Hui 蕙 (CW 32677) was seen at "Tung Huang T'ai I," line 7, and is identified with the *Melilotus arvensis*, a clover. It is also called *hsün* 薰 (CW 33051), and was burned "as incense to make the spirits descend. When worn in the girdle it is said to dispel noxious influences" (CMH, p. 262). Also, "on account of its fragrance, the plant is used for making mats, pillows, and mattresses" (*ibid.*).

Chou 綢 (CW 28208) means "to encircle," "bind around," as in *Ode* #225:

> Those ladies of good families,
> With their hair bound up straight:
> I do not see them!
> My heart is unhappy.

Where Hawkes finds "sail" in 綢, I cannot say, unless it is by analogy with 蕙帳 (CW 32677.27), or by assonance with 幬 **d'iog* "chariot curtain."

The surface sense seems clear: "Of fig creeper(?) vine my trellis-hut, bound round with *Melilotus*." The place of 蕙綢 in the political narrative is less apparent. Wang I points us to *Ode* #118 when he quotes "Round and round the thorns are bound" (one of the few times Wang I quotes directly from *any* source), but 楚 "thorn" does not necessarily mean 楚 "the kingdom of Ch'u." The suggestion of "Ch'u bound up tightly" is seductive, but not convincing.

Chou 綢 is one of a series of graphs in the family **tiok* which mean "to tie up," "to restrain."

GRAPH	ARC	MEANING
韜	*t'og	to enwrap
周	*tiog	to bind up
綢	*tiog	to restrain
舟	*tiog	to engirdle
綬	*diog	silken bonds

also:

約	*iok	to restrain in bonds
繆	*mliog	to bind up
獠	*gliog	to strangle
紐	*niog	to tie up

The whole series is generally interchangeable, and the distribution of meanings is by no means as neat as the table suggests; all the graphs may mean "to restrain" or "to bind up" in turn, depending upon the context.

Keeping in mind the general sense of "restrain" and the association of 蕙 with "excellence," as in 蕙質 (CW 32677.39) "excellent physique," and 蕙心 (CW 32677.1) "an excellent heart," we find that the last half of the line echoes the first, a common device in this text:

> The excellent one (= 柏) entwined in creepers, oh!
> The excellent one (= 蕙) restrained in bonds.

Sun 蓀 (CW 32360) with its varia 蓀 (CW 32668), 蓀 (CW 33191), 蓀 (CW 33012), and most common 荃 (CW 31681), is usually glossed "a fragrant plant." It is pronounced **swən* in all its graphic variants except 荃 (**ts'iwan*). Wang Pi 王弼 in his commentary to *Lao Tzu* (ch. 20) tells us that the *sun* "alludes to the lord." It is also so used in the *Wen Hsüan* in a number of passages that are clearly imitative. There is no text of the early period that describes the plant in any detail. Later identifications are more thorough, but not reliable for interpreting texts from earlier times. Some sources, such as those followed by Waley, equate *sun* with the *Acorus calamus* 菖蒲 , the sweet flag. Others take it to be the *Iris sibirica*, Siberian iris. The two are not distinguished in traditional sources. Both are cultivated for their sharp stiff leaves used to make brooms and for their roots: *not* to make oars, which is absurd (cf. CMH, pp. 12–13 and 221).

Jao 橈 (CW 15887), read **nog*, means "bent wood." It is borrowed for the word **niog* "oar," especially to indicate a small oar. It belongs to an interesting family of homophonous words:

GRAPH	ARC	MEANING
虐	*ngiok	maltreated
溺	*niok	depraved
謷	*ngog	vilified
蹂	*niog	trampled
怒	*niok	dissatisfied
擾	*niog	disturbed
橈	*nog	unjust

If *sun* stands, by its uprightness and fragrance, for the lord, then a piece of bent wood, with all the obnoxious connotations of "bent" suggested by the series of homophones, may stand for the oppression and vilification he sanctions by allowing the slanderers to dominate him.

Another even more startling set of homophones is:

蓀	*swən	舜	*siwən	(Shun)
橈	*niog	堯	*ngiog	(Yao)

If the correspondence with the sage kings Yao and Shun is accepted, and none may deny that the aural element would have at least been noticed by the Classical reader, then one has: (paraphrasing) "worthy Shun had his Yao, who ceded the royal power to him; I am a worthy man, but my king is no Yao."

Lan 蘭 (CW 33297) has been met earlier, above. It is an unidentified plant whose name may signify the genus *Eupatorium* among others. That is also stands metaphorically for the lord is attested by CW 33297.352 蘭蕙 which means "the lord and his worthy men" 君子賢人.

Ching 旌 (CW 13976) is a chariot banner or pennon of feathers suspended from a staff. Its figurative sense springs from the *Shu Ching* and *Mencius*:

> Point out the good with the pennon, and separate the bad from them. (*Shu Ching*, "Pi Ming," part 3; Legge 3:573)

A common man should be summoned by a plain banner [旃];
a scholar who has taken office, with one having dragons
embroidered on it [旂]; and a Great officer, with one having
feathers suspended from the top of the staff [旌]. (*Mencius*
5B:7.6; Legge 2:390)

The pennon as a distinguishing mark of the worthy is well known,
e.g.: 旌德 (CW 13796.70) "to point out the virtuous"; 旌貞 (CW
13796.l8) "to single out the upright minister": 旌賢 (CW 1379.60) the
same; 旌輿 (CW 13796.76) "the chariot with which one summons a
worthy minister"; and there are many more.

There is also an air of inappropriateness in this line. *Ching* is a
feathered pennon, not one of a plant or flower 蘭. It surmounts a
chariot, not a boat. One cannot make oars of iris. This all recalls the
continuation of the *Mencius* passage quoted previously:

When the forester was summoned with the article appropriate to the summoning of a Great officer, he would have died
rather presume to go. . . . How much more may we expect
this refusal to go, when a man of talents and virtue is
summoned in a way which is inappropriate to his character!
When a prince wishes to see a man of talents and virtue, and
does not take the proper course to get his wish, it is as if he
wished him to enter his palace, and shut the door against
him. (*Mencius* 5B:7.7−8; Legge 2:390)

Several interpretations of the whole couplet are possible, once all
these associations and allusions are taken into account:

The cypress is entangled (= I don't see the king), I am
restrained by the crooked one; all I have is a *lan*-pennon
instead of the one that summons the Great Officer.

or:

I am estranged and restrained as if in bonds. I was upright
and the crooked one maltreats me because I remonstrated
[蘭 *glan* = 諫 *klan*] about honoring the worthy.

or:

My king is tied up and helpless, I am in bonds . . . A Shun
mistreated by an inappropriate Yao.

13

	望	涔	陽	兮	極	浦
ARC	miwang	dz'iəm	diang	g'ieg	g'iək	p'wo
ANC	miwang	dz'iəm	iang	γiei	g'iək	p'uo
MSC	wang	ch'en	yang	hsi	chi	p'u
GRW	742	651	720	1241	910	102
	to look	soaked + Yang			extreme	riverbank
	afar		binome:			
			a place name			

14

	橫	大	江	兮	揚	靈
ARC	g'wang	d'ad	kung	g'ieg	diang	lieng
ANC	γwəng	d'ai	kang	γiei	iang	lieng
MSC	heng	ta	chiang	hsi	yang	ling
GSR	707	317	1172	1241	720	836
	transverse	great	a river		to raise	sorceress,
						spirit power

META: I look off toward Ch'en-yang on the far shore,
        Crossing the Great River, I display my sincerity.

PARA: I look off toward the capital, across the Kiang.
        Defying the flow of events, I made known my virtue.

The Commentaries

WANG I: *Ch'en-yang* is the name of a bank of the Kiang. It is near Ying, far away.
          P'u is "the bank of a river." *Ling* is "absolute sincerity." Ch'ü Yüan
          thinks of Ch'u. He wants to mount his light boat and ascend a lookout on
          the far shore near the mooring at Ying. In order to rid himself of his
          melancholy he crosses the Great Kiang to make known his absolute

sincerity. He hopes to be able to enlighten King Huai to order his recall to office. [2/6b4–6]

FIVE MINISTERS: {Glosses 涔 with 岑 [*ts'iəm/ts'iəm]}

Hsiang says: Ch'en-yang mooring is one far away that is close to Ying, the Ch'u capital. It says "I wander on the bank, about to cross the Great River. I make known my utmost loyalty to my prince and hope the prince will be awakened and moved to send for me." [32/18a8]

HUNG HSING-TSU: *Ch'en* sounds like 岑. *Ch'i* sounds like 祈 [*g'iər/g'jei], and is "a crooked riverbank." Today, Li-chou 澧州 has a Ch'en-yang-p'u 涔陽浦. The *River Classic* says: "The Ch'en River 涔水 rises in the south of Han-chung 漢中 county, southeast of Han-shan 旱山. It flows north to Mien-yang 沔陽 county and enters the Mien River. It is then a wide river." The *Chi Yün* says that 涔 is a river name, pronounced 郎丁 [*lieng/lieng*] and that the word sounds like 令, citing this line. It is not clear that this is true.

The *Shuo Wen* says: "*P'u* is 'a bank' 濱." The *Feng T'u Chi* 風土記 says: "When a big river has a small mouth and there are other channels, they are called *p'u*." He crosses the Great River to display his sincerity because that is where the Hsiang Chün is. [2/6b4–7]

CHU HSI: *Ch'en* sounds like 岑. Ch'en-yang is the name of a bank of the Kiang, far away. *P'u* is "a river bank." *Yang* is "to raise up his excellence" 光靈. This is a way to say that he sets out and makes plain his feelings. [2/3a8, 10]

Notes

Ch'en-yang 涔陽 (CW 17922.6) has been identified since the time of the Han dictionary *Shuo Wen* with an island in the Kiang near the site of Ying, the capital of Ch'u. When the surface narrative says "I look afar to Ch'en-yang, the far shore," it means to the far shore of the Kiang, not of the lake.

Ch'en 涔 (often misread *ts'en*) means "to soak" and "to cry." It is pronounced like 岑, according to all but Wang I, who never gives readings. The graph 岑 (GSR 657t) is read *ngiəm (MSC yin) or *tsiəm (*ch'in*) and means "a high riverbank." The sense fits the context well, but the pronunciation is at odds with common practice. *Kuang Yün* spells 溗 with 鋤針 (*dz'iəm/dz'iəm), which also yields the MSC reading *ch'in* as above. The colloquial *ch'en* or *ts'en* appear to be, as Karlgren would say, "irregular."

Ch'en-yang 溗陽, if read literally, means "the soaked Yang," an image much in harmony with the previous parts of the political interpretation: e.g., "neutralized by Yin," in line 2. Yang overcome by water (Yin) represents the royal power overcome by that of a minister; in this case, the slanderer. (Interestingly, a word for slander, 譖, is read *tsiəm, an exact homophone of 溗). The (slandered Yang?) ministers are Yin, the ruler Yang; the all-important balance between their power mirrors the dual cosmos.

The graph 甫 is often loaned for 痡 (CW 22704) in Classical texts; 痡 means "suffering," and the two graphs have identical readings in both their senses. If the reader were to hear this assonance and make the connection, the passage that would have been recalled is: "[Shou, king of Shang has] cut out the heart of the worthy man. By the use of his power killing and murdering, he has poisoned and sickened [痡] all within the four seas. His honor and confidence are given to the villanous and bad. He has driven from him his instructors and guardians. He has thrown to the winds the statutes and penal laws. He has imprisoned and enslaved the upright officer" (*Shu Ching*, "T'ai Shih," part 3; Legge 3:295).

The line paints a picture of Ch'ü Yüan wishing he could return to the capital, a theme common with many other lines in the poem. His goal is to enlighten his king, as we find below. An alternate reading of the line, "I contemplate the sodden Yang, and the extremity of suffering," is attractive within the context of the technique of homophone reading we employ in this exercise, but is not required by the interpretation. The desire to return to the capital is ubiquitous, and attested even by the usually reticent commentators in their notes to the next line.

Heng 橫 (CW 15897), which we saw above at line b.14, means either "lateral," "perverse," or "in general." In a geographic sense, "lateral" becomes "from east to west."

Heng-chiang 橫江 (CW 15897.30) means "to cross the Kiang." One must cross the Kiang at least once to get from the lake region to Ying. The diréction of travel is northwest, rather than directly west, but the general sense is clear. When the compound is interpreted "cross the Kiang," the requirement for east-west motion is weakened.

A close relative, 橫流 (CW 15897.77), means "water flowing contrary to its Tao" (i.e., against its usual direction of flow). This provides an interesting alternative. If 橫 is given its older meaning of "unorthodox" (CW 15487 丙 : 3 不順理也), one may read the compound similarly to *heng-min* 橫民 (CW 15487.18) "to incite the people to rebellion"; *heng-hsing* 橫行 (CW 15487.39) "to act in a perverse way"; *heng-cheng* 橫政 (CW 15487.91) "a cruel and oppressive government." In this sense, the phrase may be an indictment of the king: he goes against the Tao.

The image of traversing the Great Kiang suggests a battle against strong currents. This figurative view fits into the context well: the minister desires to oppose the strong current of events which separate him (like the Kiang) from his lord. In the physical dimension, he states his desire to return to the capital; in the political dimension, he states his opposition to events which have a momentum as strong as the currents of the Kiang. He makes this statement by: 揚靈.

Yang-ling 揚靈 (not in CW or DK) is variously translated:

Pfizmaier:	Ich breite rings den Geist
Harlez:	Je m'élève vers lui (ce grand Esprit)
Waley:	Lifts her godhead
Hawkes:	Waft my spirit
Liu:	My spirit form I reveal

Yang 揚 (CW 12674) means "to raise" (we saw earlier the phonetic family **diang/*dieng* "to raise"). *Ling* 靈 (CW 43483), as earlier elaborated, is either a sorceress or "spiritual power," "perspicacity." It is also a synonym of *shan* 善, as in the phrases 揚善 (CW 12674.63) "to make known good men"; and 揚美 (CW 12674.45) "to make known one's virtue," as found in the *I Ching*, hexagram #14:

君子以遏惡揚善順天休命
The superior man curbs the evil and promotes the good,
and thereby obeys the benevolent will of Heaven.

(cf. Wilhelm, p. 60)

In fact, the commentators give the same reading for it: " 靈 is 'absolute sincerity'."

In these poems the minister attempts to present himself in a flattering light so that the king will restore him to his old position. He wishes to return to the capital to awaken the king to the dangers the country faces. In order to do so he must physically and politically brave the powerful currents of events. He does so by making known his great virtue to all who will hear. The fate of his effort is revealed in the next couplet.

15

	揚	靈	兮	未	極
ARC	diang	lieng	g'ieg	miwəd	g'iək
ANC	iang	lieng	γiei	mjwei	g'iək
MSC	yang	ling	hsi	wei	chi
GSR	720	836	1241	531	910
	to raise	sorceress, spirit power		not yet	extreme

16

	女	嬋	媛	兮
ARC	nio	dian	giwan	g'ieg
ANC	niwo	ziän	jiwän	γiei
MSC	nü	ch'an	yüan	hsi
GSR	94	147	255	1241
	female	capti-vating	distracted	

capti- +
binome: beautiful

	爲	余	太	息
ARC	gwia	dio	t'ad	siək
ANC	jwie	iwo	t'ai	siək
MSC	wei	yü	t'ai	hsi
GSR	27	82	317	925
	to cause	me	great	to sigh

META: I display my sincerity, but to no avail.
My sister dissuades me, sighing for me a great sigh.

PARA: I made known my virtue, but it did no good.
My king was led like a cow on a tether; it makes me heave a great sigh.

The Commentaries

WANG I: *Chi* is "end." *Nü* is Nü-hsü 女嬃 the elder sister of Ch'ü Yüan. *Ch'an-yüan* is like 牽引 "to pull along." The line says that he has made known his utmost sincerity but has exhausted himself without avail. So Nü-hsü leads him along and scolds him. Her sighs are numerous and he is remorseful. She wants him to change his nature and be at ease with his fate, as is the custom. [2/6b7–9]

FIVE MINISTERS: {Glosses 媛 with 爰 [*giwan/jiwən]}

Han says: *Nü* refers to Ch'ü P'ing's sister. The line says "I show forth my utmost sincerity without result. Nü-hsü leads me along in order to prevent me from giving in to inferiors. I will never get my desire; she heaves a big sigh." [32/18a9; 19b1]

HUNG HSING-TSU: For *ch'an-yüan* see the *Li Sao*. [Note from *Li Sao*, line 66:] The *Shuo Wen* says that 嬃 is a "female word." It sounds like 須 [*siu/siu*]. Chia I says that the Ch'u people call a woman *hsü* 嬃. In the Former Han it was taken for a name. *Ch'an-yüan* sounds like 蟬爰 [*dian-giwan/ziän-jiwən*]. The *River Classic* quotes Yüan Sung 袁崧, who says: "Ch'ü Yüan had a wise elder sister who heard he was banished and also came to console with him. All the people of the area saw this and its results and therefore named it Chih-kuei 秭歸 county. Ch'ü Yüan's old home is in the north of it. In the northeast there is the Nü-hsü Temple." Wang I says Nü-hsü scolds Ch'ü Yüan for not going along with the crowd. This does not represent the idea of the *chün*. It is wrong. [1/15a3–5]

CHU HSI: *Chi* is "extent." *Wei-chi* is "not to have attained one's goal." *Nü shan-yüan* indicates that the onlookers, seeing the sincerity and fondness of his desire to return, are moved to affection and sigh for him. [2/3b1–2]

Notes

The commentators explain that *wei-chi* 未極 means "not to attain one's goal" 無從達 or 未得所止也. Thus, "I make known my sincerity but do not attain my goal."

This is the same in the surface narrative as in the political interpretation.

The second line has tested the translators as well as the commentators:

> Pfizamier: Die Weiber zieh'n an sich die Neigung, sie trauren tief um mich.
>
> Harlez: Qu'une nymphe gracieuse m'y conduise et dirige des soucis vers moi.
>
> Waley: Reluctant, her handmaidens follow her, for my sake heave a great sigh.
>
> Hawkes: And the maiden many a sigh heaves for me.
>
> Liu: Tenderly, my maiden heaves for me a great sigh.

Nü 女 (CW 6170) "woman" is often used in ancient texts as a loan for a homophone, "you," which was later differentiated by a second borrowing 汝. Wang I says that *nü* 女 is Nü-hsü, allegedly the elder sister of the poet. The Five Ministers concur. Hung's long note is more ethnographic than exegetic.

The central problem is the interpretation of *ch'an-yüan* 嬋媛 (CW 6878.5). The first definition in CW is "it depicts beauty." However, Wang I and the Five Ministers clearly prefer the second definition (which unhappily originates in their own notes to this line) "to pull along like a cow on a rope" (CW 20502.4) 牽引. The phrase 牽引 frequently bears a political connotation, as in *Tso Chuan*, Duke Hsiang year 13: [A minister, speaking to his king of a foreign ambassador:] "If you send him back, and thus frustrate the object of his mission, he will resent the conduct of his ruler, and be at emnity with the great officers and *lead them along*; would not this be a better course?" (based on Legge 4:458; emphasis added).

This binome is variously written:

嬋媛	*dian-giwan
繟緩	*t'ian-g'wan
嬋娟	*dian-iwan
撣援	*dian-giwan

The various graphs when read literally yield interesting alternate readings for the same basic words:

嬋媛	captivated and distracted
繟緩	indulgent and remiss
嬋娟	captivated and bewitched
撣援	autocratic and undisciplined

When these readings are coupled with the preferred sense of 牽 "to be pulled along like a cow on a rope," one has quite a full catalog of sins. The reader well acquainted with his written language would see multiple accusations:

You are:
$$\left.\begin{array}{l}\text{led around on a tether,} \\ \text{captivated and distracted,} \\ \text{indulgent and remiss,} \\ \text{captivated and bewitched,} \\ \text{autocratic and undisciplined,}\end{array}\right\}\text{it makes me sigh!}$$

We have seen before how a whole family of graphs may spring from a single basic word to differentiate some of its various readings or finer senses. In this case, the binome *dian-giwan*, with the basic sense of looseness and captivation, gives us the tenor of the line. The surface narrative seems to say that the sister has (captivated and distracted =) taken Ch'ü Yüan's mind off his troubles in an effort to dissuade him from his course.

Reading 女 as "you" as it is read elsewhere in the poem (v. line 36) may indicate the slanderer, as it is often used among equals, according to Wang I's note at *Li Sao*, line 111: "*Nü* 女 is Yin 陰, ministers use it as an epithet for their peers." In this case, the line would suggest: "You are leading the king along (in your despicable schemes), it makes me sigh."

Either way, the line is an unflattering statement about the king and his dependence upon the "bewitching" advice of the poet's enemies at court.

17

	橫	流	涕	兮	潺	湲
ARC	kwang	liog	t'iər	g'ieg	dz'ian	giwan
ANC	γwang	liəu	t'iei	γiei	dz'iän	jiwän
MSC	heng	liu	t'i	hsi	ch'an	yüan
GSR	707	1104	591	1241	208	255
	transverse	to flow	tears		flow	+	flow
	loan:				binome: to flow
	copious				

18

	隱	思	君	兮	悱	側
ARC	iən	siəg	kiwən	g'ieg	b'iwər	tsiək
ANC	iən	si	kiuən	γiei	b'jwei	tsiək
MSC	yin	ssu	chun	hsi	fei	ts'e
GSR	449	973	459	1241	579	906
	grieved	to think	lord		to conceal + side-leaning
					binome: in mean
					surroundings

META: Copiously flow my tears, without ceasing;
          From my rude exile, I think of the lady.

PARA: Copiously flow my tears, without ceasing;
          I conceal my thoughts of the king, who is no fit match for Yao.

The Commentaries

WANG I: *Ch'an-yüan* depicts flowing water. Ch'ü Yüan is touched by the words of
          Nü-hsü. He desires to change his firm resolve but he cannot change his
          inner feelings. Inside, he is sorely wounded and his tears flow copiously.
          Chün refers to King Huai. *Fei* is "vile and rustic." The line says that
          although he has been banished and is hiding in mountains and waste-
          lands, he still thinks of his lord, even in these mean surroundings
          側陋中. [2/7a1−3]

FIVE MINISTERS: {Glosses 潺 with 仕連 [*dzian/dz'iän*], 湲 with 爲元 [*giwan/jiwən*], and 悱 with 符沸 [*b'iwəd/b'jwei*]}

Liang says: *Ch'an-yüan* depicts flowing water. *Fei* is "vile and rustic." Moved by Nü-hsü's words, he cries. His tears flow copiously. Even though he is hiding in mean surroundings, he yet is thinking of his lord. [32/18b2, 4]

HUNG HSING-TSU; *Ch'an* is pronounced either 仕連 or 鉏山 [*dz'an/dz'an*]. *Yüan* sounds like 爰. *Yin* is "pained." *Mencius* calls it "a feeling of commiseration." *Fei* is pronounced 符沸. [2/7a1–3]

CHU HSI: *Ch'an* is pronounced 仕連, also 鉏山. *Yüan* sounds like 爰. *Fei* is pronounced 符沸. For the rhyme, *ts'e* 側 is pronounced 札力 [*tsiək/tsiək*]. *Ch'an-yuan* depicts flowing water. *Yin* is "pained." *Chun* is the Hsiang Chün. *Fei* is "hidden." *Ts'e* is "restless." [2/3b1–2]

Notes

In this context, 橫 is best read *kwang*, meaning "intense," "copious." *Ch'an-yüan* 潺湲 (CW 18653.4) means "tears flowing without ceasing," which sounds suspiciously as though it originates in the very note we are trying to understand. The surface meaning is quite transparent: "My tears flow copiously, flow without ceasing."

Wang I says the poet cries because his sister's words have touched him, even though he is unable to change his loyal behavior. In a political reading of the text he has sufficient cause as well, so the sense of the line is perfectly well suited to either interpretation.

Yin 隱 (CW 42825) is taken by Wang I and the Five Ministers to mean "hidden," presumably a reference to his banishment. Hung (and thus Chu) take it to mean "pained" 痛 as in *Mencius*, obligingly quoted by Hung: "Without a heart that feels pain and distress (for the sufferings of others), one is not human" (Legge 2:202) 無惻隱之心非人也.

Continuing in this interpretation, Hung (and Chu) read 悱 = 隱, and 側 = 惻 giving the repetitive paraphrase 隱思君兮隱惻 or "With a commiserating heart, I think of the lord, commiserating." This is not convincing, although Hung and Chu assert it in plain Chinese. Such vapid formulations are not uncommon in the surface narrative, but they usually indicate something more interesting in the political interpretation, in which such luxuriously word-wasting lines are not allowed.

Wang I and the Five Ministers read 俳側 = 陋側 "vile and mean circumstances." This brings to mind the famous passage in the *Shu Ching*, "Yao Tien," where Yao chooses Shun to be his successor: "The emperor said: 'Point out some one among the illustrious, or set forth one from among the poor and mean [明揚側陋].' All in the court said to the emperor, 'There is an unmarried man among the lower people called Shun of Yü.' ... The emperor said, 'I will try him! I will wive him, and then see his behavior with my two daughters'" (Legge 3:26). Yao, Shun, and the two daughters have appeared several times before in this collection, and they are especially common in the political interpretation of this poem. Their appearance in the *locus classicus* of our phrase is not likely to have been missed by the political reader. The poet compares himself to Shun, not for the first time (cf. line 8 above), as a worthy one among the "poor and mean" to whom the king ought to turn in his time of crisis, as the wiser Yao did in antiquity.

Two additional readings of 俳側 *piwər-tsiək* are relevant. First, the homophone 悲惻 "grieved" and second, the homophone 比側 "partisan." These would suggest: "I secretly think of my lord, grieved," or "I secretly think of my lord, his ear turned away from me." Both of these are acceptable from the aural and graphical point of view and are in harmony with the political context of the poem.

The poet laments his fate, cries copiously at the thought of his helplessness to assist the king, and berates the king for his blind partiality in refusing to raise up Ch'ü Yüan from among the "low and mean" to be another Shun. This echoes line 8, above: "Compared to Yao, our king is not up to the standard." This is even more startling when 俳側 is denuded of its radicals (leaving the reading *piwər-tsək*) and read "he is not (up to) the standard (of Yao)."

19

	桂	櫂	兮	蘭	枻
ARC	kiweg	d'og	g'ieg	glan	ziad
ANC	kiwei	d'ai	γiei	lan	iäi
MSC	kuei	chao	hsi	lan	i
GSR	879	1124	1241	185	339
	cassia	oar		a plant	oar

20

	斵	冰	兮	積	雪
ARC	tuk	piəng	g'ieg	tsiek	siwat
ANC	tak	piəng	γiei	tsiäk	siwät
MSC	cho	ping	hsi	chi	hsüeh
GSR	1235	899	1241	868	297
	to chop	ice		to collect	snow

META: Cinnamon oar, thoroughwort sweep;
        I chop the ice and pile up the snow.

PARA: Nothing I did was of any use;
        I was reviled and ignored, I made no progress.

The Commentaries

WANG I: *Chao* is "an oar." *I* is "the side oar of a boat." One text has 楫. *Cho* is "to
          chop." The line says he mounts his boat and encounters extremely cold
          weather. He raises his oars to chop the ice and it congeals confusedly,
          like piled-up snow. This describes his laborious toil. One text has "I
          chop layers of ice" 斵曾冰. [2/7a3–5]

FIVE MINISTERS: {Glosses 楫 (which replaces 枻 in the text) with 翊例 [*giad/iäi]
          and 斵 with 丁角 [*tuk/tak]}
          Hsien says: *Chao* is "an oar." *I* is "the side oar of a boat." *Kuei* and
          lan are chosen for their fragrance. It says that since his intentions did
          not get through (to the king), he mounts his boat and encounters ex-

tremely cold weather. He raises his oars to chop the ice and it congeals confusedly, like piled-up snow. This is to toil diligently in vain, and to make no progress. [32/18b4–7]

HUNG HSING-TSU: *Chao* is pronounced 直教 [*d'og/d'au*]. *I* sounds like 曳 [*ziad/iäi*]. An oar is called *chao*. One text has 檝. [2/7a4]

CHU HSI: *Chao* is pronounced 直教. *I* sounds like 曳. For the rhyme it is pronounced like 泄 (*siat/siät*). This section [i.e., lines 19–24] is allusive. This song uses seeking the Spirit without a response as a simile for serving the king without being his close confidant. *Chao* is "an oar." *I* is "the side oar of a boat." *Kuei* and *lan* are chosen for their fragrance. *Cho* is "to chop." It says he mounts his boat and encounters great cold. He chops the ice and it congeals confusedly like piled-up snow. Although the boat is fragrant and pure, although he toils bitterly in his post, he makes no progress. [2/3b2–6]

Notes

This couplet is among the most famous and most often quoted in the Nine Elegies. It presents problems to the native reader as well as to the translators. Their efforts:

Pfizmaier: Vom Zimmetbaum das Ruder, die Balken von dem Lan.
Das Eis zersplittr' ich: es haüft sich gleich dem Schnee.

Harlez: Mes rames de laurier pressent les flancs de mon esquif,
Fendant les eaux auxquelles le froid donne l'aspect de naiges accumulées.

Waley: My oars of cassia-wood, my steering-plank of magnolia
Do but chip ice and pile up snow.

Hawkes: The cassia oars, the sweep of orchid
Churn the waters to foaming snow.

Liu: With cassia oars and magnolia planks,
I chop ice on piles of snow.

Kuei 桂 was discussed above at "Tung Huang T'ai I," line 8, and at line 14 of this poem; *Lan* 蘭 at "Tung Huang T'ai I," line 7, and at line 12 of this poem. *Chao* 櫂 (CW 16094) is "a long oar," also written 棹. *I* 枻 (CW 14951) is also an oar. This word, also written 栧 (both *ziad*), is homophonous with 枼 (CW 14921) "a thin board." Wang I's gloss 枻, 船傍板也 has sent several translators and modern Chinese scholars astray. Perhaps Wang confused 枼 and 枻; perhaps they were interchangeably used. The borrowing is not approved by CW. In any case, the context calls for the oar. This kind of parallel construction is not unknown in this collection; in Hebrew poetry it is the rule: "thy rod and thy staff . . ."

To translate it "sweep" may be the best choice. A sweep is a long oar which both steers and propels a small boat. This would explain the "side" 傍 of the earlier commentators' notes. Hung says "oar." Chu reverts to "side board." It remains to be shown that oars and sweeps may be made from cassia and *Eupatorium*.

The cassia, or cinnamon tree, is cultivated, as we have seen, for its bark, twigs, buds, peduncles, and oil (CMH, p. 109). No mention is made in the *Pen T'sao Kang Mu* of its wood being used for oars or any similar product. The brushy habit of the tree would argue against the possibility of oar-making, which requires long, straight, hard pieces of wood. The *Eupatorium* is a perennial flowering plant similar to the iris. Without a woody stem, it is totally unsuited to the use suggested in the commentaries and translations.

Thus a literal interpretation is untenable. Chu says these plants are chosen for their fragrance, the fragrant plants symbolizing, as always, the virtue of the good minister. Waley suggests that the sense of the line is "I am merely wasting time," as in lines 21–22 below. We will return to this point.

Chu Hsi's note that "for the rhyme, 枻 sounds like 泄" is another example of an alteration required by the Sung ear that was not needed in the T'ang or Han:

	ARC	ANC	MSC
枻	*ziad	iäi	i
雪	*siwat	siwät	hsüeh
泄	*siat	siät	hsieh

In ARC, 柤 and 雪 rhyme within the rhyme system that is common to the *Shih Ching* and the *Ch'u Tz'u*. Only in ANC and MSC do the sounds diverge.

How can one "chop ice and pile up snow" in Lake Tung-t'ing? The region has a very mild climate with a mean midwinter temperature of nearly 45°F (*Times Atlas*, p. xxi). Thus a figurative reading is again required.

Wang I and the others following him say that the poet encounters severe cold which freezes the water. His unsuccessful effort to chop his way through suggests that "he is exerting himself in diligent toil without making any progress." This image is familiar to the point of cliche. The interpretation which has the poet flying through the air over the lake is no less hampered: what are ice and snow doing piled up in the sky? Yet, what could be more Yin than ice and snow, and to encounter them in the sky, the realm of the sun (Yang) is to encounter the negative influence in the very center of the positive sphere. This is suspiciously familiar as well: the motif of "things out of place" is as much a cliché for the political situation as that of hindrance and obstruction.

Also, the boat and oars may stand for the minister's aid to his king, as in *Shu Ching*, "Yüeh Ming," part 1: [King Wu Ting says to Yüeh, his new prime minister] "Suppose me crossing a great stream: I will use you for a boat with its oars" (Legge 3:252).

Another reasonable suggestion originates in CW 1648.99 under 冰雪, which is used frequently in Han and later literature as a metaphor for the purity and excellence of a worthy literatus. An interpretation which would then be noticed by the traditional reader: "My excellence is (axed =) attacked viciously, my purity is ignored" (reading 積雪 CW 25810.107 as "snow that has lain long unmelted," an attested metaphor for ignored virtue).

Whichever interpretation one prefers, the atmosphere is one of indictment. The poet again complains of being obstructed and without any means to help his prince (= oars are useless); his goal is not reached, for evil influences restrain him (ice/snow = Yin). The clearest statement of frustration in the political context emerges from an innocuous couplet. Perhaps its role as the source of numerous allusions is more understandable in the light of the theme of political frustration.

21

	采	薜	荔	兮	水	中
ARC	ts'əg	b'ieg	lieg?	g'ieg	siwər	tiong
ANC	ts'ai	b'iei	liei	γiei	swi	tiung
MSC	ts'ai	pi	li	hsi	shui	chung
GSR	942	853	1241	1241	576	1007
	to gather	binome: a plant			water	in, middle

22

	搴	芙	蓉	兮	木	末
ARC	kian	b'iwo	diung	g'ieg	muk	mwat
ANC	kiän	b'iu	iwong	γiei	muk	muat
MSC	ch'ien	fu	yung	hsi	mu	mo
GSR	143	101	1187	1241	1212	277
	to pluck	binome: a plant			tree	branch tip

META: I pluck the fig creeper in the water,
        Pick the lotus from a tree branch.

PARA: Everything is topsy-turvy:
        The evil rule, the worthy are banished!

The Commentaries

WANG I: The *pi-li* plant is an epiphytic climber. *Ch'ien* is "to take with the hand."
Fu-yung is a lotus flower. It grows in the water. Ch'ü Yüan says that
maintaining his loyalty and sincere conduct while serving a king whose
intentions are not in agreement is like going into a pool and wading in
the water to seek the *pi-li*, and climbing up a tree on a mountain-top to
pick the *fu-yung*. Of course you cannot succeed! [2/7a6-7]

FIVE MINISTERS: Hsiang says: *Pi-li* is a fragrant plant that grows on the land. *Fu-yung* is a lotus flower that grows in the water. It says that maintaining loyalty and sincere conduct while seeking agreement with the king is like going into a pool of water to seek the *pi-li,* and climbing a mountaintop tree to get the *fu-yung.* It is an unreasonable expectation. [32/18b8–10]

HUNG HSING-TSU: *Ch'ien* sounds like 蹇 [*kian/kian*]. [2/7a7]

CHU HSI: *Ch'ien* sounds like 蹇. The *pi-li* climbs trees and now to find it in the water? The *fu-yung* grows in the water and now to find it in the treetops? These are not their proper places. It is like exerting oneself in an impossible task. [2/3b4–6]

Notes

The *pi-li* was discussed at line 11. It is an epiphytic climber, growing in trees. The *fu-yung* 芙蓉 is a lotus flower 荷華. Modern usage equates 荷 and 芙蓉 (CW 31409.10) with the East Indian lotus *Nelumbo nucifera* (CMH: *Nelumbium speciosum*).

The theme of topsy-turvyness is an ancient and honorable one in China:

> [Mencius to King Hui of Liang] You wish to enlarge your territories, to have Ch'in and Ch'u wait at your court, to rule the Middle Kingdom, and to attract to you the barbarous tribes that surround it. But doing what you do to seek for what you desire is like climbing a tree to seek for fish. (*Mencius* 1A:16–17; Legge 2:145)

> It was a fish net that was set,
> And a goose has fallen into it.
> A pleasant, genial mate she sought,
> And she has got this hunchback!
> (*Ode* #34; Legge 4:70)

> Insolent and slanderous,
> The king does not know a flaw in them.
> We, careful and feeling in peril,
> For long in unrest,
> Are constantly subject to degradation.

> As in a year of drought,
> The grass not attaining to luxuriance,
> As water plants attached to a tree,
> So do I see this country
> All going to confusion.
>
> > (*Ode* #265; Legge 2:565–66)

From the *Ch'u Tz'u*:

> Stinking weeds find a position: fragrant flowers may not come near.
> For the Dark and Light have changed places: the times are out of joint.
>
> > (*Chiu Chang*, "She Chiang," lines 32–33)

> They gather up muck to stuff their perfume bags with,
> But the pepper-shrub they say has no fragrance.
>
> > (*Li Sao*, line 139; Hawkes, p. 31)

> But why should the birds gather in the duckweed?
> And what are the nets doing in the tree-tops?
> . . .
> What are the deer doing in the court-yard?
> Or the water-dragons outside the waters?
>
> > ("Hsiang Fu Jen" lines 7–8, 13–14; Hawkes, pp. 38–39)

> The phoenix languishes in a cage,
> While hens and ducks can gambol free.
>
> > (*Ch'i Chien*, line e. 14; Hawkes, p. 70)

Things are not in their proper places, a common theme in the *Ch'u Tz'u*: universally it means that the slanderers have traduced the good minister and now have the king's ear to themselves. The good minister, who deserves the royal confidence and the place of honor, is sent off to languish in rude and mean surroundings. The rascal 小人 has taken the place of the worthy minister 賢臣.

For a striking parallel in Western literature, compare the following passage from Ovid's *Tristia* in which he writes to a traitorous former friend:

To their sources shall deep rivers flow, back from the sea, and the sun, wheeling his steeds, shall hurry backwards; the earth shall support stars and the sky shall be cloven by the plough, water shall produce flame and flame water; all things shall proceed reversing nature's laws and no part of the universe shall keep its path; everything that I once called impossible shall now take place, and there is nothing that one ought not to believe. All this I prophesy because I have been deceived by that man who I thought would bring aid to me in my wretchedness. (*Tristia* I.VIII. 1–10; Loeb Classical Library edition, p. 41)

23

心	不	同	兮	媒	勞
ARC	siəm	piug	d'ung	g'ieg	mwəg	log
ANC	siəm	piəu	d'ung	γiei	muai	lau
MSC	hsin	pu	t'ung	hsi	mei	lao
GSR	663	999	1176	1241	948	1135
	heart	not	same		match-maker	to toil

24

恩	不	甚	兮	輕	絕
ARC	ən	piug	diəm	g'ieg	k'ieng	dz'iwat
ANC	ən	piəu	ziəm	γiei	k'iäng	dz'iwät
MSC	en	pu	shen	hsi	ch'ing	chüeh
GSR	370	999	658	1241	831	296
	kindness	not	excessive		lightly	cut off

META: When hearts are not one, the matchmaker must toil;
When affection is shallow, it is easily broken off.

PARA: When intentions differ, the mediator must toil;
When royal favor is shallow, it is easily lost.

The Commentaries

WANG I: It says that the intentions and hearts of the fathers of the bride and groom are at odds. The go-between wears herself out but achieves nothing. Ch'ü Yüan alludes to the fact that his conduct differs from that of his king. Ultimately, there can be no agreement, so he wears himself out and nothing more. It says that when people first become acquainted, if their affection is not deep, then their kind feelings toward each other can be easily severed. With his king it is the same; Ch'ü Yüan is of the same clan and ancestry as the royal house and does not want to be estranged. [2/7a8–9]

FIVE MINISTERS: Han says: When the fathers of the bride and groom have dissimilar intentions, the go-between must toil. When affection is not deep,
it may be easily broken. The Tao of serving one's king is the same way.
[32/19a2–3]

HUNG HSING-TSU: no note.

CHI HSI: When the time comes to compare the horoscopes of the bride and groom,
if the desires of the parties are dissimilar, although the go-between
works hard, the wedding will not be accomplished. When friends are
distant in their relationship, even though they are friends now, they will
ultimately be easily divided. When there is a quarrel over intentions, the
union will be dissolved. When one seeks the Spirit and it does not
answer, isn't it the same? From this point on, the subtlety increases.
[2/3b6–8]

Notes

This is a fairly transparent couplet, well explained by the
commentators. It functions equally well in the ceremonial context and as
a part of the political interpretation.

Mencius discussed *en* 恩 (CW 10848), "kindness of heart," as a royal
quality:

> Therefore the carrying out his kindness of heart by a prince
> will suffice for the love and protection of all within the four
> seas, and if he do not carry it out, he will not be able to
> protect his wife and children. The way in which the ancients
> came greatly to surpass other men, was no other but this:—
> simply that they knew well how to carry out, so as to affect
> others, what they themselves did. Now your kindness is
> sufficient to reach to animals, and no benefits are extended
> from it to reach the people.—How is this? Is an exception to
> be made here? (*Mencius* 1A:7; Legge 2:143–44)

Mencius was scolding a king who, seeing the pitiful looks of an ox being led to a sacrifice, ordered a sheep substituted. His criticism, in one of *Mencius'* most famous passages, echoes our poet's: our king's *en* is not very extensive and is not sufficient to protect all within the four seas. He is far from surpassing other men and is thus no fit match for the ancients. Moreover, his royal affection is easily severed.

25

	石	瀬	兮	淺	淺
ARC	diak	lad	g'ieg	tsian	tsian
ANC	ziäk	lai	ɣiei	tsien	tsien
MSC	shih	lai	hsi	chien	chien
GSR	795	272	1241	155	155
	stone	shallows		shallow	+ shallow
				binome: rapidly	
				flowing	

26

	飛	龍	兮	翩	翩
ARC	piwər	liung	g'ieg	p'ian	p'ian
ANC	pjwei	liwong	ɣiei	p'iän	p'iän
MSC	fei	lung	hsi	p'ien	p'ien
GSR	580	1193	1241	246	246
	to fly	dragon		flutter	+ flutter
				binome: to fly to	
				and fro	

META: The rocky rapids flow rapidly;
         The flying dragon flits and flutters.

PARA: My unassailable virtue incited the slanderers [?];
         The king was beset by fawning sycophants.

The Commentaries

WANG I: *Lai* is "a torrent." *Chien-chien* depicts water flowing quickly. In his
           sorrow, Ch'ü Yüan looked down at the water of the river and saw a rocky
           torrent flowing downward rapidly and reaching its goal. Looking up-
           ward he saw a flying dragon flying to and fro and reaching its heights.
           He was wounded and discarded in the wilds, never to get any advance-
           ment. [2/7b1–3]

FIVE MINISTERS: {Glosses 淺 with 牋 [*tsian/tsian]}

> Chi says: *Lai* is "a torrent." *Chien-chien* depicts flowing water. Yüan laments and looks downward, sees the water flowing rapidly, looks upward and sees the flying dragon rising flying to and fro. He says: "Things all have their true nature, only I am unable to follow mine." [32/19a4–5]

HUNG HSING-TSU: *Lai* is pronounced 落蓋 [*glad/lai]. The *Shuo Wen* says "water flowing rapidly over sand." A note in the *Wen Hsüan* says it is "water which flows between rocks and then becomes an angry torrent." *Chien* sounds like 牋. The *Shuo Wen* says *p'ien* is "to fly rapidly." [2/7b1–3]

CHU HSI: *Chien* sounds like 牋. This section is allusive and metaphorical. It connects the previous two sections (i.e., lines 12–24) with the following one (i.e., lines 31–36) in the metaphor of seeking the Spirit without a response. *Lai* is "a torrent." *Chien-chien* depicts flowing quickly. *P'ien-p'ien* depicts flying quickly. The allusive part is to say if it is a rocky shallow then *chien-chien*, if it is a flying dragon then *p'ien-p'ien*. [2/3b9–10]

Notes

Shih-lai 石瀨 (CW 24574.1075) is a place where water rushes rapidly over stones or sand. Few other words borrow the graph 石; an allusive context (à la Chu) is difficult to detect. The rare figurative uses of 石 for 託 (*diak for *t'ak) in the *Kung-yang Chuan* is mentioned under 石 in *CW*. There is a compound 託賴 (CW 36078.60) but it is late. The two parts of the compound both mean "to rely on."

Chien-chien 淺淺 (CW 18035.29) describes "rapidly flowing water" and "insincere words," also written in this sense with the altered graph 諓諓. Alternate graphs for the same word (basically meaning "shallow") are 瀸, 濺, 餞, 濺, and 碊, all read *tsian or *dz'ian.

The commentators offer the rather unsatisfactory explanation that the poet laments the water flowing rapidly downward (i.e., following its nature, after *Mencius*) while he must endure the unnatural state of being a worthy out of office. In the absence of a more satisfying reading one must accept it. Yet a homophonous aural pun is possible: 庤厲兮諓諓 (*t'iak *liad *g'ieg *dz'ian *dz'ian) "I point out the oppressive cruelty of those whose words are insincere and shallow."

The associations of 飛龍兮翩翩 are not as obscure as those of the previous line. *Fei-lung* 飛龍 (CW 44974.274) is the emblem of the wise king (*I Ching, passim*). *P'ien-p'ien* 翩翩 (CW 29392.3), however, is not the pattern of flight of imperial dragons. It is the light fluttering of light-bodied birds.

> The Filial doves keep flying about [翩翩],
> Now soaring aloft, and now descending.
>
> (*Ode* #162; Legge 4:248)

Also the fluttering fawning of slanderers:

> With babbling mouths you go about [緝緝翩翩],
> Scheming and wishing to slander others.
> But be careful of *your* words—
> People will yet say that *you* are untruthful.
>
> (*Ode* #200; Legge 4:347)

The common borrowing of the graph 諞 for 翩, especially in the sense of "insincere words," is represented by this passage from the *Shu Ching*, "Ch'in Shih": "As to men of quibbles, skillful at cunning words [諞言], and able to make the superior man change his purposes, what have I to do with making much use of them?" (Legge 3:628).

The image of a flock of sparrows fluttering around the imperial dragon, forcing him into their distinctive manner of flight, especially as such birds often represent flattering slanderers in the *Ch'u Tz'u*, is consistent with the political context. The commonly encountered secondary sense of 翩 and 諞, "insincere words," is an additional indicator.

Unfortunately, a similarly convincing interpretation of 石瀨 is not available. Offered tentatively is a reading based on Hung's quotation from the *Wen Hsuan* note that "water flowing turbulently between rocks becomes an angry torrent." If the water (Yin) is the slanderer or his influence, then is the rock which breaks their progress and excites their wrath the unbreakable loyalty of Ch'ü Yüan?

27

	交	不	忠	兮	怨	長
ARC	kog	piug	tiong	g'ieg	iwan	t'iang
ANC	kau	piəu	tiung	γiei	iwən	t'iang
MSC	chiao	pu	chung	hsi	yüan	chang
GSR	1166	999	1007	1241	260	721
	relations	not	sincere		to resent	grow

28

	期	不	信	兮
ARC	g'iəg	piug	sien	g'ieg
ANC	g'ji	piəu	sien	γiei
MSC	ch'i	pu	hsin	hsi
GSR	952	999	384	1241
	stipulated time	not	truthful	

	告	余	以	不	閒
ARC	kog	dio	ziəg	piug	g'an
ANC	kau	iwo	i	piəu	γan
MSC	kao	yü	yi	pu	hsien
GSR	1039	82	976	999	191
	to announce	me	because	not	free time

META: Our relationship was insincere, bad feelings increased;
       At the trysting time you were faithless and said you were busy.

PARA: They served him without sincerity, my enmity grew;
       At the appointed time, he broke our agreement, deigning to inform me:
          "Urgent affairs of state."

The Commentaries

WANG I: *Chiao* is "friendship." *Chung* is "sincerity." It says that when friend-
ships are not mutually sincere, there arises mutual resentment. To keep
one's conduct loyal and sincere while being punished for these actions,
one must avoid bearing resentment against the common people.

Hsien is "leisure." It says the king previously agreed with me that we
would conduct the government together. Later, because of the slander,
he informed me that he was too busy. Then he banished me to a far-away
place. For 余, one text has 我. [2/7b4—5]

FIVE MINISTERS: {Glosses 閒 with 閑 [*g'an/γan]}
Liang says: If the king and his minister agree to be friends, but the
minister is then disloyal, the king will become angry and scold the
minister. If the prince himself is disloyal, he feigns business. His king
first agreed to conduct the government with him, afterward turned his
back. [32/19a6—9]

HUNG HSING-TSU: This says that when friendship is loyal, then one experiences
sincerity. When it is disloyal, there arises enmity. When a minister is
loyal to a king, the king should then properly be sincere. Instead, he tells
me there is not time for him to see me. This is what is referred to as:

> When you had gone halfway,
> > you turned back again;
> And instead of keeping our tryst,
> > you were of another mind.
>
> [*Chiu Chang*, line d.8, Hawkes, p. 67]

Here Ch'ü Yüan makes plain his feelings to the Hsiang Chün. *Hsien*
sounds like 閑. [2/7b6—7]

CHU HSI: {Replaces 閒 with 間 in the text}
Hsien 間 sounds like 閑, but for the rhyme is pronounced like 賢
[*g'ien/γien]. Whenever friendship is without loyalty, then enmity must
grow. When one is insincere at the appointed time, then there must be
the announcement "I am too busy," breaking the agreement. The metaphor is to seek the Spirit and not to get an answer. For the significance,
see the previous section. The reader is invited to look back there.
[2/3b9—4a1]

Notes

Chiao 交 (CW 294) means "crossed legs," and by extension "inter-course," "relationship." As a prerequisite of the king and his minister, we find in the Classics:

> Superior and inferior unite [交] and they are of one will. (*I Ching*, hexagram #11; cf. Wilhelm, p. 441)

> To feed a scholar and not love him, is to treat [交] him as a pig. (*Mencius* 7A:37; Legge 2:471)

> The reason why the superior man was reduced to straits between Ch'en and Ts'ai was because neither the princes nor their ministers had anything to do with him [交]. (*Mencius* 7B:18; Legge 2:486)

Chung 忠 (CW 10647) means "sincere," "loyal," "unselfish," and serves for a host of related ideas. One difficulty in the interpretation of 忠交 as "faithful friendship" (Waley, Hawkes) is that king and minister do not relate to each other with *chung*. The proper place for *chung* is between friends (= faithful) and from inferior to superior (= loyalty). From the *Lun Yü*:

> [Tseng-tzu said:] "I daily examine myself on three points:— whether, in transacting business for others, I may have been not faithful [忠];—whether, in intercourse [交] with friends, I may have been not sincere;—whether I may have not mastered and practised the instructions of my teacher." (*Lun Yü* 1.4; Legge 1:139)

> A prince should employ his ministers according to the rules of propriety; ministers should serve their prince with faithfulness [忠]. (*Lun Yü* 3.19; Legge 1:161)

In a passage from *Mencius*, quoted earlier in fuller form, *chung* describes the "utmost":

> [He] proceeds to do his utmost [忠], but still the perversity and unreasonableness of the other are repeated. On this the

superior man says, "This is a man utterly lost indeed! . . .
Why should I go to contend with a brute?" (*Mencius*
4B:28.6; Legge 2:334)

In a political context, *chung* must refer to the behavior of a minister
toward his prince. Ch'ü Yüan cannot be indicting his prince for failure to
behave in what would be an inappropriate manner. He cannot either be
indicting his own failure to be loyal. The obvious intention is to impugn
the unseemly conduct of his enemies: "Their service of you was
disloyal."

The word **iwan*, meaning "to hate," is written variously: 怨, 苑, 冤,
悁, 惌, 愠, 夗, 屌, 夗, and 蘊. A special use of this word (CW 10739.II
and −.46) is *yüan-wang* 怨望 "to have a complaint against a superior," as
in *Ode* #255:

> King Wen said, "Alas!
> Alas! You sovereign of Yin-shang,
> You show a strong fierce will in the center of the kingdom,
> And consider the contracting of enmities a proof of virtue.
> All unintelligent are you of your proper virtue,
> And so you have no good men behind you, nor by your side.
> Without any intelligence of your proper virtue,
> You have no good intimate advisor nor minister."
>
> (Legge 4:507)

Ch'i 期 (CW 14701) means "appointment," "agreement to meet." *Hsin*
信 (CW 653) is a synonym of *chung* with the special meaning, in this
context, of "fidélité à tenir un engagement" (Cd. 41a), as in the *Tao Te
Ching*: 夫輕諾必寡信 "On tient rarement une promesse donnée à la
légère."

Kao 告 (CW 3494) means "to manifest," "instruct" and more specifically "a superior's order to an inferior." The *Shih Ming* (ex. CW)
explains: 上敕下曰告．告，覺也．使覺悟知己意也 "A superior's
order to an inferior is called *kao* 告. *Kao* 告 is to make known; to cause
one's intention to be realized and known."

Pu-hsien 不閒 (CW 24.888) is glossed by Wang I to mean 無暇 "no
leisure." This formula is found in the *Tso Chuan*, Duke Chao year 30.
An envoy of Cheng explains his king's laxity in observing a funeral
custom: "On occasions of death among the rulers of Chin [晉], when there

was leisure in our poor State, our former rulers have at times assisted, and held the traces of the bier. If there was no leisure [若其不閒], even an officer [士] or great officer [大夫] have not been seen, as the letter of the rule required" (Legge 4:734a). The idea is that the rules of propriety may be violated when the press of events dictates: a diplomatic excuse—"called away on urgent business." This is a particularly weak excuse in the context of traditional politics, one that would no doubt be rejected by the gentleman familiar with the rules of propriety.

29

	鼂	騁	騖	兮	江	皐
ARC	d'iog	t'ieng	miug	g'ieg	kung	kog
ANC	d'iäu	t'iäng	miu	γiei	kang	kau
MSC	ch'ao	ch'eng	wu	hsi	chiang	kao
GSR	1147	817	1109	1241	1172	1040
	a frog *loan*: dawn	to gallop	to hasten		a river	marsh

30

	夕	弭	節	兮	北	渚
ARC	dziak	miar	tsiet	g'ieg	pək	tio
ANC	ziäk	mjie	tsiet	γiei	pək	tsiwo
MSC	hsi	mi	chieh	hsi	pei	chu
GSR	796	360	399	1241	909	45
	night	finish	juncture		north	islet

META: At dawn I gallop along the marshes of the Great River.
At dusk I stop to rest at the Northern Island.

PARA: When I was in power, I exerted myself in the king's service.
Now, while others are in control, I must rot in a southern exile.

The Commentaries

WANG I: *Ch'ao* is to allude to the abundant brightness. A crooked swamp is called *kao*. It says he wishes at dawn that he could be young and healthy and gallop quiçkly with a heavy burden in order to conduct himself according to the Tao and its Te. For *ch'ao* one text has 朝.

Mi is "at rest." *Chu* is "the bank of a river." *Hsi* is to allude to decay. It says that in the evening, when it is almost dark, he is already old and his emotions are stilled. His thoughts peaceful; he is ending his days in the wild wastes. [2/7b8–9]

FIVE MINISTERS: {Adds "Morning is to allude to flourishing" before "It says he wishes . . ." in Wang I's note.}

Hsien says: Evening alludes to the fact that when one is young and healthy, one wants to exert oneself mightily before one's king, but when one is retiring because of age, on the contrary, one must quiet one's thoughts in the wilderness. It is a phrase of self-lament. *Ch'eng-wu* is "to go quickly." *Mi-chieh* is "to quiet one's thoughts." [32/19b1–2]

HUNG HSING-TSU: *Ch'ao* is pronounced 陟遙 [*tiog/tiäu] and means "early." *Ch'eng* sounds like 逞 [*t'ieng/tiäng]. *Wu* sounds like 鶩 [*miug/miu]. The *Shuo Wen* says: "*Ch'eng* is 'to gallop in an orderly way'; *wu* is 'to gallop in a disorderly way'." To gallop furiously and rest one's pace, never leaving the area between the Kiang marshes and the Northern Island, is to be distressed at not being able to live at court. *Chu* is an islet in a stream. The *Erh Ya* says: "A small island is called *chu*." The *Han Shih Chang Chü* 韓詩章句 says: "One bank of a river is called *chu*." [2/7b8–11]

CHU HSI: *Ch'ao* is the same as 朝, pronounced 陟遙 . *Ch'eng* sounds like 逞 . *Wu* sounds like 救 . *Ch'ao* is "early." *Ch'eng* is "to gallop in an orderly manner," *wu* is "to gallop in a disorderly manner." *Mi* is "at rest." *Chu* is a riverbank. This says that "since the Spirit didn't come, I will retire and wander, sighing, in order to take my rest." [2/4a1–3]

Notes

Wang I, followed by the others, provides *ch'ao* 鼂 (*d'iog) = 朝 (*tiog) "morning." Karlgren (GSR 1147a) gives the intriguing information that only Han or later examples of *ch'ao* exist in its basic sense of "frog" (CW 49259), yet in the *Ch'u Tz'u* (allegedly ca. 300 B.C.) it is already a loan for 朝.

The *Shuo Wen* says: "*Ch'ao* is the *yen-ch'ao* 匽鼂 ." There is no entry for this binome in either CW or DK. *Yen* 匽 (CW 2732) means "hidden." The *Shuo Wen* continues: "It is read like 朝. Yang Hsiung says *yen-ch'ao* is the name of a reptile. Tu Lin considers it to be 'morning' but this is wrong. It is written with 旦 and 黽 ." Hsü Shen explicitly denies the equation 鼂 = 朝 .

Later notes to this passage in the *Shuo Wen* say the animal resembles the *ch'ü-pi* 鼀鼄 , a great tortoise whose carapace was used for divination.

Couvreur (following *Kang Hsi Tzu Tien*) says: "Grenouille qui vit sur le bord de la mer et crie toute la nuit; nom d'une tortue marine dont la chair est grasse et bonne à manger." Tuan Yü-ts'ai's note to the *Shuo Wen* says: "Probably also a large-bellied reptile, since it is written with 黽 ; the reason why it is written with 旦 is impossible to explain."

Yet there is almost universal agreement on the formula *ch'ao* 鼂 = 朝. Hung (and so Chu) even gives the pronunciation of *ch'ao* (properly *$^*d'iog$*) by 陟遙 (= *$^*tiog$*) to reinforce the identity with 朝 (*$^*tiog$*). The two sounds are close enough to qualify as homophones within the guidelines established by Karlgren.

Ch'eng 騁 and *wu* 騖, according to the *Shuo Wen*, are "to gallop in an orderly manner" and "disorderly manner," respectively. The commentators say "galloping wildly" for the compound. As tempting as it is to denude it of radicals: 粤敄 "I speak frankly about maltreatment" (*$^*t'ieng-miug$* becoming *$^*p'ieng-miug$*), the phonetic rules do not support it, although the presence or absence of radicals in the early script was a matter of uncertainty.

Kao 皐 (CW 30788) is a script variant of 臯 (CW 23231), which means "a marsh," and more particularly the edge of a marsh. It is loaned regularly for its homophone (also *$^*kog$*) "to announce," "call out," variously written: 告, 誥, 皋, 号, 號, 譹, 効, 効, and 哮.

The commentators read it "edge of a marsh," taking the words of the lines in their literal senses, reserving their attention to the allegory for a consideration of the couplet as a unit.

Hsi 夕 (CW 5857) is dusk, the opposite of (鼂 =) 旦 dawn. The pair *ch'ao-hsi* 朝夕 (CW 14705.8) is well known in the Classics: A king charges his minister: "Morning and evening present your instructions to aid my virtue. Suppose me a weapon of steel;—I will use you for a whetstone. Suppose me crossing a great stream;—I will use you for a boat with its oars" (*Shu Ching*, "Yüeh Ming I"; Legge 3 : 252).

From this originates the common sense of "morning and evening audience" for *ch'ao-hsi* found in *Ode* #194:

> The honored House of Chou is nearly extinguished,
> And there is no means of stopping or settling the troubles.
> The Heads of the officers have left their places,
> And no one knows my toil.
> The three high ministers, and other great officers,
> Are unwilling to attend to their duties early and late.
> The lords of the various States
> Are unwilling to appear at court morning and evening.
> If he would indeed turn to good,—
> But on the contrary he proceeds to greater evil.
>
> (Legge 4 : 326)

The suggestion of the minister's daily service at court reinforces the figurative context favored by the commentaries, which will be dealt with below.

Mi 弭 (CW 9988), also written 彌, 弬, and 敉, is a bow with bone-capped nocks. By extension it means "end." Here, the commentators give the synonym 安 or 按 meaning "to rest" or "stopped." *Mi-chieh* 弭節 (CW 9988.13) thus means "to halt one's steps" or "move slowly." This is its use in the *Li Sao*, line 96 (Hawkes, p. 28): 吾令羲和弭節兮 "I ordered Hsi-ho to stay (the sunsteeds' gallop)."

Chieh 節 in this context has the significance "period of time," giving the narrative meaning of "At dusk, my allotted time is completed . . ."

Pei chu 北渚 "Northern Island" appears prominently in "Hsiang Fu Jen," line 1, where Wang I places it in the Hsiang River, the deathplace of Shun's two wives. If Wang is correct, Northern Island is in fact *south* of the lake proper as the Hsiang flows roughly northward for a hundred kilometers, passing Ch'ang-sha, entering the lake at its southernmost extent. In his book *The Divine Woman*, Schafer describes the area and the island in some detail (pp. 57–59, q.v.).

Wang I and the Five Ministers take the couplet figuratively: (at dawn =) when I was young and vigorous I could gallop quickly under heavy burdens. I served my king and my conduct was virtuous. Now (at dusk =) I am old and banished, my emotions must be stilled, here in the wilderness with my ruined ambition.

Hung adds a geographical sense to this. Since the area bounded by the Kiang's marshy bank on the north and the Northern Island on the south encompasses roughly the area of Lake Tung-t'ing and no more, Ch'ü Yüan is saying: "I gallop around in my exile, frustrated at being confined in this area, unable to live at court." Ying, the capital, is over 150 kilometers northwest of the lake, far beyond the area defined by the geographical clues in the line.

The parallelism of 鼂 (朝) and 夕 adds a further element: while he is banished, the daily audiences are going on without his participation.

The composite image of the line is of the banished minister, chafing at his exile. He laments his estrangement, his absence from court and hence his powerlessness and inability to participate in the important duty of advising the king. He also laments his ageing, in a figurative way, and compares it to his political fate.

31

	鳥	次	兮	屋	上
ARC	tiog	ts'iər	g'ieg	uk	diang
ANC	tieu	ts'i	γiei	uk	ziang
MSC	niao	tz'u	hsi	wu	shang
GSR	1116	555	1241	1204	726
	bird	to take position		roof	top

32

	水	周	兮	堂	下
ARC	siwər	tiog	g'ieg	d'ang	g'a
ANC	swi	tsiəu	γiei	d'ang	γa
MSC	shui	chou	hsi	t'ang	hsia
GSR	576	1083	1241	725	35
	water	around		hall	bottom

META: Birds nest on my roof.
Water swirls beneath my house.

PARA: Evil portents indict the king!
Evil influences pervade the ministries!

The Commentaries

WANG I: *Tz'u* is "to lodge." To spend two nights is called *hsin* 信; to exceed this is called *tz'u*. *Chou* is "all around." It says that where he dwells is in the middle of lakes and marshes [cf. lines 29–30]. Many birds nest on top of his roof. The flowing water flows around below his hall. "In my self-pity, I have for companions birds and animals, fish and turtles." [2/8a2–3]

FIVE MINISTERS: Hsiang says: "I dwell between the Kiang and the lake. Birds lodge on my roof, the water surrounds my hall." [32/19b2–4]

HUNG HSING-TSU: *Hsia* sounds like 戶 [*g'o/ɣuo*].

CHU HSI: *Hsia* is pronounced for the rhyme like 戶. *Tz'u* is "to lodge." *Chou* is "everywhere." [2/4a1–3]

Notes

Since these lines are in plain Chinese, so to speak, the commentators are sparing in their comments. Ch'ü Yüan is complaining about the rude surroundings in which he finds himself, but says he has the local wildlife for company.

These lines are charged with symbols. The *Han Shu* (quoted from CW 7864.4 屋上) reports a portent: "a yellow sparrow landed on the roof of the prime minister's office."

Wu-shang 屋上 may also designate the king's section of the audience hall (= *t'ang-shang* 堂上) and be in antithesis with *t'ang-hsia* 堂下, the ministers' section. If the imperial animal is the dragon 龍, what can it mean if *birds* roost there in its stead? The king is not a true king. Or, perhaps, we are to recall the fluttering slanderers which were described as birds above in line 26 (q.v.). If the birds have roosted there for longer than three days, the slanderers are installed permanently.

For other bird portents see *Han Shih Wai Chuan* 3/31 (Hightower, pp. 89–91); *Tso Chuan*, Duke Ch'ao year 25 (Legge 4:709ab). Also, *Tso Chuan*, Duke Hsi year 16 (Legge 4:171); and *Shu Ching*, "Mu Shih" (Legge 3:302).

From the *Shu Ching*, "Kao Tsung Yung Jih" (Legge 3:264): "On the day of the supplementary sacrifice of Kao Tsung there appeared a crowing pheasant. Tsu Chi said, 'To rectify this affair, the king must first be corrected.'"

Water is the essence of Yin. The image of water revolving in the lower hall, the part reserved for the ministers, is clear in the political context: evil influence pervades the ministries.

In fact, we have a portrait of the court as the poet sees it. The king is overshadowed by his advisor, the bird whose roosting above the royal place is an evil portent. When such a thing occurs, one must correct the situation by correcting the king. The influence of this noxious advisor has pervaded the ministries; there is an excess of Yin in the lower audience chamber.

33

	捐	余	玦	兮	江	中
ARC	giwan	dio	kiwat	g'ieg	kung	tiong
ANC	iwän	iwo	kiwet	γiei	kang	tiung
MSC	yüan	yü	chüeh	hsi	chiang	chung
GSR	228	82	312	1241	1172	1007
	to abandon	me, my	pendant		a river	in, middle
			gap-circle			

34

	遺	余	佩	兮	醴	浦
ARC	giwed	dio	b'wɔg	g'ieg	liər	p'wo
ANC	iwi	iwo	b'uai	γiei	liei	p'uo
MSC	i	yü	p'ei	hsi	li	p'u
GSR	540	82	951	1241	597	102
	to leave	my	pendant		a river	bank
			girdle			

META: I throw my jade semicircle into the Great River.
          I abandon my girdle on the banks of the Li.

PARA: I throw my symbol of dismissal into the Kiang.
          I abandon my insignia of office on the bank of the Li.

The Commentaries

WANG I: *Chüeh* is a jade pendant. It is the jade token with which the Ancient
          Kings gave orders to the ministers. With a *huan* 環 they were recalled,
          with a *chüeh* they were banished. *I* is "to leave." *P'ei* is like 瓊 and 琚
          parts of the girdle. It says that although he has experienced banishment,
          he often thinks of the king. Now he is about to make a long journey. He
          discards his token gem on the banks of the Kiang, hoping that the king
          will search for him and issue the order to return. For *p'ei* one text has 珮.
          For 醴 one text has 澧. [2/8a4–6]

FIVE MINISTERS: {Glosses 玦 with 决 [*kiwat/kiwat*]. In the text, 醴 is replaced with 澧 which is glossed 禮 [*liər/liei*]}

Chi says: *yüan* and *i* are both "to place." *Chüeh* and *p'ei* are ornaments on court dress. He places them on the banks of the Kiang and Li in the hope that the king will summon him that he may yet be of service. [32/19b4–6]

HUNG HSING-TSU: *Yüan* sounds like 沿 [*diwan/iwän*]. *Chüeh* is pronounced 古穴 [*kiwet/kiwet*]. It looks like a *huan* but it has a gap. The *Tso Chuan* says: "This golden semicircle for the girdle shows the abandonment of kindly feeling." *Hsün Tzu* says: "One cuts off one's dealings with a man by means of a *chüeh*." Both take the meaning to be "to cut off and abandon." *Chuang Tzu* says: "One who gets a *chüeh* for his girdle is put out of office and cut off." The *Shih Chi* says: "He held up a *chüeh* pendant and displayed it." Both of these take the meaning to be "decided," "fixed." To abandon his *chüeh* and leave behind his *p'ei* means the same as in *Li Sao* [line 113]: "I took off my belt as a pledge of my suit to her." It alludes to seeking the worthy. *I* is read in the even tone. A note to the *Fang Yen* 方言 says: "The Li River is in Ch'ang-sha." The *River Classic* says: "The Li River has its source at Wu Ling Ch'ung 武陵充 county." The "Yü Kung" 禹貢 says: "Flowing eastward, it met with the Li." The *Shih Chi* writes it 醴. K'ung An-kuo 孔安國, Ma Jung 馬融 and Wang Su 王肅 all take it to be the name of a river. Cheng Hsüan 鄭玄 says that Li is the name of a hill [*ling* 陵]. There is a Li-ling county near Ch'ang-sha. 澧 and 醴 were formerly written the same. Today the *Li-chou* 澧州 has a *P'ei-p'u* 佩浦 named for the *Ch'u Tz'u*. [2/8a4–9]

CHU HSI: *Yüan* sounds like 沿. *Chüeh* is pronounced 古穴. *I* is read in the even tone. For *p'ei*, one text has 珮. For *pi*, one text has 醴.

The *chüeh* is like a *huan* only with a gap. He abandons his pendant and leaves his girdle in order to present them to the Hsiang Chün. The Li River rises in Wu Ling Ch'ung 武陵充 county and flows into Lake Tung-t'ing. The *Shih Chi* writes it 醴. [2/4a5–6]

Notes

Chüeh 玦 (CW 21336) has confused some of the translators:

Pfizmaier: meinen Perlschmuck

Harlez: mes sceaux

Waley: ivory thumb ring

Hawkes: thumb-ring

Liu: jade ring

"Jade ring" is the most prudent choice, though Pfizmaier and Harlez are closer to the ceremonial gem mentioned by the commentators.

Hung's quotation from the *Tso Chuan* is from Duke Min year 2 (Legge 5:130). The marquis of Ch'in has disowned his eldest son by presenting him with symbolic gifts. The son's charioteer, Hu T'u, explains their meaning: "The symbol is the manifestation of the feeling. Were there a real interest in the expedition, the order for it would have come earlier; the robe for his person would have been one of color; and the proper feeling would have given the proper symbol for the girdle. This parti-colored robe shows a wish to remove his person; this golden semicircle for the girdle shows the abandonment of kindly feeling.... The gold semicircle shows a wish that he should not return;—though he do return, of what good would it be? The duke has his mind made up."

Chüeh 夬 means "breach," and from it comes the family:

GRAPH	ARC	MEANING
夬	*kwad	breach
	*kiwat	archer's thimble
決	*kiwat	archer's thimble (i.a.)
玦	*kiwat	jade gap-circle/archer's thimble
缺	*k'iwat	defective, incomplete

The kinship between the sound *kwad* or *kiwat* and the idea of incompleteness is not limited to cousins of 夬:

GRAPH	ARC	MEANING
泬	*χiwet	empty space
戉	*χmiwat	utterly destroyed
闋	*k'iwat	breach
越	*giwat	hole
豁	*χwat	empty
窟	*k'wət	hole

The circular pendant with a gap (here called a "gap-circle"), the token of dismissal, is clearly demanded by the context. The image of Ch'ü Yüan throwing it into the Kiang must have been very moving and powerful for the decorous, sometimes timorous Chinese scholar-officials. Would a banished minister be more likely to carry an archer's thumb-ring? It strains one's sense of the possible.

His abandonment of his insignia of office 佩 on the riverbank, according to Wang I, is a gesture of disgust with his king, which nevertheless leaves open the possibility of recall, since he does not throw it into the river as well.

Chu Hsi takes the more ethnographic route. He says that the tokens are a gift for the river Spirit, but his earlier comments outlining the political/allusive sense are still in force.

The location of the Li River, much remarked upon by Hung, is not central to the interpretation. Modern maps clearly show a Li River between the Kiang and the Yüan River, flowing southeastward into the lake.

As the poet nears the end of his remonstrance, he becomes more open and decisive. Discarding the badge of dismissal shows his contempt for the benighted king, under the sway of the poet's enemy. Abandoning his court insignia on a riverbank (perhaps prefiguring his later suicide) represents his break with the court. Even so, there is still some hope that the king might reverse his act and recall him with a *huan* 環 **g'wan* (= 還 **g'wan* "return"), just as he was dismissed with a *chüeh* 玦 **kiwat* (= 夬 **kiwat* "there is a breach"/"it is decided").

35

	采	芳	洲	兮	杜	若
ARC	ts'əg	p'iwang	tiog	g'ieg	d'o	niak
ANC	ts'ai	p'iwang	tsiəu	ɣiei	d'uo	nziak
MSC	ts'ai	fang	chou	hsi	tu	jo
GSR	942	740	1086	1241	62	777
	to gather	fragrant	island		a plant + a plant
					binome: a plant	

36

	將	以	遺	兮	下	女
ARC	tsiang	ziəg	giwed	g'ieg	g'a	nio
SNC	tsiang	i	iwi	ɣiei	ɣa	niwo
MSC	chiang	i	i	hsi	hsia	nü
GSR	727	976	540	1241	35	94
	about to	therewith	to transmit		inferior	woman

META: I pluck ginger on the fragrant island.
        Which I shall pass on to the ones who follow.

PARA: I have chosen these examples of my virtue:
        I bequeath them to posterity, to the worthies who will follow.

The Commentaries

WANG I: *Fang-chou* is a place where fragrant plants grow thickly in the water. *I* is
          "to give." *Nü* is *yin* 陰. It is to allude to the way ministers address their
          peers. It says he wants to go to a fragrant exotic island to pick *tu-jo* to
          give to a true and upright person who is of the same mind and will never
          change. [2/8a9—8b2]

FIVE MINISTERS: Liang says: *Fang-chou* is where many fragrant plants grow. Thus,
          in such a place, he will pick the *tu-jo*. *Hsia-nü* alludes to the worthy
          ministers to whom he wants to bequeath his own excellent virtue,
          worthy ministers of like mind who will some day restore good govern-
          ment. [32/19b8—9]

HUNG HSING-TSU: *I* is pronounced in the going tone. Since he gave the 玦 and 佩 to the Hsiang Chün, he also bequeaths *tu-jo* to the *hsia-nü*. To bequeath them to *hsia-nü* is to honor the worthy without end.

The *Li Sao* says: "I look for one to follow to whom I can give it." [2/8a9—8b2]

CHU HSI: *I* is pronounced in the going tone. *Tu-jo* leaves resemble the ginger but with a striped pattern. For *hsia-nü*, see the *Li Sao*. [2/4a4—7] [Wang I's note on *hsia-nü* from *Li Sao*, line 111: He wants to pass them on to the worthy men of the world 天下賢人 so they may therewith serve the king. Hung's supplementary note: *Hsia-nü* alludes to the worthy men who will follow.]

Notes

Fang 芳, as seen above, means "fragrant," and by extension "the excellence of a wise and virtuous minister" (CW 31393.VI and VIII). It is ubiquitous in compounds. Typical are: 芳名 (CW 31393.13) "a worthy reputation"; 芳草 (CW 31393.71) "men of excellent virtue"; and 芳躅 (CW 31393.161) "the heritage of previous worthies." 洲 (CW 17731) means "island," and is often loaned for 州 (CW 8870). 洲 and 州 may both be "congregation": 洲聚也，人所聚息之處也 (from the *Shuo Wen*).

Tu-jo 杜若 (CW 14796.151) [*d'o-niak*] also called *tu-heng* 杜衡 and 杜蘅 [*d'o-g'ang*] or *ch'u-heng* 楚衡 [*ts'ia-g'ang*], is variously identified as *Pollia japonica* (Hawkes, CMH, CW); various types of *Asarum sp.* (GSR, CMH); *Alpina officinarum* (CMH referring to an erroneous identification). This scheme is finally proposed by CMH to account for the various species:

杜若	*Pollia japonica*	"Pollia"
杜衡	*Asarum forbesii*	"Wild Ginger"
若	*Alpinia officinarum*	"Wild Ginger"
薑	*Zingiber officinale*	"Ginger"

In any case, all are zingiberaceous plants: "gingers," strikingly fragrant, and thereby representative of his strikingly virtuous reputation.

In this line, as the Five Ministers say, he wants to bequeath his excellent virtue to worthy ministers of like mind who will restore good government.

I 遺 (CW 40002), read in the going tone as Hung and Chu suggest, means "to offer a gift." Read in the level tone, it means "to bequeath." Since little is known for certain about tones in Archaic Chinese, neither reading may be safely preferred on grounds of tone alone. However, the various readings are not sufficiently divergent to present a problem in this line.

Hsia-nü 下女 (CW 11.21), as also in *Li Sao*, line 111, means (lowly woman =) "serving maid." In their notes at *Li Sao*, line 111, as well as here, the commentators are adamant about the figurative meaning: *nü* is Yin; ministers use this Yin word as an epithet or term of address for their peers. The king is Yang; only when Yin and Yang are in their proper balance will good government prevail. Thus, there is nothing incongruous about the Yin word *nü* as an epithet for the minister's peers. *Hsia-nü* is thus "future worthy ministers": 下女喻賢人在下者也 (Hung's note to *Li Sao*, line 111). Wang I elaborates that the poet wishes to pass on these examples of his virtue (presumably these poems) so that future ministers may find something in them that they may use in restoring good government.

37

	昔	不	可	兮	再	得
ARC	diəg	piug	k'a	g'ieg	tsəg	tək
ANC	zi	piəu	k'a	γiei	tsai	tək
MSC	shih	pu	k'o	hsi	tsai	te
GSR	961	999	1	1241	941	905
	time	not	able		twice	to obtain

38

	聊	逍	遙	兮	容	與
ARC	liog	siog	diog	g'ieg	diung	zio
ANC	lieu	siäu	iäu	γiei	iwong	iwo
MSC	liao	hsiao	yao	hsi	yung	yü
GSR	1114	1149	1144	1241	1187	89
	ringing in ear, *loan*: awhile	saunter +	saunter binome: to be at ease		at ease +	together binome: to wander aimlessly

META: This opportunity cannot be had twice;
So for a while I will take my ease, aimlessly wandering.

PARA: My opportunity is lost, it will never come again;
But I will endure this decline in dignified idleness.

The Commentaries

WANG I: It says the sun is not twice at its zenith, one's years are not twice in their vigor. For 昔, one text has 時. *Hsiao-yao* is to wander at one's pleasure. The *Ode* says: "In your fox fur you saunter about." It says that Heaven's seasons do not come twice. A man's life has not two flourishings. He is already old and missed his crucial opportunity. Therefore, for the time being he will wander at ease, be without cares and enjoy himself until the end of his allotted span. [2/8b3–4]

FIVE MINISTERS: Hsien says: He says he is saddened, and has decided upon death. Once he is dead, he will not be able to live again. How then could he again await the orders of his king, hoping to strive to do his best with a sincere heart? [32/20a1–2]

HUNG HSING-TSU: no note.

CHU HSI: 旹 is the old graph for 時. One text has 時. *Hsiao-yao* and *yung-yü* both mean "to wander at ease and enjoy oneself." This couplet says that the Hsiang Chün didn't even appear, but the heart that loves and respects cannot forget. So he untied his *chüeh* and *p'ei* to be a gift. Yet, the *chün* still did not appear in spite of the fact that he had given them for her to adorn her body. So all he could do was dispose of them in the water as if they were discarded and lost. This is to say: "My thoughts and hopes are here, take these as a betrothal gift." When a guest is about to depart, he goes between the pillars of the inn and unties the four pelts and ties up his cotton cloak; the guest does not present them to the host, and the host does not make a salutation to the guest.

He is still afraid he will not obtain any advancement, so he picks fragrant flowers to give her serving maids to make known: "My thoughts are respectful and diligent, I gave you my *chüeh* and *p'ei* to use. Take them with my tender and respectful thoughts." In spite of this, still nothing is certain. So he wanders at ease and tries to enjoy himself, awaiting her and never able to forget. [2/4a5, 7–10]

Notes

Shih 旹 (CW 14138) is a script variant of *shih* 時 (CW 14222). In this case *shih* has the particular significance of "crucial time" or "opportunity." One may not experience such an opportunity twice in a lifetime, says the line. Ch'ü Yüan expresses in these closing lines his resolve to face his failure, hoping his example will profit his successors.

Liao 聊 (CW 29689) means "ringing in the ears" but is borrowed to mean "temporarily," just as its synonym *ch'ieh* 且 is used in 姑且 "for now."

Hsiao-yao 逍遙 (CW 39756.2) is "to saunter about." It could be a derogatory phrase describing one who flouts propriety, such as the king who is the subject of *Ode* #146:

In your lamb's fur you saunter about:
In your fox's fur you hold your court.
How should I not think anxiously about you:
My toiled heart is full of grief.

(Legge 4:215)

In this poem, several previously mentioned images reappear: the toiling heart 勞心 , the arrogant swaggering of the man who defies propriety, and things out of place (the wrong robes worn at court).

Hsiao-yao also means "to idle." This is the opinion of the commentators. It is associated with the righteous minister who abandons the service of an unworthy ruler in *Ode* #186. By his care for the resigned minister, represented by the white colt, the author shames his king for his indifference:

Let the brilliant white colt
Feed on the young growth of my vegetable garden.
Tether it by the foot, tie it by the collar,
To prolong this morning.
So may its owner of whom I think
Spend his time here at his ease [於焉逍遙]!

(Legge 4:299)

The author of this couplet is not criticizing the king, except by indirection: he speaks of his withdrawal from court (when in fact he has been expelled) and his enforced idleness. The reasons need not be repeated endlessly.

Yung-yü 容與 (CW 7331.99) is treated as a kind of synonym of *hsiao-yao*, "to enjoy oneself," but in a very dignified way. These binomes for "enjoy oneself," such as *yung-yü* 容與, *hsiao-yao*, and the like, may have been differentiated more clearly in former times, but today we are left with nothing when we confront a line like 聊逍遙兮容與 and find it reduced by the glosses to the insipid and redundant "he enjoys himself." The basic question of why this word and not that one cannot be answered convincingly in these cases.

The poet ends with his intention to spend his days in dignified idleness. This befits a virtuous man, forced from office by a benighted ruler, when he has tried everything to no avail. The sense of despair and defeat is shattering. The classically educated reader, knowing of the poet's eventual suicide, cannot have been unmoved.

Selected Bibliography
Index

Selected Bibliography

Aoki Masaru, "Soji Kyūka no Bukyokuteki Kekkō," *Shinagaku* 7 (1934).

Barnard, Noel. *The Ch'u Silk Manuscript*. Canberra: The Australian National University, 1973. Part III.

Barnard, Noel. "A Preliminary Study of the Ch'u Silk Manuscript." *Monumenta Serica* 19 (1960).

Biallas, F. X. "Aus den neun Liedern des K'ü Yüan." *Bulletin of the Catholic University of Peking* (1934), pp. 171–82.

Biallas, F. X. "K'ü Yüan, His Life and Poems." *Journal of the Royal Asiatic Society, North China Branch*, New Series 59 (1892): 248–49.

Bischoff, F. A. *Interpreting the Fu: A Study in Chinese Literary Rhetoric*. Münchener Ostasiatische Studien, 13. Wiesbaden: Steiner, 1976.

Bishop, C. W. "The Chronology of Ancient China." *Journal of the American Oriental Society* 52 (1930): 232–47.

Bodman, Nicholas C. *A Linguistic Analysis of the Shih Ming*. Cambridge: Harvard University Press, 1954.

Chan Kuo Ts'e. Trans. J. I. Crump, Jr. Oxford: Clarendon Press, 1970.

Chen Chi-li. *Ch'ü Sung Ku Yin I*. Ch'eng-tu: Ssu Ch'uan Jen Min Ch'u Pan She, 1957.

Chen Shih-hsiang. "On Structural Analysis of the Ch'u Tz'u Nine Songs." *Tamkang Review* 2 (April 1971): 3–14.

Ch'eng Kuang-yü. *Chung Kuo Li Shih Ti T'u Chi*. Shanghai: Chung Hua Shu Chü, 1961.

Chiang Liang-fu. *Ch'u Tz'u Shu Mu Wu Chung*. Peking: Chung Hua Shu Chü, 1961.

Chmielewski, Janusz. "Remarques sur le problème des mots dissyllabiques en chinois archaïque." In *Melanges*. Paris: Institut des hautes études chinoises, 1957.

Chou Fa-kao, editor. *A Pronouncing Dictionary of Chinese Characters in Archaic & Ancient Chinese, Mandarin & Cantonese*. Rev. ed. Hong Kong: The Chinese University Press, 1979.

Chou Li. *Le Tcheou-li ou rites des Tcheou*. Trans. Edouard Biot. 3 vols. Paris: Imprimerie nationale, 1851.

Chow Tse-tung. "The Early History of the Chinese Word *Shih* (Poetry)." In *Wen-lin: Studies in the Chinese Humanities*. Madison: University of Wisconsin Press, 1968.

Chu Hsi. *Ch'u Tz'u Chi Chu*. In *Ku I Ts'ung Shu*, collected and published by Li Shu-ch'ang, vols. 19–20. Tsun I Li Shih block print edition, 1884.

Chuang Tzu. *The Sayings of Chuang Chou*. Trans. James R. Ware. New York: Mentor, 1963.

Chung Kuo Jen Ming Ta Tz'u Tien. Hong Kong: T'ai Hsing Shu Chü, 1931.

Chung Wen Ta Tz'u Tien. Taipei: Lien Ho Ch'u Pan She, 1962–68.

Coral-Rémusat, Gilberte de. "Animaux fantastiques de l'Indochine, de l'Insulinde et de la Chine." *Bulletin de l'Ecole française de l'Extrême Orient* 36 (1936): 427–35.

Crump, J. I., Jr. *Intrigues: Studies of the Chan Kuo Ts'e*. Ann Arbor: University of Michigan Press, 1964.

Couvreur, Seraphin. *Dictionnaire classique de la langue chinoise*. 3rd ed. Hou Kien Fou: Imprimerie de la Mission catholique, 1911; rpt. Taipei: World Book Company, 1963.

Das, Sarat Chandra. *A Tibetan-English Dictionary with Sanskrit Synonyms*. Calcutta: Bengal Secretariat Book Depot, 1902.

Diény, Jean-Pierre. *Aux Origines de la poésie classique en Chine*. Leiden: E. J. Brill, 1968.

Diény, Jean-Pierre. *Les Dix-neuf Poèmes anciens*. Paris: Presses Universitaires de France, 1963.

Dobson, W. A. C. H. *Early Archaic Chinese*. Toronto: University of Toronto Press, 1962.

Dobson, W. A. C. H. *The Language of the Book of Songs*. Toronto: University of Toronto Press, 1968.

Dobson, W. A. C. H. *Late Archaic Chinese*. Toronto: University of Toronto Press, 1959.

Dobson, W. A. C. H. *Late Han Chinese*. Toronto: University of Toronto Press, 1964.

Doré, Henri. *Recherches sur les superstitions en Chine*. 18 vols. Shanghai: Imprimerie de la Mission catholique, 1911–28.

Eberhard, Wolfram. *Lokalkulturen im alten China.* Part I: *T'oung Pao* supplement 37 (Leiden, 1942); Part II: *Monumenta Serica,* Monograph 3 (Peking, 1942).

Fish, Michael B. "Mythological Themes in the Poetry of Li Ho." Ph.D. diss., Indiana University, 1973.

Forke, Alfred. *The World-conception of the Chinese.* London: Probsthain, 1925.

Franke, Otto. *Geschichte des chinesischen Reiches.* 5 vols. Berlin: De Gruyter and Company, 1930–52.

Giles, Herbert A. *A Chinese Biographical Dictionary.* London: B. Quartich; Shanghai: Kelly & Walsh, 1898.

Giles, Herbert A. *Gems of Chinese Literature.* New York: Paragon Book Reprint Company, 1965.

Govinda, Anagarika Brahmacari. *The Way of the White Clouds.* London: Hutchinson, 1966.

Graham, A. C. "The Prosody of the *Sao* Poems in the *Ch'u Tz'u.*" *Asia Major* 10 (1963): 119–61.

Granet, Marcel. *La Civilisation chinoise.* Paris: Albin Michel, 1950.

Granet, Marcel. *Danses et légendes de la Chine ancienne.* 2 vols. Paris: Presses Universitaires de France, 1926.

Granet, Marcel. *Fêtes et chansons anciennes de la Chine.* 2nd ed. Paris: Ernest Leroux, 1929.

Granet, Marcel. *La Pensée chinoise.* Paris: Albin Michel, 1950.

Groot, Jan Jakob Maria de. *Universismus: Die Grundlage der Religion und Ethik, des Staatswesens und der Wissenschaften Chinas.* Berlin: G. Reimer, 1918.

Han Ying. *Han Shih Wai Chuan.* Trans. James R. Hightower. Cambridge: Harvard University Press, 1952.

Harlez, C. de. "La Poésie chinoise." *Bulletins de l'Académie royal de Belgique* 24 (1892): 200–208; and 25 (1893): 148–56.

Hartman, Charles. "Language and Allusion in the Poetry of Han Yü: The 'Autumn Sentiments'." Ph.D. diss., Indiana University, 1974.

Hartman, Louis F., and A. L. Oppenheim. "On Beer and Brewing Techniques in Ancient Mesopotamia." *Journal of the American Oriental Society,* supplement 10 (1950).

Harvard-Yenching Sinological Index Series. Taipei: CMRASC, Inc., 1966.
    Indices: vol. 17: Index to the *Water Classic*
                 vol. 27: Index to *Li Chi*
                 vol. 37: Index to *Chou Li*

Supplements: vol. 9: Concordance to *Shih Ching*
              vol. 10: Concordance to *I Ching*
              vol. 11: Combined Concordance to *Ch'un-ch'iu, Kung-yang, Ku-liang,* and *Tso-chuan*
              vol. 16: Concordance to the *Analects*
              vol. 17: Concordance to *Meng Tzu*
              vol. 18: Index to *Erh Ya*
              vol. 20: Concordance to *Chuang Tzu*
              vol. 21: Concordance to *Mo Tzu*
              vol. 22: Concordance to *Hsün Tzu*

Hawkes, David, translator. *Ch'u Tz'u: The Songs of the South.* Oxford: Clarendon Press, 1959.

Hawkes. David, "The Problem of Date and Authorship of Ch'u Tz'u." Ph.D. diss., Oxford University, 1955.

Hawkes, David. "The Supernatural in Chinese Poetry." In *The Far East: China and Japan.* University of Toronto Quarterly Supplements, No. 5, 1961, pp. 311–24.

Hervouet, Yves. *Un Poète de cour sous les Han: Sseu-ma Siang-jou.* Paris: Presses Universitaires de France, 1964.

d'Hervy-Saint-Denys, Marquis. *Le Li-sao, poème du IIIe siècle avant notre ère, traduit du chinois.* Paris: Adrian Maisonneuve, 1970.

Holzman, Donald. *Poetry and Politics: The Life and Times of Juan Chi.* Cambridge: Cambridge University Press, 1976.

Hsiao T'ung. *Sung Pen Liu Ch'en Chu Wen Hsüan.* Taipei: Kuang Wen Shu Chü, 1964.

Hsiao T'ung. *Die chinesische Anthologie.* Trans. Erwin von Zach. 2 vols. Cambridge: Harvard University Press, 1958.

Hughes, E. R. *Two Chinese Poets: Vignettes of Han Life and Thought.* Princeton: Princeton University Press, 1960.

Hung Hsing-tsu. *Ch'u Tz'u Pu Chu. Ssu Pu Pei Yao* edition. Shanghai: Chung Hua Shu Chü, 1927–35.

I Ching. Trans. Richard Wilhelm. Princeton: Princeton University Press, 1967.

I Li. *The I-li or Book of Etiquette and Ceremonial.* Trans. John Steele. 2 vols. London: Probsthain & Co., 1917.

Karlgren, Bernhard. "The Authenticity of Ancient Chinese Texts." *BMFEA* 1 (1929): 165–84.

Karlgren, Bernhard. "The Book of Documents." *BMFEA* 22 (1950): 1–82.

Karlgren, Bernhard. "Cognate Words in the Chinese Phonetic Series." *BMFEA* 28 (1956): 1–18.

Karlgren, Bernhard. "Compendium of Phonetics in Ancient and Archaic Chinese." *BMFEA* 26 (1954): 211–368.

Karlgren, Bernhard. "Das T'ien-wen des K'üh Yüan." *Orientalische Literaturzeitung* 34 (1931), columns 815–18.

Karlgren, Bernhard. "The Early History of the Chou Li and Tso Chuan Texts." *BMFEA* 3 (1931): 1–60.

Karlgren, Bernhard. *Etudes sur la phonologie chinoise.* Leiden: E. J. Brill, 1915–26.

Karlgren, Bernhard. "Glosses on the Book of Documents." Part I: *BMFEA* 20 (1948): 39–315; Part II: *BMFEA* 22 (1950): 63–206.

Karlgren, Bernhard. "Glosses on the Siao Ya Odes." *BMFEA* 16 (1944): 25–170.

Karlgren, Bernhard. "Glosses on the Ta Ya and Sung Odes." *BMFEA* 18 (1946): 1–198.

Karlgren, Bernhard. *Grammata Serica Recensa.* Stockholm: Museum of Far Eastern Antiquities, 1957.

Karlgren, Bernhard. "Legends and Cults in Ancient China." *BMFEA* 18 (1946): 199–366.

Karlgren, Bernhard. "Loan Characters in pre-Han Texts." Part I: *BMFEA* 35 (1963): 1–128; Part II: *BMFEA* 36 (1964): 1–106; Part III: *BMFEA* 37 (1965): 1–136; Part IV: *BMFEA* 38 (1966): 1–82.

Karlgren, Bernhard. "On the Script of the Chou Dynasty." *BMFEA* 8 (1936): 157–78.

Karlgren, Bernhard. *Philology and Ancient China.* Oslo: H. Aschehoug and Co., 1926.

Karlgren, Bernhard. "Shi King Researches." *BMFEA* 4 (1932): 117–86.

Karlgren, Bernhard. *Sound & Symbol in Chinese.* London: Oxford University Press, 1923.

Karlgren, Bernhard. "Tones in Archaic Chinese." *BMFEA* 32 (196): 113–42.

Knechtges, David R. *The Han Rhapsody: A Study of the Fu of Yang Hsiung.* Cambridge and New York: Cambridge University Press, 1976.

K'uai Shu-p'ing. "Notes on the Li Sao Riddle." *Studia Serica* 8 (1949): 103–6.

Kuller, Janet A. H. "The 'Fu' of the *Hsün Tzu* as an anti-Taoist Polemic." *Monumenta Serica* 31 (1974–75).

Lausberg, Heinrich. *Handbuch der literarischen Rhetorik.* 2 vols. Munich: Max Heuber, 1960.

Legge, James. *The Chinese Classics*. 5 vols. 1861–72; rpt. Hong Kong: Hong Kong University Press, 1960.

Legge, James. "The *Li Sao* Poem and Its Author." *Journal of the Royal Asiatic Society* 47 (1895): 839–64.

Li Chi: Book of Rites. Trans. James Legge. 1885; rpt. New York: University Books, 1967.

Li Chi. *Li Ki ou mémoires sur les bienséances et les cérémonies*. Trans. S. Couvreur. 2 vols. Ho Kien Fou: Imprimerie de la Mission catholique, 1913.

Li Sao. *The Li Sao*. Trans. Lim Boon Keng. Shanghai: Commercial Press, 1929.

Lin Yutang. *The Gay Genius: The Life and Times of Su Tung-p'o*. New York: John Day, 1947.

Liu Chün-jen, editor. *Chung Kuo Ti Ming Ta Tz'u Tien*. Taipei: Wen Ha, 1967.

Liu Hsieh. *Wen Hsin Tiao Lung*. Trans. Vincent Yu-chung Shih. *The Literary Mind and the Carving of Dragons*. New York: Columbia University Press, 1959; rpt Taipei: Chung Hwa Book Company, 1970.

Liu Wu-chi. *An Introduction to Chinese Literature*. Bloomington: Indiana University Press, 1966.

Margouliès, George. *Le "Fou" dans le Wen-siuan*. Paris: Geuthner, 1926.

Maspero, Henri. "Légendes mythologiques dans le Chou King." *Journal Asiatique* 204 (1924): 1–100.

Mathews, R. H. *A Chinese-English Dictionary*. Cambridge: Harvard University Press, 1947.

Mayers, William Frederick. *The Chinese Reader's Manual*. London: Trubner and Co., 1874.

Medhurst, W. H. *Theology of the Chinese*. Shanghai: Mission Press, 1847.

Morohashi Tetsuji, compiler. *Dai Kan-wa Jiten*. Tokyo: Dai Shukan Shoten, 1955–60.

Needham, Joseph. *Science and Civilisation in China*. 4 vols. Cambridge: Cambridge University Press, 1954–65.

Nienhauser, William H. "An Interpretation of the Literary and Historical Aspects of the *Hsi-ching Tsa-chi*." Ph.D. diss., Indiana University, 1972.

The Oxford English Dictionary. 12 vols. Oxford: Clarendon Press, 1933.

P'ei Wen Yün Fu. Shanghai: Commercial Press, 1937.

Petillion, Corentin, S. J. *Allusions littéraires*. 2nd ed. Shanghai: Imprimerie de la Mission catholique, 1910.

Pfizmaier, August. *Das Li-sao und die neun Gesänge.* Vienna: Kaiserlich-königliche Hof- und Staatsdruckerei, 1852.

Richards, I. A. *Mencius on the Mind.* London: Kegan Paul, Trench, Trubner, & Co., 1932.

Schafer, Edward H. *The Divine Woman.* Berkeley: University of California Press, 1973.

Schlegel, Gustaaf, *Uranographie chinoise.* 1875; rpt. Taipei: Ch'eng Wen Publishing Company, 1967.

Serruys, Paul L-M. *The Chinese Dialects of Han Time according to Fang Yen.* Berkeley: University of California Press, 1959.

Shiba Rokurō. *Mongen Sakuin.* 4 vols. Kyoto: Kyoto Daigaku Jimbun Kagaku Kenkyusho, 1957–59.

Shirokogoroff, Sergei Mikhailovich. *Psychomental Complex of the Tungus.* London: Kegan Paul, 1935.

Shu Ching. *Chou King.* Trans. Seraphin Couvreur. Sien Hsien: Imprimerie de la Mission catholique, 1934.

Smith, Arthur H. *Proverbs and Common Sayings from the Chinese.* 1914; rpt. New York: Paragon and Dover, 1965.

Smith, F. Porter, and G. A. Stuart, translators. *Chinese Medicinal Herbs.* San Francisco: Georgetown Press, 1973.

Ssu-ma Ch'ien. *Les Mémoires historiques de Se-ma-ts'ien.* Trans. Edouard Chavannes. 5 vols. Paris: Ernest Leroux, 1895–1905.

Ssu-ma Ch'ien. *Records of the Grand Historian.* Trans. Burton Watson. 2 vols. New York: Columbia University Press, 1961.

Suzuki Torao. *Fu Shi Taiyo.* Tokyo: Fusanobu, 1936.

Suzuki Torao. *Sōji to Kyūka.* Tokyo: Shina Bungaku Kenkyū, 1925.

Takeji Sadao. *A Concordance to Ch'u Tz'u.* Tokushima: Tokushima Daigaku, 1964.

Tchang, Mathias. *Synchronismes chinois.* Shanghai: Imprimerie de la Mission catholique, 1905.

Thiel, Joseph. "Schamanismus im alten China." *Sinologica* 10 (1968): 149–204.

The Times Atlas of China. New York: Quadrangle Press, 1974.

Waley, Arthur. *The Nine Songs: A Study of Shamanism in Ancient China.* London: Allen & Unwin, 1955.

Watson, Burton. *Early Chinese Literature.* New York: Columbia University Press, 1962.

Wilhelm, Helmut. "The Scholar's Frustration: Notes on a Type of *'Fu'*." In *Chinese Thought and Institutions*. Ed. John K. Fairbank. Chicago: University of Chicago Press, 1957.

Yu Kuo-en, editor. *Li Sao Tsuan I*. Peking: Chung Hua Shu Chü, 1980.

Yu Kuo-en, editor. *T'ien Wen Tsuan I*. Peking: Chung Hua Shu Chü, 1982.

von Zach, Erwin. "Verbesserungen zu Couvreur's Dictionnaire Classique." In *Sinologische Beiträge*. Batavia: Druckerei Tong An, 1930.

Index

DESIGNED BY CAMERON POULTER
COMPOSED BY ASCO TRADE TYPESETTING LIMITED
NORTH POINT, HONG KONG
MANUFACTURED BY CUSHING MALLOY, INC.
ANN ARBOR, MICHIGAN
TEXT AND DISPLAY LINES ARE SET IN APOLLO

Library of Congress Cataloging-in-Publication Data
Waters, Geoffrey R., 1948–
Three elegies of Ch'u.
Includes translations of three elegies of Ch'u tz'u.
Bibliography: pp. 213–220.
Includes index.
1. Ch'u tz'u. 2. Chinese poetry—To 221 B.C.—
History and criticism. 3. Chinese poetry—Ch'in and
Han dynasties, 221 B.C.—220 A.D.—History and criticism.
I. Ch'u tz'u. English. Selections. 1985. II. Title.
PL2521. C54W38   1985   895.1'11   84–40505
ISBN 0-299-10030-8